HOLY ENVY

Holy Envy

WRITING IN THE JEWISH CHRISTIAN BORDERZONE

Maeera Y. Shreiber

FORDHAM UNIVERSITY PRESS NEW YORK 2022

Copyright © 2022 Fordham University Press

All rights reserved. No part of this publication may be reproduced, stored in a retrieval system, or transmitted in any form or by any means—electronic, mechanical, photocopy, recording, or any other—except for brief quotations in printed reviews, without the prior permission of the publisher.

Fordham University Press has no responsibility for the persistence or accuracy of URLs for external or third-party Internet websites referred to in this publication and does not guarantee that any content on such websites is, or will remain, accurate or appropriate.

Fordham University Press also publishes its books in a variety of electronic formats. Some content that appears in print may not be available in electronic books.

Visit us online at www.fordhampress.com.

Library of Congress Cataloging-in-Publication Data available online at https://catalog.loc.gov.

Printed in the United States of America
24 23 22   5 4 3 2 1

First edition

Contents

PREFACE   vii

ACKNOWLEDGMENTS   xix

1   Holy Envy: Writing in the Jewish Christian Borderzone   1

2   Lives of the Saints: Mina Loy and Gertrude Stein   27

3   Hiding in Plain Sight: Louis Zukofsky, Shame, and the Sorrows of Yiddish   54

4   Unholy Envy: Karl Shapiro and the Problem of "Judeo-Christianity"   80

5   The Certainty of Wings: Denise Levertov and the Legacy of Her Hebrew-Christian Father   108

6   Coda: Holy Insecurity   133

NOTES   143

WORKS CITED   151

INDEX   163

Preface

Eight years ago, I attended the annual conference of the American Association of Religious Studies. Reading through the program, I noticed that an old friend from college, Marc Brettler, was speaking. I didn't pay much attention to what he was talking about, but I knew that since he had a stellar reputation as a Hebrew Bible scholar it was bound to be interesting. However, nothing prepared me for the swell of intellectual energy filling the packed room, generated by an august gathering of Jewish and Christian scholars debating the then newly published *Jewish Annotated New Testament* (*JANT*)—co-edited by Marc and Amy-Jill Levine. I took a deep breath, looked around, and wondered: What interest could the New Testament possibly hold for *Jewish Studies* scholars? Yes, at that point, I was one of them: a relatively literate, actively identified Jew whose knowledge of the New Testament didn't extend much beyond the first verse of the Gospel of John—for the idea of the originary Word, or *Logos*, is a staple in literary studies. After the session, I went straight to the book exhibit and bought a copy of *JANT*—the first step in an intellectual journey that resulted in the book you have now before you.

Like many intellectual projects, this one is rooted in a personal narrative— one that I have decided to risk telling because it informs the major conceptual scaffolding upon which the project depends. The idea of the "border zone" (and its variants) has been part of academic discourse for a long time. Although I won't trouble you with a lengthy genealogy, I do want to remind you of a few landmark works. In 1987 Gloria Anzaldúa introduced the term "borderlands" to identify discomforting, volatile spaces, often characterized by violence and dark feelings such as hatred and anger. Even while remaining keenly focused on a specific slice of land separating Mexico and the US Southwest where disparate cultures "edge each other," Anzaldúa recognizes the power of "borderlands" as a potent metaphor for describing spaces where worlds "grate" and "bleed" into one another (25). With its focus on fluidity, the term became central to the then-nascent field of postcolonial studies. In this field, scholars such as Mary Louise Pratt taught us to think about "contact zones" or spaces of "transculturation," where disparate "cultures meet, clash, and grapple with each other, often in contexts of highly asymmetrical relations of power" (34). And then there is Homi Bhabha's important identification of the "Third Space," the "'inter'—the cutting edge of translation and negotiation, the *in-between* space—that carries the burden of culture" (38). Focusing on the essential hybridity of cultures, Bhabha is interested in showing how "borders"—which are constructed in the interest of disguising or effacing this hybridity—actually prove to be the spaces where its composite, variegated nature is most evident.

These theoretical breakthroughs certainly helped me, as a scholar of modern poetry, identify new ways of thinking about modes of textual production and how poems make meaning. But it took longer for me to recognize that the constructed nature of boundaries and the spaces in between cultures, especially religious ones, mattered to me quite personally and intellectually—and merited deeper consideration.

Jews have long had a vexed relation to borders and boundaries. Early in the Hebrew Bible, the Israelites are known by others as *Ivrim* ("Hebrews" in the Anglicized version)—that is, the "crosser-overs" who traversed the Euphrates River (Genesis 14:13). Interestingly enough, this term appears only when *Ivrim* interact with non-*Ivrim*; in other words, there is something distinctive, different, about being a border-crosser, something that sets this group apart from others. Despite this designation, or perhaps because of it, Jews are a people obsessed with setting firm boundaries—dietary boundaries, temporal boundaries, and interpersonal boundaries—particularly when it comes to relationships with non-Jewish others. For all of our well-intentioned rhetoric about "welcoming the stranger" (an injunction based on our own long sojourns in foreign lands), we, too, have struggled for most of our history with a fear of the Other. Indeed, we should note that the word *Ivrim* shares the same root (*eiyn, vet, resh*) as *Aveira*—meaning "transgression"—a violation of a sacred boundary. Many of the more injurious *avarot* (transgressions) are occasioned by Jewish/non-Jewish interaction.

For many years my Judaism was grounded in this particular linguistic variation—crossing as transgression—a stain to be studiously avoided. From my mid-teens well into my thirties, I lived as an Orthodox Jew. My world was defined by boundaries. I strictly observed the laws of Shabbat, including those dictating that on Shabbat one can carry objects only within an area demarcated by an *eruv*—a boundaried space determined according to Jewish law. But long before I took it upon myself to observe these strictures, I knew that certain boundaries were inviolate, specifically boundaries between Jews and non-Jews. I didn't grow up in an Orthodox family. My father was an ardent, secular Zionist who sent me to an Orthodox day school so that I could learn Hebrew—but he insisted firmly that I not try and foist all that *Narishkeit* (nonsense) on him. My mother, in particular, who grew up in one of only five Jewish families in Shawnee, Oklahoma, is very social—and she had many non-Jewish friends. Nonetheless, I grew up with a clear sense of difference: "us" and "them"—Jews and *goyim*.

Perhaps in the interest of ensuring that our identities remained intact, my parents tolerated and maybe even encouraged a certain amount of religious intolerance. Once, while we were on a family trip, we stayed at St. Andrew's Hospice in Jerusalem. Today it is an upscale hotel with few ecclesiastical markings, but back in those days, the Hospice was still part of an active Scottish church, and many crucifixes adorned the property, including the guest rooms. My younger sister and I were completely horrified and instructed our father to cover these "offensive" objects with sheets. He obliged. On the same trip, we went to Rome, and when the Pope came out on his balcony to bless the assembled crowd gathered at the Vatican, my sister and I put our fingers in our ears and said the *Shema* out loud—as if we could fend off the Trinity by reciting this affirmation of God's singularity. One more memory: I was in my twenties and standing at my grandmother's graveside as her body was about to be buried. As is customary, family and friends lined up to help shovel dirt over the casket—a sign of love and deep respect. A non-Jewish friend took up the shovel. My father grabbed the shovel out of the friend's hand and shoved him aside—for, according to *halacha* (Jewish law), Jews should be buried only by other Jews. I want to stress here that my father had exquisite manners and was a secular Jew—but his own schooling in the primacy of Jewish/non-Jewish boundaries was so deeply ingrained that it overrode all other courtesies and considerations.

I have thought about this moment many times over the years and am only now beginning to understand the consequences of being schooled in a worldview that insisted upon inviolate religious boundaries—a perspective informed by an acute ambivalence (even hostility) toward the non-Jewish Other. I am also beginning to understand a bit more about what informs this ambivalence. Being in relation to someone who is different—truly Other—means that you will have to change, and so will your understanding of your religion. This knowledge is derived not merely from mining the work of Jewish writers and scholars who probe the fissures in the walls separating Judaism from Christianity, but from my own decision to "marry out"—to craft an intimate relationship with a non-Jew, and to dwell in what a formidable Jewish feminist theorist once described (in an essay about the moral and ethical implications of my marriage) as a "borderland."

About twenty-five years ago, while living and working in Los Angeles, a city that (as a friend says) "is in love with cultural negotiations," I met Vincent Cheng. A literary scholar who has himself written very beautifully about identity formation, Vince was genuinely interested in learning about my commitment to Judaism and astonishingly supported my need to establish a Jewish home (but don't ask him how he feels about giving up beer for Passover). That said, he was neither interested in becoming Jewish nor in identifying with any other faith tradition (he was raised Catholic). Now, this was more than twenty years ago, when intermarriage was still a seismic affair in the Jewish world. To the members of my liberal but observant Jewish community, all of this was rather shocking. After all, I was a serious, well-educated, strongly identified Jew. If it could happen to me, it could happen to anybody. My community (many of whom were either Rabbis or scholars of Jewish studies), not to mention my family, struggled hard to overcome the fears and anxieties stirred up by our decision to marry. Happily, most were able to see their way to attending a memorable ceremony that we wrote to honor our love and our differences—and joyfully celebrate with us. But one thing still haunts me about what was otherwise an exuberant, full-hearted coming together of disparate cultures, sensibilities, and deeply-held beliefs. Our friend, a well-known Jewish feminist theologian whom we had asked to facilitate the ceremony, began by welcoming the assembled guests to what she described as an occasion of "dialogic transgression." Now, she didn't mean to offend; rather, she was being scrupulously honest. It *was* a dialogic occasion insofar as the relationship and the wedding ceremony were byproducts of lots of cross-religious and cross-cultural negotiation. Lots. And, it was surely "transgressive"—an *aveira*. In marrying Vince, I had chosen to "cross over," to enter a borderzone, an in-between space that violated Jewish law. But to hear our wedding described as a "transgressive" occasion caused me to feel deep *shame* since the word highlighted the problematic, maybe even offensive, nature of our relationship.

I tell this story because it may help my readers understand more fully why I am invested in the language of "borderzones" when it comes to talking about the spaces where Jewishness meets Christianity, and why I am interested in *affect*—that is, the often unacknowledged emotional charges coloring the aesthetic expressions born out of these unstable constructs. Indeed, as readers familiar with the well-meaning but often fraught language of interfaith exchange know, cross-religious encounters are often represented as unmapped terrain, where one can find oneself unknowingly stumbling onto someone else's turf. Christopher Leighton, for example, begins his account of "Christian Theology after the *Shoah*" by noting that "Christians walk a path that repeatedly crosses Jewish boundaries. There is no way around this stubborn fact" (*Christianity in Jewish Terms*, 36). Carefully observing the rules of the road as dictated by the Jewish Other by using the word "Shoah" instead of "Holocaust" to describe a catastrophe that primarily targeted Jews, Leighton quickly acknowledges that while Jews and Christians "share a common spiritual ancestry," the boundaries between the two are absolute. As a contemporary theologian writing in the interest of advancing respectful cross-religious relations and trying to redress almost two thousand years of lethal misunderstandings, he is understandably not invested in dwelling much on the first four centuries of this long and tangled narrative when these two "religions" were far from distinct. (In other words, "good fences make good neighbors.") But I want to suggest another, more complementary approach. Rather than hurrying over this turbulent story of intense interaction, I want to explore what Daniel Boyarin describes as "the boundaries that were also crossing points" (*Border Lines*, 7)—by testing them against modern literary texts produced in these interspaces. To be clear, I am drawn to these texts not because I want to make a case for the dissolution of boundaries (religious or otherwise), but because I think that by examining the psychosocial conditions under which the Jewish "self" comes into relation with the Christian "other"—and by considering not only what kinds of feelings these encounters activate, but the aesthetic expressions that they engender—we might be in a better position to challenge that deep-seated tendency to polarize and simplify the relationship between "Us" and "Them."

At this point, I also want to say something about the kind of texts upon which I have chosen to focus. Although I briefly look at prose fiction in the opening chapter, poetry is what guides this project. It is not merely a matter of leveraging my particular field of scholarly expertise, for I think the conditions of poetry are especially well suited to the questions I want to pursue. To start, poetry, particularly modern and contemporary verse, often depends on the art of drawing lines. Line breaks are a strategic means of making meaning, defining space, and constructing borderzones or borderlands where alternate meanings may swell and gather. Mina Loy, for example (see Chapter 2), a poet who lives between Jewishness and Christianity, uses enjambment lavishly, cutting lines off long before normative sense dictates, forcing a reader to enter the unmapped spaces where meanings and identities are unfixed. Perhaps more pointedly, poetry—especially the lyric kind, as initiated by an "I" speaker—is a distinctively relational literary form. For a long time, the tendency was to think of lyric in narrow, monologic terms—as a "confession of private thoughts," a refuge from ordinary social demands, or a strategy for constructing (however briefly) a coherent, autonomous self. However, over the last thirty years or so, these claims have been subject to extensive revision, with both poets and critics insisting otherwise. Susan Stewart, for example, offers a counternarrative, maintaining that the "history of lyric is a history of a relation *between* pronouns" (*Poetry and the Fate*, 46; emphasis mine). Even more emphatically, Allen Grossman declares: "Poetry is the least solitary of enterprises. It pitches persons toward another full of news. Its purpose is to realize the self; *and its law is that this can only be done by bringing the other to light*" (*Sighted Singer*, x; emphasis mine). This last point speaks especially to my interests here since I think that one of the ways the religious self comes to know its own contours is by crafting a dynamic relationship with a religious Other. In this way, poems themselves are borderzones, spaces where one religious entity meets, interacts with, or otherwise engages the religious Other, in the course of realizing or articulating a version of the Self. Such encounters are notably intense. Indeed, in most of the cases considered here, the feelings aroused by the Other are decidedly negative; anxiety, shame, distrust, and envy are particularly conspicuous. Like the borderzones these poems inhabit, the feelings they make manifest are often overlooked for fear that perhaps they will disrupt interfaith harmony.[1]

    The first half of my title is "Holy Envy"—a phrase that has garnered much attention since 1985 when Swiss theologian Krister Stendahl coined the term as part of a broader effort to quell interreligious hostilities. Just recently (2019) Barbara Brown Taylor, an Episcopal priest and Religious Studies professor, published a popular trade book called *Holy Envy: Finding God in the Faith of Others*. At first I panicked, convinced that I had been "scooped," or at the very least that I would have to come up with a new title. But after spending some time with the volume, I decided to stay my course—since Taylor's account is so strikingly, and more importantly, different from my own. Based on her experiences teaching an undergraduate course in World Religions, Taylor takes the reader on a tour of four non-Christian faith traditions, drawing heavily on land-based metaphors to make her argument. Traveling through an array of religions, each with its own "well-tended" fields and "pastures," all defined by well-established "fences," she pauses to admire each scene of spiritual engagement, reminding her reader to keep their hands to themselves, and to refrain from poaching or trespassing. (This last warning is self-directed, as she reflects on her own "bad" habit of "spiritual shoplifting"—of casually acquiring such religious objects as Muslim prayer rugs, Tibetan singing bowls, and Jewish spice boxes, largely because they were aesthetically pleasing—with little regard for their spiritual functions.) Even while recognizing this acquisitive impulse as an expression of "envy," she quickly mutes the darker valences of this

affective field, urging her readers to encounter the religious Other "without *feeling* compelled to defeat or destroy them" (76; emphasis mine).
 These negative feelings and states are so very troubling that at one point Taylor imagines a world altogether free of such boundaries, where "turf" would "no longer be the reigning metaphor" and where religious boundaries would give way to one single pool, a body of "deep waters" that exceeds the claim of human sovereignty. Before, however, rushing to embrace such a vision of nonsectarian bliss, I would ask us to pause and consider the all-important adjective, "Holy," a term inextricably bound up with the notion of difference: in Judaism, for example, *lekadesh* ("to make holy") is a performative utterance marking difference and transforming the essential status of objects, bodies, or actions as the boundary between the ordinary and the sacred is traversed. That is, to speak of the "holy" is to speak of difference-making, of distinguishing one thing or one condition of being from one another—acts which necessarily produce boundaries. So rather than envisioning a world devoid of difference, and thus of holiness, I suggest that we consider more fully the art of boundary negotiation. As the poems I discuss here make vivid, this can be a messy business, and often quite painful. But poised at the seams of religious contiguities, they offer profound opportunities for spiritual, intellectual, and cultural growth.

Mapping the "Jewish Christian Borderzone"

What follows is a brief overview of this study. I start with a bit of contextualizing, focusing particularly on several defining and emotionally charged moments in the history of Jewish Christian scholarship to explain what makes the site of Jewish Christian encounters so alluring, productive, and sometimes incendiary. With this frame in place, I consider two modern novelists whose works animate many of this study's central concerns and tensions. Sholem Asch, the controversial Yiddish writer, devotes the end of his career to writing in the Jewish Christian borderzone, excavating this terrain in the interest of mitigating the ravages of anti-Semitism. (To illuminate the deeply provocative nature of Asch's project, I turn briefly also to poets Jacob Glatstein and Paul Celan.) While Asch is driven largely by partisan concerns, Henry Roth, long regarded as a paradigmatic *Jewish* American modernist writer, wades deep into the space in between Jewishness and Christianity, seeking liberation from aesthetic and generic constraints.

 The liberatory nature of the Jewish Christian borderzone is on full display as I then turn, in the next chapter, to two high modernist poets: Mina Loy and Gertrude Stein. Drawn together by a fondness for linguistic innovation and "religious knickknacks," each affords a different take on what can be gained by traversing religious boundaries. Of the two, Loy is much more theologically inclined. Born to a Jewish father and an Anglican mother, Loy, in her long quasi-autobiographical poem "Anglo-Mongrels and the Rose," showcases how Jewishness serves as a way of renegotiating a relationship with Christianity. More specifically, she shows how, from a mystical vantage, that great dividing wall known as "incarnational thought" becomes less formidable, less absolute. For her part, Gertrude Stein is decidedly not interested in religion—at least not in any conventional doctrinal sense. Yet while much attention has been paid to her status as a "Jewish," albeit secular, poet, relatively little has been said about what specifically draws her so steadily to Christian tropes, liturgical forms, rhythms, and, perhaps most obviously, Christian figures such as St. Teresa of Avila. Like Loy, Stein is deeply interested in language as a material presence. But what draws her to St. Teresa, as rendered in Stein's wildly successful opera *Four Saints*, is something quite personal, perhaps even surprising, in light of the poet's daunting reputation and literary prowess—for the saint serves as the ongoing embodiment of happiness.

If Stein and Loy find Christianity to be a restorative, expansive resource—emotionally as well as aesthetically—Louis Zukofsky's forays into the Jewish Christian borderzone reveal a rockier terrain. In 1926, the young poet bursts onto the literary scene, brashly taking on the dominant—aka Christian—culture, with a long poem crafted in the service of excavating a space for his own "mongrel" poetics. Yiddish—the *mame loshen*, or mother tongue—is central to the effort. While other writers, including perhaps even Sholem Asch, view Yiddish as somewhat provincial, Zukofsky sees it as a portal, a means of gaining some purchase on a much larger stage. Underwriting this aesthetic objective is a complex emotional tangle that erupts when he sets out to write his epic, known simply as "A." Focusing on the earliest installments (or "cantos") constituting what is a very long poem, I show how Zukofsky deploys Yiddish (by way of translation) to negotiate his desire for the Christian Other—as embodied by Johann Sebastian Bach—only to have his lofty investments curdle and become a source of shame.

While my account of Zukofsky ends with the poet shamefacedly turning away from the "Jewish" language upon which he had invested so much in his efforts to access Western (Christian) culture, the next chapter finds another poet, Karl Shapiro, furiously battling against the steady rise of that problematic construction known as "Judeo-Christianity." The Christianizing narrative that Zukofsky, writing in the early decades of the twentieth century, finds so irksome (and desirable) becomes, in the '40s and '50s, an institutional phenomenon. Further aggravated by what he experiences as the formal endorsement of anti-Semitism, Shapiro begins to articulate the long-buried disappointments coloring his own relationship with Jewishness. This recognition unleashes a profoundly "ugly" emotional and aesthetic reaction to religious differences. Writing out of that dark place we call "envy," Shapiro's poems offer a sobering opportunity to reflect more deeply on the role which that noxious feeling, envy, might play in interfaith encounters—for Shapiro's poems are far from "holy."

Toward the end of his painful confrontation with the aesthetic implications of religious difference (and their emotional fallout), Shapiro imagines (albeit briefly) the dissolution of all such boundaries. This is a fitting introduction to the poet with whom I conclude this study, Denise Levertov—who grew up in the world of "Hebrew-Christianity" as constructed by her father, Paul Philip Levertoff, known by his disciples as a "Christian Chasid." (In this way, she is wholly unique; for even Mina Loy, who was the product of a "mixed" marriage, was formally raised solely as an Anglican.) This challenging inheritance informs his daughter's efforts to craft what I call a "poetics of the in-between," whereby the text serves as the site of connection—between persons and traditions. At this point, the philosopher-theologian Martin Buber's work comes into play— both because he affords insight into the traumatic nature of a relational and spiritual landscape pocked with uncertainty, and because he deepens our understanding of the affinities linking Christianity and Judaism, connections which are central to Paul Levertoff's own synthetic vision. Even as Denise Levertov's poetry is rife with disappointment born out of unfulfilled spiritual longings—or what Buber might call scenes of chronic "mismeetings"—she teaches us much about the desire for the Other (human and divine) who is Other than the self, a presence that can be found residing in the Jewish Christian borderzone.

Finally, this study ends with a coda in which I briefly explore yet another way of entering into a relationship with the religious Other. Such encounters, which can be at once uncomfortable and generative, mean entering into a borderzone region that Martin Buber evocatively recognizes as "the kingdom of holy insecurity." In the interest of asking what sorts of expressions and experiences this unstable space might engender, I begin by taking up Leonard Cohen's ecumenical prayer/song "Hallelujah," paying particular attention to how it has been received and claimed by disparate religious traditions. But the book ultimately ends as it began, on a personal note—as I recount how, while attending a Passover "seder" hosted by Christians, I learned just how disquieting such spaces—the spaces of "holy insecurity"—can be.

The Cover: Reliquaries and the Boundaries of Holiness

"Reliquary II" is part of a series designed and assembled by the artist Beth Krensky. The work was commissioned by the Orchard Street Shul Cultural Project, a collaborative exhibition sponsored by the New Haven Historical

Society seeking to honor this historic site. Established in 1913, the Orchard Street Shul had once been at the heart of a large Jewish immigrant community. At the time of the exhibit, the building was empty and in acute disrepair.

Prior to writing this book, I would not have known what to make of this object: a simple bronze box, with just a hint of gold trim surrounding an opening containing a *tallit* (a Jewish prayer shawl), entitled "Reliquary II." I might have felt slightly discomforted and I might have looked away. I might even have dismissed it as an ill-conceived travesty, or at least a barbed provocation, for the word "reliquary" brings to mind slow meandering walks through shadowy cathedrals, peering at elaborate, jewel-encrusted constructions containing bones, hair, or bits of fabric belonging to a saint or a holy figure. My viewings were mostly colored by a mixture of schooled respect, bewilderment, and, to be honest, a smidgen of distaste—for the idea of revering a person, much less part of a corpse, seemed wholly alien to my account of holiness, which has little to do with revering bodies, or even objects (other than books or scrolls containing one of the Hebrew names of God).

But after having spent so much time in the Jewish Christian borderzone, I felt obliged to look more closely and think more deeply about Krensky's piece. A reliquary containing a clearly recognizable Jewish prayer garment and crafted to honor a once-thriving Jewish place of worship demanded attention. Krensky's short artist statement concerning her turn to the "Catholic tradition's use of reliquaries" as "a conceptual structure" for "sanctifying" the memory and continuity of this frayed community heightened my interest. Never having given such objects much thought before, I was moved to learn that rather than simply fetishizing the dead (as I, in my ignorance, had surmised), reliquaries (a religious and aesthetic tradition that hearkens back to the fourth century) are believed to have a restorative, indeed transformative, function. For they began as a response to the traumas suffered by early Christian martyrs whose bodies were often subjected to such acts of desecration as burning and fragmentation (Byam and Gerson, https://www.jstor.org/stable/767274?seq=1#meta data_info_tab_contents). By enshrining the remains, reliquaries served a sacred function, compensating for the trauma by providing a sacred space whereby wholeness can be restored, and access to the divine can be achieved (Hahn, 10). Serving to enclose that which is of the divine, reliquaries conceal as much as they reveal (many such constructions are mostly opaque, providing only a small aperture through which the sacred object can be partially viewed), making vivid the intimate and ultimately mysterious nature of the divine encounter.

Turning back to "Reliquary II," I now stop clenching my jaw and begin to see. The bronze case itself is small, less than a foot high. The window is covered with mica—a prayer-thin mineral to which Krensky is drawn not only because of its translucence but also because of its metaphysical resonances. In the world of gemstones, mica is believed to help one see (the self, as well as others) more clearly and without judgment. In this instance, the choice seems especially opportune, since so much of this book (and my own intellectual/psychological process) has been about learning to see the religious other as dispassionately and fully as possible—even when the writers I consider are caught up in dense webs of emotion. While traditional reliquaries are often thickly covered in gold and encrusted with jewels, Krensky's rendition pointedly takes a lighter approach; just a bit of gold leaf trims the window. That is, Krensky casts her "reliquary" in thoughtful dialogue with Catholic tradition, refraining from wholesale appropriation to achieve her own aesthetic or theological ends.

So what of the *tallit*, the prayer shawl, contained within? It is unclear where this particular *tallit* originates. There is nothing to indicate if it once belonged to a member of the Orchard Street Shul or if the artist acquired it elsewhere. Indeed, the anonymity of this ritual prayer garment seems to be precisely the point. Unlike the bits of bone or scraps of cloth housed within a traditional reliquary, the *tallit* does not signify the presence of any particular holy person. In its plainest meaning, the shawl signifies prayer, an act of sacred encounter with the divine other (the blessing to be said upon donning this garment is worked into the top of the piece). Typically, most Jews (men and, increasingly, women) wear a *tallit* while praying. Hurrying to join or start the service, many (myself included) often say the prayer quickly under their breaths while wrapping the *tallit* around their shoulders, focusing on what lies ahead. We take little time to consider how the act of enwrapping enacts, symbolically, a moment of holy reparation, a way of setting to right one's relation with the divine Other (see Schonfield, 86–89). Indeed, I confess that I knew little about this weighty meaning—that is, *until* I saw a *tallit* as part of a "reliquary," an enclosure meant to serve as the site of sacred restoration. It was then that I felt compelled to learn more about the ritual garment, one of which I have worn regularly for more than twenty years. So it seems appropriate to open with "Reliquary II," a borderzone artifact that dwells in a space between Jewishness and Christianity—a space that is alive with new meanings.

Acknowledgments

Even as this book is grounded in my love for and sustaining interest in both poetry and Jewish texts, it also took me into unfamiliar waters: the world of Jewish Christian relations. I want to thank the many friends and colleagues who have helped me navigate these sometimes rough seas, and have kept me on course: Andrea White, Allison Schachter, Norman Finkelstein, Dean Franco, Brandon Peterson, Ursula Rudnick, Scott Black, Barry Weller, Kate Coles, Anita Norich, Kimberly Johnson, Marjorie Perloff, Craig Dworkin, Sarit Katan, Naomi Seidman, Shaul Magid, Ernest Rubenstein, Malgo Bakalarz Duverger, David Levinsky, Eric Huntsman, Steven Feldman, Judith Grossman, Jonathan Freedman, Charles Bernstein, K. Anne Amienne, Jeff Gottesfeld, and Mary Anne Berzins. Much thanks go to Marc Brettler, who believed in this project from the outset and who generously read the manuscript for the press (along with another anonymous reader). And I am grateful to Beth Krensky for generously allowing me to use the inspiring image that graces the cover.

I want also to acknowledge the Tanner Humanities Center at the University of Utah for giving me the time and space to focus on the book, as well as the many other institutions that invited me to speak about the work as it was being developed: the University of Haifa, the Hebrew University of Jerusalem, the Frankel Center for Judaic Studies at the University of Michigan, the Center for Jewish History, Fordham University, and the Graduate Theological Union. I want also to express my appreciation for the Marriott Library at the University of Utah and its fine librarians who made research possible during the first dark months of the COVID-19 pandemic.

Finally, I want to thank my editor at Fordham University Press, Fredric Nachbaur, who embraced this project and saw it through completion; every writer should have the opportunity to work with someone as responsive, responsible, and engaged.

This book is dedicated with love and deep appreciation to Vincent Cheng.

HOLY ENVY

1
Holy Envy
Writing in the Jewish Christian Borderzone

"Holy envy." This is what is missing from most interfaith encounters, at least according to the prominent theologian Krister Stendahl. Calling for a more active, demanding, and affective condition than the dispassionate tolerance that typically presides over such meetings, Stendahl challenges us to be genuinely vulnerable and to recognize that there may be something about another faith that is genuinely lacking in one's own. He challenges us thus to risk experiencing, in all its pain and discomfort, the shameful condition we call *envy*.

I first came across this arresting locution while reading the editors' introduction to *The Jewish Annotated New Testament* (*JANT*), in which they—Amy-Jill Levine and Marc Zvi Brettler—confess to having experienced this malaise as a result of immersing themselves in the world and wisdom of the New Testament. The volume is indeed quite remarkable. By presenting the New Revised Standard edition of the text with a running commentary by a group of fifty Jewish scholars of Christian and Jewish antiquity, along with a set of essays exploring different topics such as "Jesus in Modern Jewish Thought" and "Midrash and Parables in the New Testament," the editors provide greater access to important new developments in Jewish Christian inquiry. Indeed, the very existence of such a project—not to mention its warm reception (*JANT* is now out in a second edition)—speaks to a new moment in Jewish Christian relations and to a renewed commitment to interfaith exchange grounded in textual literacy—an occasion informed by many developments both within and outside the academy.[1]

Judaism and Christianity: of course, these two traditions have long been engaged in much messier, more interesting kinds of theological and cultural entanglement. In this sense, *JANT* potentially offers useful strategies for sorting out a more nuanced relationship between Judaism and Christianity. But this is not the dominant argument fueling *JANT* (2011), which has been celebrated in Jewish publications such as the *Jewish Review of Books* and *Tablet* magazine as an "epochal" achievement heralding a new moment in interfaith relations and even more extravagantly as "a small miracle."[2] Instead, the target audience skews decidedly Jewish (at least according to the book's Introduction), effectively blunting the disquieting feelings it means to provoke.

We are told at the outset that readers of *JANT* may be in a position to be better "neighbors," part of a larger fellowship of goodwill. But there is more. It seems that *JANT* may make "us" (Jews) better consumers of Western (high) culture: "to appreciate fully Bach's masterpieces, it helps to know the texts upon which they are based; familiarity with the infancy narratives in the Gospels of Matthew and Luke helps readers to appreciate the magnificent portraits of the Madonna and her child"—and so on (xiv). Moreover, the editors suggest that *JANT* may make us better Jews, as we will discover "why most Jews did not follow Jesus or the movement that developed in his name" (in other words, we made the right choice!). Even as they note that there are all kinds of real wisdom and insight within these pages, many of these passages are renderings of "basic, ongoing Jewish values" (like love of God, love of neighbor, and repair of the world) (xiv). *JANT* invites us to engage the Christian Other as a rather cozy version of the Jewish self—a move that may reopen the door to universalism even as that is far from what the editors intend. That said, this is the sort of vulnerable relational stance underwriting the invoked, evocative, and complex notion known as "holy envy." With this term, the Swedish bishop Stendahl (who coined it) means us to understand that real interfaith encounters require more than mutual tolerance. Instead, such meetings demand that one be not merely open to recognizing what is admirable about a faith tradition (other than one's own), but also open to actively recognizing that a different tradition has features absent from one's own faith, thus acknowledging a genuine lack and recognizing an object of envy. Sometimes such cross-religious forays, as we shall see, can be more challenging, more painful, and finally more risky.

"A radical parting of the ways." "A fundamentally asymmetrical relationship." Up until twenty years ago or so, these phrases dominated most academic accounts of the relationship between Judaism and Christianity, especially in the annals of early Jewish history. But this model has been thoroughly revised recently by scholars such as Daniel Boyarin (author of *Border Lines: The Partitions of Judaeo-Christianity*), Philip Alexander, Martha Himmelfarb, Paula Fredriksen, and Peter Schäfer (author of *The Jewish Jesus: How Judaism and Christianity Shaped Each Other*). They have been busily mining the depths of writings in the tannaitic period (spanning roughly from the first century to the early part of the third century) to show how what was once described as a radical "parting of the ways"—a static model of relationship which cast Judaism as the "parent" of Christianity, the "child" who left home without looking back—is a considerably messier, more fluid, and more interestingly dynamic mode of relation. Boyarin likens the relationship to that of "twins, joined at the hip"—with no surgeon in sight (5). In the wake of this paradigm shift, several disciplinary fields, including theology and modern Jewish history, have begun reexamining their own respective accounts of Jewish Christian inquiry.

But this revisionary model has yet to have any real impact on Jewish literary studies—especially when it comes to modernism, one of my fields of interest. Rather than understanding the interaction as one characterized by vibrant interplay, most modernist literary accounts still presume an antagonistic model whereby each of these religions vies for sovereignty. In other words, we haven't progressed much beyond Leslie Fiedler's harsh take on writers who forsake "authentically Jewish tradition" and instead turn toward what he describes as "Jewish Christology" in search of a mythological frame for celebrating the suffering *artiste* (70–71). Consider, for example, poet-critic Rachel Blau DuPlessis's recent call for a "careful investigation" of how modern literary culture embodies a "Christianizing structure of feeling"—a culture dominated, of course, by T. S. Eliot and his "callow mix of universalist-yet-exclusionary aims" ("Midrashic Sensibilities," 202). Although separated by more than thirty years, DuPlessis, like Fiedler, seems to assume that these traditions are wholly separable from—and fundamentally at odds with—each other.

While I am drawn to DuPlessis's "call," I don't envision placing "Jewish" texts on some kind of continuum between Judaism and Christianity in the interest of assessing how far they have strayed or to what extent a given piece of work may have submitted to the oppressive "Christian" narrative underwriting literary modernism. Instead of viewing Christianity as an aesthetically coercive force to be indulged or resisted, I propose a more nuanced approach. As scholars have repeatedly observed, these religious borders, long viewed as absolute, are produced through discursive, linguistically deft acts. By exploring literary texts that flourish in the fissures marking the Jewish Christian borderzone—texts that dwell in this place of in-betweenness, in the interstices between languages, cultures, and religions—I mean to pursue Boyarin's important question: "What creative use can be made of problematic desire [which is how he casts the Jewish/Christian interaction]—not only what pleasures does it engender but also what *utile* can it be in the world" (ix)? And what aches, I might add. That is, how do these texts deepen our understanding of the challenges, demands, and rewards of engaging the religious Other? What is to be gained, and what is to be lost, by engaging the religious Other?

"Problematic desire." Indeed. As it turns out, the Jewish Christian borderzone is rife with the language of affect—provoking emotions such as desire, envy, anxiety, fury, and more. Let me illustrate briefly, through a case study, just how high emotions run in this debate. Among the many scholars excavating this rough terrain, Boyarin has been especially articulate in naming how emotionally demanding these sorts of forays can be. Even as I am indebted to him for helping revise an important chapter in the history of religion, I am also fascinated by the large contours of his academic journey and how it speaks to my own concerns. Twenty-four years ago, Boyarin—known then mostly as a remarkably innovative reader of Talmudic texts—took it upon himself to "wrestle" with the letters of Paul. This encounter, as chronicled in A *Radical Jew: Paul and the Politics of Identity*, is notably "antagonistic" since Boyarin, an orthodox Jew, approaches Paul as one of Judaism's most powerful *internal* interlocutors. The book, now a classic in religious studies, helps initiate important new ways of thinking about Paul's role in shaping Christian thought. But it also marks a significant shift in Boyarin's scholarly pursuits: what could have been just an intellectual detour, a brief respite from the hard work of standard Talmudic inquiry, becomes a major preoccupation—a passion verging on an obsession. Five years later finds Boyarin in the thick of it since, in the opening pages of *Dying for God: Martyrdom and the Making of Christianity and Judaism*, he struggles mightily to cast off such familial metaphors as the well-rehearsed account of Christianity as the "daughter" of Judaism, in search of something more dynamic, less stable—some metaphor that will capture his own complicated feelings about a religion that he had been taught to regard as reliably Other. While none of the proposed alternatives seem to take root, his appetite for making visible the messy interstitial spaces where Judaism and Christianity meet grows exponentially.

Five more years, and *Border Lines: The Partition of Judaeo-Christianity* (2004) appears. Boyarin, who is given to confessional interpolations, or what he describes as a predilection for wearing his "heart on his sleeve," decides now to "come out" and confess to a "strange attraction," to being "in love with some manifestations of Christianity." It is a "problematic desire" "not entirely unlike the 'love' that binds an abusive couple to each other"—"a love that (almost) would not dare to say its name, the love of an Orthodox Jew for Christianity" (xi). Like most lovers, Boyarin wants to share his story with the world.

This impulse informs his next expedition, *The Jewish Gospels: The Story of the Jewish Christ* (2012), a more "accessible" rendition of his academic efforts to blunt the idea of Jesus as a divine savior, in favor of something much less scary or off-putting (at least to a Jewish readership). He effectively upends Christian doctrine, redefining the well-known locution "Son of Man" to mean divine redeemer—arguing that many of Christianity's core beliefs, including that of the resurrection, originate in pre-Christian Jewish thought. To put it another way, it is a love that knows no limits. Writing out of a desire to make vivid just how blurry the boundaries between Judaism and Christianity really are, Boyarin comes close to erasing the differences altogether. Upon publication, *The Jewish Gospels* sets off a firestorm as another esteemed scholar of late antiquity, Peter Schäfer, lets loose, writing in the pages of *The New Republic*, grieving how this "wildly speculative" and "highly idiosyncratic" book leaves him "irritated and sad": for by charting a surprisingly smooth path between the two traditions, *The Jewish Gospels* short-circuits the more challenging, complicated narrative—of which, ironically enough, Boyarin himself has been a principal author.

To be sure, Schäfer's objections are thoroughly grounded in sound scholarship and mounted in the interest of academic integrity. But there is, I think, also something deeply personal that can get triggered for those who traffic in the unruly, fundamentally unmappable spaces demarcating Jewishness and Christianity. Boyarin describes his tangled desire for Christianity as a kind of "nostalgia"—a yearning not so much for a different place as for a different time, a time when the boundaries between these two traditions seemed less absolute. This longing is painfully aroused by Schäfer's study, *Jesus in the Talmud*, which represents rabbinic Judaism (first century CE) embroiled in a "fight to the death," an "all-out war" with Christianity. Schäfer, a German-born, non-Jewish scholar, walks a difficult line, arguing that the Talmud (written in the sixth century CE) is riddled with caustic accusations of sexual immorality lodged against Christianity as part of an ill-fated power struggle. Two years before *The Jewish Gospels* appeared, Boyarin himself wrote a long and pointed critique of this study.[3] Grieving Schäfer's account and its potential impact on interfaith relations, Boyarin counters Schäfer's claims with a set of redemptive readings of Talmudic texts. Now, such exchanges are hardly unique in academia, where highly charged interactions are part of the landscape. But the extent to which emotions become part of the discursive landscape when Jewish Christian convergences and divergences are at stake is truly noteworthy. The last ten years have seen a virtual "bumper crop" of books devoted to deciphering the complex history surrounding the earliest days of Jewish Christian relations.

These debates, as I have suggested, go well beyond the usual academic feuding: the stakes here are high, and often personal.

Thus far, I have been looking at current trends in Jewish Christian scholarship. But the idea of a more fluid mode of cross-religious interaction is itself not all that new. When first embarking on this project, I thought that this revolutionary development in the narrative of first century Jewish-Christianity was wholly original to the field of early Jewish/Christian history and Bible. And I wondered about its potential impact on my field of expertise: modern Jewish writing (especially poetry). But it turns out that I had missed an important step in mapping my cross-historical account. While it is certainly true that current scholarship has done much to correct outdated notions of how a supposedly stale, spiritless religion (Judaism) gave way to something more vital and less punitive (Christianity) by deploying careful textual analysis to show how unstable and fluid the boundaries between these two religious orientations were, it is also true that these boundaries have long been the site of discussion. For example, in a short survey entitled "Jesus in Modern Jewish Thought," Susannah Heschel discusses how recent scholarship belongs to what she calls the "Third Quest" for the historical Jesus (JANT, 736–40). Although, as I will suggest, I am not entirely sure that the complex interactions characteristic of Jewish/Christian history can be so neatly contained, what Heschel calls the first of such quests was initiated in the eighteenth century in the interest of mounting a defense of Judaism and continued well into the first part of the nineteenth century. Fueled by the anxious recognition that Judaism was fast losing ground to Christianity, scholars such as Moses Mendelssohn insisted that Judaism—a religion he claimed to be grounded in reason—was fundamentally incompatible with Christian mysteries (Heschel, "Jesus in Modern Jewish Thought," 737). Another significant shift occurred in the mid–nineteenth century with historian Abraham Geiger's *The Original Text and Versions of the Bible*, which marks the beginning of the "second quest." Taking it upon himself to prove that Jesus was indeed a liberal Pharisee—that is, a left-leaning, liberal Jew (assigning him an identity position closer to that of a Reform Jew than that of a Protestant Christian)—Geiger practices history with an agenda. Working to "boost Judaism's flagging self-esteem," Geiger charts a course for many leaders of Reform Judaism, including his student Emil Hirsch, senior Rabbi at Chicago's Sinai Temple (known especially for its radical stance on religious inclusion), who, during one of his standing-room-only Sunday (!) sermons, preached to his rapt congregation: "Jesus is so thoroughly Jewish that you are at a loss to find originality in him" (Hirsch, *My Religion*, 46). The point was, I think, that when it came down to it, Christianity was simply not worthy of Jewish desire. Particularly since, when it came to suffering, Judaism had far outstripped its competitors. After concluding that Jesus was nothing more than another Jew, Rabbi Hirsch suggests that this paradigmatic figure of divine suffering wasn't all that exceptional. Comparing Judaism's Rabbi Akiva, whose gruesome death is graphically detailed, to that of Jesus, the latter's martyrdom pales alongside that of the former. While Jesus whined, "Eli, Eli, why hast thou forsaken me?," Rabbi Akiva courageously affirmed his faith, reciting the traditional *Shemah*: "Hear, Oh Israel, the Lord is God, the Lord is One" (46).

Even as they insist on Jesus's Jewishness, neither Geiger nor Hirsch seems particularly interested in testing the boundaries between Judaism and Christianity. Instead, both are focused on curbing any real interest in the Christian Other as a spiritual alternative and on fixing the Jewish gaze squarely on its own tradition. It may well be that throughout much of the nineteenth century, the borders between the two faiths remained largely intact, as per Heschel's account—or at least it is possible to claim as much. Indeed, the nineteenth-century American poet Emma Lazarus (1849–1887)—best known for the Statue of Liberty sonnet—affirms these boundaries, planting herself firmly "Outside the Church" (1872). In this poem, a litany comprising emphatically complete sestets, Lazarus ventures briefly into the "cloistered limitations of the 'Mother-Church,'" only to flee, "estranged, unsatisfied" (Schor, *Emma Lazarus*, 273). Once outside, the poet-speaker finds solace in open spaces, with each "bush a God"—a secularized variation, perhaps, on Moses's blazing encounter with the divine. A few years later, she takes a decidedly more aggressive stance in "The Crowing of the Red Cock"—a poem written in response to harrowing reports about the Russian pogroms which are beginning to fill American newspapers. There she accuses "The folk of Christ" not only of betraying the Jews but of defaming Christ himself, whom she pointedly identifies only as "The Son of Man," focusing thus on his profound humanity rather than on his divine status (285).

With this move made in the service of securing boundaries, Lazarus anticipates a steady destabilizing of what had seemed to be a fixed state of affairs, as cracks in the walls setting the two religions firmly apart begin to emerge. It is not so much a matter of there being some kind of clear assault on these cultural/religious/institutional fortifications as it is that prevailing conditions now make manifest these fissures, these leakages that were always there. By "conditions," I mean the steady rise of European anti-Semitism—a dynamic that, as Jean-Paul Sartre explains, turns on the idea of perceiving an Other not as a distinct presence but rather as an alienated image of the self, or as Homi Bhabha puts it, a subject onto whom one projects "the otherness of the Self" (Bhabha, *The Location of Culture*, 44). Indeed, as Lazarus intuits, one powerful way of disabling this lethal mindset is to remind readers of Jesus's Jewish lineage. Beginning in the early 1900s, all kinds of Yiddish writers, including Lamed Shapiro, Itsik Manger, and the Ukrainian-born Hebrew poet Uri Zvi Greenberg, deployed this strategy, reaching for the image of Christ on the Cross to protest the horrors of anti-Semitism.[4]

The image also finds its way into the realm of the visual arts. Marc Chagall, who most famously and over a period of nearly thirty years returns repeatedly to the "Jewish Jesus," offers a strikingly complicated example of how the same figure serves sometimes to blur the boundaries between the "self" and the "other," and sometimes to ensure their stability. Early in his career, the young artist is interested in a Jesus whom he identifies as the embodiment of Western "light" —as a way of gaining access to the broader culture (Hoffman, 209). The most famous example is probably his 1938 painting "The White Crucifixion," one of at least twenty images of his featuring the Jewish Jesus. However, with the rise of anti-Semitism, this universalizing function gives way to something much more ethnically specific. Reflecting upon "White Crucifixion," Chagall later says, "For me, Christ always symbolized the true type of the Jewish martyr. That is how I understood him in 1908 when I used this figure for the first time. . . . It was under the influence of the pogroms" (Amishai-Maisel, 143). That is, Chagall works to jam the machinery of anti-Semitism by confronting his largely Christian audience with an image that—since his Jesus Christ is so clearly marked as Jewish—will disable the kind of essentialist Othering underwriting anti-Semitic violence by forcing the Christian Self to recognize both Jesus and oneself in the Semite Other. To be sure, this is an arresting, even shocking move. Nonetheless, the religious categories "Christian" and "Jewish" remain more or less intact, at least as far as the artist is concerned. But the painting's contemporary reception suggests that a more complex account may be in order. A few years ago the Art Institute of Chicago, where the painting now hangs, announced that they were shipping the work to Florence at the request of Pope Francis, who has proclaimed "White Crucifixion" (1938) to be his favorite work of art, and he specifically asked that it be included in a show devoted to "Divine Beauty."[5] That is, even as an artist may claim to be invested in shoring up religious boundaries, the viewer's gaze can work to very different ends. These boundaries—as with most boundaries—are fundamentally unstable.[6]

While for Chagall "Christian" and "Jewish" ultimately remain separate, boundaried categories, Chagall's good friend, the writer Sholem Asch, envisions a more nuanced, muddled, and ambiguous model of interaction; it is an effort that arguably costs him dearly. Born in a small Polish town in 1880, Asch turned away early from his traditional Jewish upbringing and joined the ranks of the secular Yiddish literati. Heralded as a *wunderkind*, Asch became known as a gifted storyteller and, above all, a dramatist. Even as he delighted his readership with idyllic tales of traditional Jewish life, it seems that he was always drawn to cultural borderzones. In the summer of 1906 he wrote *The God of Vengeance*, a Yiddish-language play featuring what has been described as "Broadway's First Lesbian Kiss." Situating his tale in a Jewish-owned brothel, Asch bundles same-sex attraction, interfaith relations, and illicit sexual dalliances into one tragic affair. As one might imagine, the play generated strong responses. New York audiences threw eggs, while tastemakers such as Abe Cahan (editor of the Yiddish newspaper the *Forverts*) championed Asch's bold and artful achievement.

Undeterred by this decidedly mixed response, Asch became even more prolific. As if energized by controversy, he published more than thirty works of fiction and dramatic art between 1906 and 1939—when he came out with *The Nazarene*, the first installment in his "Christological" trilogy. The novel, along with its companions, *Mary* and *The Apostle*, precipitated a storm of abuse that made the response to *The God of Vengeance* look like a summer shower, at least as far as Asch's Yiddish readership was concerned. Indeed, the novel first appeared in English—a move which, as Anita Norich explains, was at least as infuriating as the narrative itself. It was bad enough that a Jewish writer would devote himself to mining the intersections between Judaism and early Christianity, but to offer up such an account in English was seen as an act of high treason. At a moment when Yiddish culture was struggling to withstand that tidal wave called "Judeo-Christianity," Asch's turn to English—the language of the universalizing Other—was devastating (Norich, "Sholem Asch," 252–53). Informed by a worldview in which this idea of a hyphenated, "Jewish-Christian" culture had already taken root, English-language Jewish intellectuals such as Philip Rhav and Alfred Kazin wrote kind but restrained accounts of Asch's efforts to infuse the "Christian epic" with a sense of "Jewish loneliness" ("Jew as Modern Writer," 375). Turning, however, to the realm of Yiddish letters, one discovers a world ablaze—as Abe Cahan declares "war" on the author who was once a star player for the home team. Among the many shots fired, Cahan is most often quoted for wickedly observing that Asch's *"yidishkayt iz yezuskayt"*—that is, his "Jewishness is Jesusness." The attacks continue, culminating with Chaim Lieberman's three hundred–page assault. Published first in Yiddish, then translated into English, it begins: "Americans have their Ezra Pound. . . . Jews have Sholem Asch" (Lieberman, *The Christianity of Sholem Asch*, 9). Lieberman directs much of his firepower at Asch's failure to point up the various instances upon which the New Testament misrepresents Judaism, but buried in all the ire are some real insights into what fuels this kind of vitriol and what makes Asch's effort compelling. Lieberman writes: "Asch's offense was not only against his people and their faith, but against the principles of his very art. From a purely artistic standpoint it was a serious error to *blur the very sharp distinctions between the two viewpoints*. His work would have gained considerably in stature had he dared speak up for Judaism with boldness, meeting the Christian issue squarely. His pages should have been flaming with warfare—with the clash of ideas, concepts, biblical passages, even of single verses" (64; emphasis mine).

The ironies here are staggering, maybe even profound. Yiddish, the stuff out of which Asch wove his tales, is a "language of fusion" to begin with—a polylingual, mongrel construction born in the borderzones between several cultures, classes, national affiliations, and linguistic registers. By its very nature, it seems that Yiddish should have been hospitable to the kinds of border crossings upon which Asch embarked.[7] This is especially true since Asch was writing in America, where Yiddish authors were often in dialogue with other aesthetic movements, and some, most notably those who called themselves the "Introspectivists," found themselves in the American poetic vanguard. Along with a penchant for aesthetic innovation, many of these writers routinely pushed the boundaries of their received literary culture by turning to non-Jewish writers and thinkers (including T. S. Eliot, James Joyce, and others) as sources of inspiration. These forays, however, slowed down considerably when the scope of the catastrophic injuries suffered by European Jewry began to be understood. Jacob Glatstein's most famous poem, "Good Night, World" (1943), provides one of the strongest examples of the enraged rejection of modernity and the desperate, tortured, and deeply ambivalent turn toward traditional Judaism (*yiddishkeit*) that this knowledge engendered. The poem has been translated many times over, but the version I cite here is that of Benjamin and Barbara Harshav since it goes a long way in capturing the complex range of bitterness, defensiveness, defiance, and loss that makes the poem so very searing. Here is the last installment in the speaker's protest, lodged against those icons of Western civilization which have betrayed him so thoroughly:

> Good night. I grant you, world,
> All my liberators.
> Take the Jesusmarxes, choke on their courage.
> Drop dead on a drop of our baptized blood.
> . . . .
> I do not need consolation.
> I go back to my four walls,

From Wagner's pagan music—to tune, to humming.
I kiss you, tangled Jewish life. . . .

(Harshav, *Sing, Stranger*, 453)

As the Jewish world begins to grasp the full extent of the horror, Glatstein begins redrawing the cultural/religious boundaries that, as a modernist poet, he had happily abandoned. Yet as Norich points out, "Good Night, World" finds the poet directing his fury toward *both* Jews and Christians alike for falling prey to the seductive visions of those "Jesusmarxes" (Norich, *Writing in Tongues*, 487). Six years later, however, any nonpartisan impulses have thoroughly dissipated, along with any pangs of doubt he may have suffered—as, in a subsequent poem ("How Much Christian"), he pointedly refuses to participate in any of the easy pieties offered on behalf of those who had suffered, scoffing bitterly: "How much Christian, so to speak, can I get / How much pity was left me / And what I can I forgive?" (Harshav, 487) And to those who would murmur sympathetically and suggest that perhaps something like "Christian" forgiveness is in order, Glatstein's speaker concedes: "So much pity / They can still get out of me / For the children of my leprous enemies / This pinch of sympathy—take it from me, toss." That, however, is as far as he can go. As the last line makes clear, he adamantly refuses to indulge in any of the Christianizing symbols which typically present themselves as universalizing gestures of goodwill: "But do not shadow my heart / With a pitiful cross" (Harshav, 488). The issue, for Glatstein, is not so much one of religious devotion; he remains—like so many Yiddish writers—staunchly secular. Instead, thoroughly convinced that Nazi ideology was deeply bound up with Christian doctrine, Glatstein insists on laying blame where it belongs.

Betrayed utterly by the promise of a secular culture grounded in unspecified, noncontroversial "Jewish-Christian" ideals such as love, tolerance, and forgiveness, Jacob Glatstein ultimately draws a firm boundary between these two Western religions. But for a ground-leveling response to the horrors of anti-Semitism and what that means for interfaith engagement, we have to look—even if briefly—at Paul Celan, a writer who troubles the Jewish Christian borderzone to devastating ends. Writing thirteen years after the end of World War II, Celan gives us "Tenebrae," a poem that finds that since neither Judaism nor Christianity is a reliable source of meaning, the border between them is vulnerable to total collapse. Like Glatstein's "Good Night, World," "Tenebrae" has been translated repeatedly—each version charged with different religious meanings. Indeed, as Naomi Seidman has so deftly argued, translation has played a central role in the story of Jewish Christian relations, especially when it comes to understanding "the constructedness of Holocaust discourse" (Seidman,

Faithful Renderings, 200). The choices made in the interest of producing an English rendering of Celan's harrowing poem demonstrate powerfully how translation operates as a contact zone, a site of Jewish Christian cultural/religious negotiations. I begin here with John Felstiner's translation, which appears in 1995 as part of his book-length study *Paul Celan: Poet, Survivor, Jew*:

Tenebrae

Near are we, Lord,
near and graspable.

Grasped already, Lord,
clawed into each other, as if
each of our bodies were
your body, Lord.

Pray, Lord,
pray to us,
we are near.

Wind-skewed we went there,
went there to bend
over pit and crater.

Went to the water-trough, Lord.

It was blood, it was
what you shed, Lord.

It shined.
It cast your image into our eyes, Lord. Eyes and mouth stand so open
    and void, Lord.

We have drunk, Lord.
The blood and the image that was in the blood, Lord.

Pray, Lord.
We are near. (101)

The title "Tenebrae," of course, invokes a Christological frame: for it is the name of the Catholic liturgical service included as part of evening prayers during the last three days of Holy Week. Centermost to the service is the sequential extinguishing of fifteen candles until the chapel is in total darkness, hence the name "Tenebrae"—Latin for "darkness." Thus worshippers symbolically mark Jesus's death—and prepare spiritually for Easter, the day of his rebirth when light was restored to the world. Not surprisingly, before Vatican II (1962–65) the ceremony was linked explicitly to a strong anti-Semitic predisposition. In the eighteenth century, Pope Benedict XIV declared: "On the three days before Easter, Lauds follow immediately on Matins, which in this occasion terminate with the close of day, in order to signify the setting of the Sun of Justice and the darkness of the Jewish people who knew not our lord and condemned him to the gibbet of the cross" (*New Advent Catholic Encyclopedia*). Indeed, Celan's poem was initially celebrated by what critic John Felstiner calls "sympathetic German" readers, valuing it especially as an "enhancement" of Christian liturgical practice—with little regard for, or interest in, Celan's own Jewishness (nor for his traumatic experiences during the Holocaust) (104). This bias persists, as evidenced by Hans-Georg Gadamer's 1997 translation of the same poem:

> We are near, Lord,
> Near and graspable.
>
> Grasped already, Lord,
> Clutching one another, as if
> The body of each of us were
> Your body, Lord.
>
> Pray, Lord,
> Pray to us
> we are near.
>
> Wind-awry we went there,
> We went there to bend
> Over hollow and ditch
>
> To the watering-hole we went, Lord.
>
> It was blood, it was
> What you poured out, Lord
>
> It glistened.
> It cast your image into our eyes, Lord,
> Eyes and mouth stand so open and empty, Lord.
> We have drunk, Lord.
> The blood and image that was in the blood, Lord.
>
> Pray, Lord
> we are near. (173)

In an accompanying essay, Gadamer shows his hand by posing, up front, what turns out to be a rhetorical question: Should "Tenebrae" "be understood as a blasphemous poem or as a Christian poem?" What follows is a detailed effort to show how the "poem approaches the ultimate intention of the Christian doctrine of the incarnation, *with which Christianity rises above the other known world religions: no God who is not human, no God who does not bear dying upon himself, can provide hope and redemption for the faithful*" (*Who Am I and Who Are You?*, 176; emphasis mine). Even as he stops short of arguing for the poem as an out-and-out celebration of Christian resurrection, Gadamer firmly insists on reading the poem as a sturdy testament to Jesus, our "Lord." Arguably this reading informs his decision to give us a poem that strikes a softer, more universalizing note—in contrast to Felstiner's viciously sharp-edged rendering. Consider, for example, the difference between Gadamer's "clutching" to Felstiner's "clawing," or Gadamer's "hollow and ditch" to Felstiner's "pit and crater," or the latter rendition's "wind-awry" to the former's "wind-skewed."

Indeed, Felstiner's translation is explicitly crafted to counter the kind of Christianizing narrative deployed by Gadamer. Deeply troubled by what he views as resistance to reading Celan as a "Jewish" poet, Felstiner focuses upon "Tenebrae" as the site of a kind of religious tug-of-war, with Jewishness finally winning the day. To this end, he proposes that although the poem may have been initially inspired by François Couperin's *Leçons de Ténèbres*, Hebrew Biblical references to darkness, including lines from Genesis, Exodus, Deuteronomy, and Job, are more resonant sources. Many of these suggestions strike me as rather oblique. But there is one Biblical text, not on Felstiner's list, with strong echoes. In Deuteronomy, Chapter 30, a portion which many Jews read annually as part of the Yom Kippur (Day of Atonement) morning service, God says: "Surely this Instruction which I enjoin upon you this day is not too baffling for you, nor is it beyond you. It is not in heaven that you should say, 'Who among us can go to the heavens and get it for us and impart it to us, that we may observe it?' Neither is it beyond the sea, that you should say, 'Who among us can cross to the other side of the sea, and get it for us and impart it to us, that we may observe it?' No, the thing is very close to you, in your mouth and in your heart to observe it" (Deuteronomy 30:11–14; *JPS*).

Importantly, these lines appear as part of a guaranteed reaffirmation of the sacred covenant binding the people of Israel to God in a privileged relationship—a promise that is most sorely tested by the Holocaust. These are the lines that I hear vibrating behind the poem's chilling opening and its haunting close: "Near are we, Lord / near and graspable. . . . Pray, Lord / We are near." The profound loss of relation—Celan's wrenching focus—is similarly at stake in

Lamentations, the Biblical poem of mourning, which is chanted during the darkest days in both the Jewish and Christian traditions. For Jews, Lamentations belongs to the Ninth of Av—the day commemorating the destruction of the Temple, the material manifestation of the sacred relationship, and the site requisite to its maintenance. For Christians, this Biblical poem of mourning belongs to Holy Week—the period when God's light is at its most remote. This is not to say, however, that Celan's poem is an ecumenical tribute to "Jewish-Christianity." On the contrary, it discovers how, in the wake of catastrophic destruction, neither system of meaning is accessible or useable.

The poem itself is notably sparse; not only are there few words, but the vocabulary is limited, and there is a great deal of repetition. This linguistic poverty is made especially vivid in Celan's poem when read alongside the German poet Hölderlin's long and densely worded hymn "Patmos," which famously begins: "God is near." Indeed, this very knowing (that God is near) sponsors Hölderlin's confident fluency. As Elaine Scarry explains, language depends on a stable connection between the would-be speaker and the material world he or she inhabits. A body in acute pain, one estranged from the world, necessarily resists language—for "pain actively destroys language" (42). Focusing on the image of acute corporeal anguish ("Grasped already Lord, / Clawed into each other, as if each of our bodies were / your body, Lord"), Felstiner insistently links these lines to the "brute fact" of a gas chamber ceiling "dug into by fingernails"—as portrayed in Alan Resnais's historic documentary *Night and Fog*, for which Celan wrote the German commentary. In Felstiner's account, this truth trumps any sort of Christological valence; he writes: "Not Golgotha now but Belzec, Sobibor, Chelmno, Maidenick, Treblinka, Auschwitz—sites of human being so broken that it bows down divinity" (Felstiner, "Clawed into Each Other," 202). But even as it is likely that this horrific site is folded into the poem, Felstiner's singular focus preempts a fuller understanding of just what makes "Tenebrae" so excruciating and its language so unbearable.

Celan is widely known as a "difficult" poet. Like Emily Dickinson, Gerard Manley Hopkins, or Gertrude Stein, Celan asks much of us. In a beautifully attentive essay, Joanna Klink patiently sorts out how Celan is more intensely oriented toward what she calls the "real" rather than the "actual." The actual is the literal appearance of things—such as fingernail markings on ceilings; the real is "the source of meaning which sponsors existence in this world" (Klink, "Introduction to Paul Celan," 3). As Klink understands it, "difficult poetries" are those linguistic artifacts that reach toward the real. To be sure, most poems have some vestiges of the actual; otherwise, they would be nearly unintelligible, a heap of syllables. In this poem, the actual informs our sense of the way it is engaged with the destruction of the Holy Temple,

Christ's crucifixion, and the Holocaust—all occasions in which sources of meaning were leveled. But to focus on any one of these elements—and to claim the poem as Jewish or Christian, or even Jewish-Christian—is to miss understanding Celan's real gift to us as a poet of what Klink calls "radical doubt." Celan writes out of the deep conviction that there is no single cultural, religious, or spiritual tradition upon which he can rely as a way of structuring his relation to the world. Neither the Jewish God's promise of eternal access nor the Christian God's promise of redemptive sacrifice holds up. Reading through the lens of Felstiner's translation, we encounter a stark instance of a writer whose travels into the Jewish Christian borderzone reveal a landscape more akin to a demilitarized zone, the site of a religious stalemate, where all prospects of exchange or dialogue are rendered impossible.

Taken together, Glatstein and Celan provide an important frame for understanding just why Sholem Asch's project was so incendiary. Asch took it upon himself to blur boundaries in the interest of imagining a redemptive solution to a world drenched in violence. His response ran counter to the fury and outrage that seized the larger Jewish community; it seemed, indeed, to smack of the naïve, assimilationist mindset that may have helped the disaster to spread so widely and quickly. Yet it was neither a matter of willful ignorance nor disregard that drove Asch to write not one but three lengthy novels in service of such "blurring" of boundaries between Judaism and Christianity. Quite the contrary. While living in France, he addressed a large anti-Nazi protest rally in 1933—and continued to live in Europe on and off until 1939, when it became clear that staying would be impossible. He also visited Palestine, first in 1927 and then again in 1939, and was warmly appreciative of the youthful, pioneering spirit he encountered there among the Zionist settlers. But he didn't embrace Zionism as a "solution to the perennial 'Jewish problem.'" As Dan Miron explains, Asch didn't view the emerging state as the only viable answer to an embattled Jewish consciousness. Even more important, he rejected the "weak" Messianism underwriting the establishment of a Jewish homeland, which argued for global salvation as the "natural" outcome of a seemingly "ordinary" turn of events. Instead, he believed ardently in what he calls "the messianic mystery" requisite to humanity's redemption (Miron, 186). This conviction informs his passionate endorsement of the "Jewish-Christian" ideal. Writing in his 1945 book-length essay, *One Destiny: An Epistle to the Christians*, he explains: "The first, most important reason for hatred of the Jews is the separate faith which has isolated them" (39). The best way to remedy this desperate state of affairs is to focus not merely on what Judaism and Christianity have in common (he has little interest in Islam) but to insist that the two religions need each other not just to survive, but to thrive:

> The preservation of Israel and the preservation of the Nazarene are one phenomenon. They depend on each other. The stream must run dry when the spring becomes clogged, and Christianity would become petrified if the Jews, God forbid, should cease to exist. And just as the spring loses its value, becomes spoiled and moldy when it has lost its mission and does not water the stream, so would Jewry itself become petrified, barren and dry if there were no Christendom to fructify it. ... The two are one. (9)

Asch does his part to reanimate this fluid model of relationship with his "Christological" trilogy, beginning with *The Nazarene*—the most readable of the three novels, but also the longest. Weighing in at almost seven hundred pages, *The Nazarene* makes for some demanding reading. It is a decidedly odd combination of historical fiction and fantasy, with an elaborate frame that ultimately collapses under the weight of the epic narrative it seeks to contain.

The Nazarene is difficult to summarize. The novel begins in Warsaw, sometime during the early part of the twentieth century. The narrator, a young, unnamed Jewish scholar, meets Pan Viadomsky, an elderly, notoriously untrustworthy, brilliant, and viciously anti-Semitic scholar of ancient Near East texts who needs help translating a mysterious, newly discovered scroll. But before learning any of this, the reader encounters a strange little meditation on a well-known *midrash* or exegetical story. *The Nazarene* begins thus:

> Not the power to remember, but its very opposite, the power to forget, is a necessary condition of our existence. If the lore of the transmigration of souls is a true one, then these, between their exchange of bodies, must pass through the sea of forgetfulness. According to the Jewish view we make the transition under the over-lordship of the Angel of Forgetfulness. But it sometimes happens that the Angel of Forgetfulness himself forgets to remove from our memories the record of the former world; and then our senses are haunted by fragmentary recollections of another life. (*The Nazarene*, 3)

This kind of preface notifies the reader that the narrative to follow is highly unreliable, and one should quickly dismiss any expectation of historical veracity. By foregrounding the highly speculative nature of the narrative, Asch quickly introduces elements of both uncertainty and speculative possibility into the narrative, key features of so much writing that dwells in the Jewish Christian borderzone. A few pages into *The Nazarene*, the fantastical element becomes quite pronounced. Inspired perhaps by James Joyce's deployment of "metempsychosis" in *Ulysses* (what Leopold Bloom defines as "the transmigration of souls" and "reincarnation") as the key concept in Joyce's characters' efforts to escape what Stephen Dedalus famously calls "the nightmare of history," Asch reaches for a similar strategy—in order to imagine an alternative to the history of horrific violence that has long colored Jewish Christian relations. In *The Nazarene*, Viadomsky reveals to the young Jewish translator that he is actually Cornelius, Ciliarch of the Antoni in Jerusalem, second in command to Pontius Pilate—reincarnated. And it was actually he who had "directed the execution of that mysterious personality whose nature has remained unexplained down to our day" (25). Unsatisfied with that cryptic disclosure, the Jewish translator presses for an answer and learns, to no surprise, that we are talking about "Yeshua of Nazareth, he who is called Jesus Christ." The next 625 pages are given over to an elaborate imagining of the young charismatic rabbi's rise from an especially compelling itinerant teacher to a political/religious force with which to be reckoned. But there is more. Imbuing this "Rabbi of Galilee" with nearly superhuman powers (even while he is wearing all the proper Jewish prayer garb and observing Jewish law and traditions), Asch tests that boundary between Jewishness and Christianity which depends on wholesale belief in or rejection of divine Incarnation. It is an arresting move but, importantly, not without precedent. As Shaul Magid demonstrates, the idea that the gulf between God and the human may be traversable and that perhaps God is "*in* the human" is woven throughout early Jewish mysticism. This belief becomes quite pronounced in the seventeenth century with the flowering of Hasidism (53–55). In other words, Asch extends an opportunity to reexamine entrenched assumptions about what sorts of beliefs are and are not "authentically" Jewish, affording a space where these kinds of revisionary accounts become more visible—so that some of the basic "mysteries" and precepts of the Roman Church might not be fully original and distinct from earlier Jewish precedents.

Asch's interest in expanding the Jewish Christian borderzone, a space where distinctions become less absolute, arguably overrides his aesthetic sensibilities. While Asch was typically known for his well-crafted but conventionally structured stories and novels, *The Nazarene* seems to demand of the reader something else altogether. So Asch goes to great lengths to dismantle that framing device that would have afforded the reader some sort of ironizing distance. About two-thirds through the novel, the Jewish translator/narrator is prodded by the "wizardry of Viadomsky's own memory" into recalling his own repressed past. That is, the frame collapses entirely as the narrator becomes an active participant. The rest of the novel is presented as a collaborative affair crafted out of both Viadomsky/Cornelius's recollections of the fateful days leading up to the crucifixion and those of the translator himself, who, it turns out, is a reincarnation of "Johannan," a pupil of "Rabbi Nicodemon" and a witness to Yeshua's "last days." While Asch doesn't go as far as making Johannan one of the Nazarene's actual disciples (even though his name conjures *Johannes* or John), he is certainly most sympathetic to the miracle worker's alluring vision.

To leave it here might suggest that Asch's representation of the Jewish Jesus is richly detailed but, finally, not all that different from other artists, including Chagall, who seek to disable anti-Semitism by reminding viewers of the shared history linking perpetrator to victim. Chagall's image of Jesus on the Cross is clearly situated in a readily recognizable Jewish environment: a *shtetl* complete with a burning *shtiebel* (synagogue) and a hunted man carrying a Torah scroll. As such, the Jewish-Christian divide remains intact. But Asch's account of Yeshua's last moments makes for something much more unruly, less easily contained. Dying on the cross, "the Rabbi lifted his eyes to heaven, and moaned bitterly, and from his lips came the cry: *Eli, Eli, lama sabachtani*" (685; "My God, My God, why hast thou forsaken me?"). So far, all is according to "history," as scripted in the New Testament. But this is not where the "Rabbi's" story ends. According to Asch, this famous cry is only Jesus's penultimate utterance and not his last words. *The Nazarene* reads thus: "Upon hearing the Rabbi's anguish an unidentified woman answers his cry with words of comfort: *tinoki, tinoki!* My little one! My little one!" The Rabbi's "despair" and "death terror" then give way to calm, and "with a last effort he looked up again at the heavens, and in a loud, clear voice called: 'Hear, O Israel, the Lord our God, the Lord is One.'" In other words, Jesus is saying the *Shema*, the best-known of Hebrew prayers, which is also traditionally uttered at the moment of death. With this radically inclusive scene, a scene that effectively unfixes Yeshua's identity as definitively either Jew or Christian—for here Jesus melds into Rabbi Akiva—Asch undoes the very binary that polemicists such as Rabbi Hirsch invoke in the service of making the case for Jewish exceptionalism. It is a decidedly disorienting conclusion, as Asch writes purposively against what Homi Bhabha might call a "homogenizing history," seeking to dismantle the powerfully destructive forces that all too often fuel efforts to secure religious difference. Asch's penchant for nuanced equivocations makes for a particularly sly conclusion, one that finds the narrator celebrating Jesus as a "saint" instead of recognizing him as either "Son of God" or a "righteous man" (in Yiddish, a *zaddik*). In this way, Asch neatly avoids landing hard on one side or the other of the religious divide.

As we have seen, the novel garnered harsh reviews in the world of Yiddish letters, while the English readership was mostly unruffled. Indeed, as noted previously, this incendiary borderzone narrative first appeared in English translation—a move that tested Asch's Yiddish readership sorely. But there is more to this decision than a desire for an expanded audience or a penchant for controversy, for it also reflects Asch's deep conviction that, although he was distressed by American materialism, he also believed that America was "the healthiest country in a sick world." It was, therefore, the most likely place for the "Jewish-Christian ideal" to take root and thrive. In the very last sentence of *One Destiny*, Asch makes it passionately clear why he was willing to risk so much by writing not just one but three novels exploring the Jewish Christian borderzone. He writes: "It is upon America, young and strong in her faith, that the mission has been placed of renewing the Jewish-Christian ideal as the only means of salvation for a world in flames. . . . In our own time, humanity has been brought to the level of beasts. The dignity of the human being, that sacred position bestowed on him by the Jewish-Christian religion, can be restored only by acceptance and submission to its teachings" (87–88). The word "submission" here is especially arresting because it suggests something about the kind of struggle that negotiating this landscape—which from certain vantages can be seen as a contact zone and from others as more like a combat zone—may entail. The contrast between Celan, for whom the nexus between Jewishness and Christianity bristles with hostility, and Asch, who casts this relation in restorative terms, helps set the stage for what is to follow in this study. In subsequent chapters, we will see how a widely diverse set of twentieth-century American poets map this terrain quite differently as they explore what the borderzone means for their own writing. In this way, each one deepens our understanding of this aesthetically productive, compelling, and emotionally charged hybrid construction.

But before turning to these poets, I want to look at one more novel—Henry Roth's *Call It Sleep*—as a paradigmatic example of a borderzone text that invites us to consider how religious unmooring may fuel aesthetic innovation. Now occupying a revered position in the annals of Jewish modernism, this celebrated novel has had an uneven history. Initially heralded as the great American inheritor of modernist innovation (*à la* James Joyce), *Call It Sleep* quickly fell out of print and virtually disappeared for twenty-five years. Alfred Kazin and Leslie Fiedler are widely credited with recovering the novel, championing it not merely as a dazzling example of American modernism but (to quote Fiedler) as a "specifically Jewish book, the best single book by a Jew about Jewishness written by an American." More recently, in *Call It English: The Languages of Jewish American Literature*, Hana Wirth-Nesher carefully elaborates on what makes the novel a distinctively *Jewish American* modernist achievement, detailing how linguistic and religious border crossing implicate each other. Although her account is much more nuanced and is not nearly as partisan as Fiedler's, Wirth-Nesher is similarly invested in addressing what makes the novel distinctively Jewish American—an ethnic or cultural identification. In her account, religion is largely a placeholder, or a marker, of a cultural position rather than a substantive entity. While this approach is certainly sanctioned by the long-standing accounts of modernism as a secular enterprise, I want to focus on how in Roth's world the boundaries between "Jewishness" and Christianity as distinct religions become increasingly porous—as he mines a new space for his expressive project.

Call It Sleep features a young boy, David Schearl, who, in the first part of the novel, is found basking in the glow of his mother's love. Cocooned in Yiddish, the mother tongue (rendered by Roth as beautifully lyrical English), this perfect dyad lives in exquisitely idealized intimacy. Set off against this maternal domain is the world of the Father: the world of the street, and the world of the *cheder* (the classic afternoon, supplementary Hebrew school) to which he trudges at his "father's decree." Each realm is rife with its own secrets, challenges, and promises. For David, who maps his world according to different linguistic registers, the *cheder* is linked to the mysteries of Hebrew, "God's tongue," thus holding out the potential for a God-sighting. Maybe even a conversation.

But instead of divine intimacy, David discovers a world where the light fades to a "blank pallor" and the stagnant air is filled with the rabbi's curses and the harsh whack of his rod. Although not nearly as irredeemably grim as Michael Gold's 1930 portrait of the *cheder* as a "hellhole of Jewish piety," Roth's rendition is still pretty bleak. Even the rabbi's praise for David's sharp mind, his "iron head" (in Yiddish, an *eiszener kop*), adds little in the way of either levity or relief. Indeed, poor Mendel, David's classmate—a loutish boy suffering from a large carbuncle on his neck, whose rendition of the Hebrew prayers is dismissively described as a "swift sputter of gibberish"—only adds to the bleakness of the place. After David tries (and fails) to keep up with Mendel's hurried chanting, David's thoughts begin to roam, ending up in a muddled meditation on that most impenetrable yet profoundly material aspect of Jewishness— dietary restrictions: "Why do you have to read chumish. . . . no fun. First you read, Adonai elahenoo abababa, and then you say, And Moses said you say, you mustn't and then you read some more abababa and then you say mustn't eat in the traif butcher store" (226). With this short but potent passage, Roth sketches out the aesthetic challenge awaiting his protagonist. The question guiding David's subsequent moves can be understood thus: How does one break out of a world confined by referential language (such as "elahenoo"/*Elohenu*, our Lord)—whereby the meaning of a given word takes precedence over its sound— and gain access to a region where sound and meaning are wholly of a piece ("abababa")? This is, as the linguistic theorist Roman Jakobson has noted, the province of poetry.[8]

An answer begins to take shape when the rabbi interrupts Mendel's droning and David's reverie to roughly parse the story found in Chapter 6 of the Book of Isaiah—which, happily enough, constitutes the bulk of the haftorah portion assigned to David for his upcoming Bar Mitzvah. Now, I am hardly the first among Roth's many readers to find the novelist's choice of text especially significant, but my take on its appeal is somewhat different. I am interested in how this narrative, relaying how Isaiah is called to prophecy, serves a conjunctive function affording David access to the Jewish Christian borderzone, an in-between space where he can realize his poetic potential. Not everyone, however, shares this perspective. Recently, for example, Josh Lambert declaims that "it is not the authority of Judaism or Christianity that makes the imagery in *Isaiah 6* meaningful"; rather, he argues, Roth's interest in Isaiah must largely be understood in the context of his use of modernist frameworks of allusion and referentiality (as in Eliot and Joyce). Following Wirth-Nesher's line of thought, Lambert argues that, with its focus on purification, redemption, and prophecy, the Biblical text appeals to Roth largely as a weighty mythic narrative that could provide the kind of authoritative scaffolding requisite to an epic endeavor the likes of *Ulysses* or "The Waste Land" (which Roth claimed to have memorized!). Furthermore, Lambert argues that Isaiah's preoccupation with purity (especially according to the rabbi's rather liberal translations of the biblical text) reflects Roth's deep interest in modernist juxtapositions of the pure and the nasty, the sacred and the profane (*Unclean Lips*, 84). This focus on linguistic strategy is instructive, but in the end, I think that such a reading shortchanges Roth's effort—for Roth is after more than just joining his august elders with a proto-mythic modernist narrative of his own. He is navigating new terrain in search of something closer to the radical, linguistic free-for-all that is the stuff of *Finnegans Wake*—that groundbreaking, supremely avant-garde text in which eloquence and nonsense are placed on a total collision course (and are indistinguishable).

The question is: How to get there? To be sure, this kind of revolutionary mode of making demands a visionary space free of constraints—including those imposed by religious institutions. For Roth, the answer begins with *Isaiah*, since his protagonist not only needs to find his way out of the narrows of Jewish doctrine (with all of its "musn'ts"), but he also needs to work through his desire for Christian otherness. Even as Christianity extends the promise of light—which his goyish/Irish-Catholic buddy Leo tells him is "'way bigger. Bigger den Jewish light'"—it could also seriously impede David's poetic growth (as I will suggest). Even as David is deeply drawn to Leo's Catholic "scapiller" ("scapular": a holy image worn like a necklace under one's shirt) engraved with a "'pitcher o' de Holy Muddy an Chil,'" this kind of smothering maternal attachment, with all of its cloying lyrical obligations, must be finally discarded if David is to realize his aesthetic objective (Roth's portrayal of the artist as a young boy). Happily enough, Leo refuses to give David his scapular, offering him, instead, an old rosary, telling him that "it's way way holier"—a sacred object better suited to David's story because the cross on the rosary prefigures the self-sacrifice and rebirth awaiting David, but it also underscores the necessarily solitary nature of his venture.

Isaiah figures large in Roth's imaginative process as a profoundly liminal text; David's *haftorah* portion, which includes Chapter 6 of *Isaiah*, as well as a bit of Chapter 9, is a strong example of a borderzone text, figuring large for both Judaism and Christianity. On the one hand, the narrative occupies an important role in Jewish thought, treasured especially by the rabbinic tradition, as a source of important proof texts when it comes to issues of social and economic justice. On the other hand, *Isaiah* is also central to Christian theology because the story of his call to prophecy culminates with the promise of Messianic redemption: "Surely a child has been born to us / a son has been given us / And authority has settled on his shoulders . . . " (9:6). *Isaiah*'s role in spreading Christian gospel is so central that, in the second century, the Catholic historian Jerome was moved to celebrate Isaiah not merely as Christ's prophet but as Christ's evangelist. The book's status as a site of religious contiguity is especially pronounced when it comes to liturgical practice. For example, Chapter 6, verse 3 is the primary source text for the *Kedushah* (Sanctification), the high point of the *Amidah* (the core of the Jewish prayer, where worshippers proclaim: "Holy, Holy, Holy / The Lord of Hosts! / His presence fills all the earth"). As it turns out, the very same verse, Isaiah 6:3, becomes a central part of traditional Eucharistic prayers (the *Sanctus*) and the source for many church songs. Just as the language of the *kedusha* (holy, holy, holy) is central to Jewish liturgy, so it appears as a key part of the Christian liturgy, as a hymn known as the *Sanctus* (antiphonally chanted three times during Mass: *Sanctus, sanctus, sanctus* [holy, holy, holy]).

As the novel moves toward its climatic conclusion, David catapults furiously between the Old World and the New, between Jewishness and Christianity, between maternal love and paternal rage, between the sacred and the profane—and the wordplay begins to go wild as these binaries begin to collide and collapse. Things finally come to a head when Albert (David's father) learns that his son has lied to the rabbi, telling him that his real father was a gentile "orghaneest." The oafish, and often violent, milkman turns on his son in rage. Driven both by mortal fear and spiritual longing, David rushes out into the street, snatches his father's metal milk dipper, and shoves it down between two of the streetcar rails, causing a huge electrical short circuit—actions inspired by his hero Isaiah, who was rendered pure when an angel seared the prophet's lips with a live coal—and electrocutes himself in the process. Despite the rabbi's mocking insistence that "God's light is not between car-tracks," David knows better—and is justly rewarded with a fantastic shower of sparks, followed by lyrically lush outpouring:

> *Power.*
> *Power, like a paw, titanic power*
> *ripped through the earth and slammed*
> *against his body and shackled him*
> *where he stood. Power! Incredible,*
> *barbaric power! A blast, a siren of light*
> *within him, rending, quaking, fusing his brain*
> *and blood to a fountain of flame, vast rockets in a searing spray!*
> *Power! . . .*
> *. . . Terrific rams of dark-*
> *ness collided; out of their shock space*
> *toppled into havoc. A thin scream wobbled*
> *through the spirals of oblivion, fell like*
> *a brand on water, his-s-s-s-s-ed— —*
>   (419; the passage goes on for a good twenty more lines)

To be sure, these are fine lines, but, frankly, they are not really all that remarkable or fresh. The alliterations, the repetitions, the images are the stuff out of which much of what we call poetry is made. But as we shall see, Roth is only getting started. As the street crowd swells around David's unconscious body, voices rise overlapping one another, words begin to tumble out, and the difference between nonreferent sound and referent sound begins to blur.

> Khir-r-r-r-f S-s-s-s. . . . Khir-r-r-r-f S-s-s-s. . . . Khir-r-r-r-f S-s-s-s. . . . (423)

What we are looking at—or sounding out—can be best described by invoking the poet-critic Charles Bernstein, who uses the term "anti-absorbative" to describe poetic strategies deployed in the interest of blocking—or short-circuiting?—the facile consumption of language. With its aggressive crudities and unpronounceable sonic eruptions, the final pages of *Call It Sleep* take us into new terrain—poetically and theologically (Bernstein, "Artifice of Absorption"). Anti-absorption can trouble not only our relation to language, but also our relation to those institutions in which that language operates.

This kind of trouble happens pointedly toward the very end of Roth's volcanic performance:

Kh-r-r-rf! S-s-s-s.

(Wall sunlit, white washed. Chadgodya! Moaned the man in the wires. One kid only kid. And the wall dwindled and was a square of pavement with a footprint in it—half green, half black, "I too have trodden there.")

It is more of the same: a collage of sounds and phrases that send us scurrying to parse. Among the linguistic debris, Jewish readers may find themselves latching onto a shard of the familiar when stumbling upon "*Chadgodya* . . . One kid only kid": fragments of the well-known song from the Passover Haggadah, which is, of course, typically sung at the end of the Seder. Immediately we think of Passover (*Chad Gadya*), Easter (Christ's rebirth), Jewishness and Christianity vying for the same space. But the dynamic is even more complicated and interesting: it turns out that the Haggadah (a composite work compiled and revised over at least eight centuries) is itself a borderzone text, a by-product of Jewish Christian dialogue. One might even call it a textual combat zone. "Dayyenu," for example, that most beloved hymn of praise that many Jews regard as *the* point of the Passover seder, may not only have been inspired by a Christian doxology predating the Hebrew song, but was actually crafted as a response to Christian complaints about ungrateful Jews (Yuval, *Two Nations*, 71). More generally, recent scholarship has shown that numerous parts of the now-standardized Haggadah began with Christian thinkers seeking a story to frame the new meanings linked to Passover. In response, the rabbis overwrote this effort, (re)claiming the holiday as an occasion to remember the Jewish exodus. In other words, the Christian Last Supper, in turn, gives birth to the modern Seder Haggadah in an effort to reclaim the Seder from its Christian appropriation. This theological tug-of-war results in textual production. Indeed, even "Had Gadya," which some read as an allegory celebrating Jewish survival triumphalism at the expense of all sorts of enemies, may have originated as a bit of Christian folklore (see Siedler, "Reading Chad Gadya," 337). In other words, the Haggadah (allusions to which are seeded throughout Roth's novel), like *Isaiah* itself, dwells in the borderzone of Jewish Christian interactions and interpenetrations. These are the texts that fuel Roth's astonishing foray into that most generative zone—a zone that is occupied to compelling and extraordinary ends by modernist poets Mina Loy and Gertrude Stein—who are the focus of my next chapter.

2
Lives of the Saints
Mina Loy and Gertrude Stein

Jewish saints? Jewish female mystics? If the latter notion strikes you as unfamiliar, it is for good reason. Among the world's three Abrahamic religions—Judaism, Christianity, and Islam—only Judaism can claim the dubious distinction of lacking a single one. This occlusion merits a range of explanations. But two reasons stand out. First, Jewish women were simply not allowed to study the texts comprising mystic knowledge. Second, because Jewish mysticism uniquely depends upon an understanding of physical purity as a precondition of divine intimacy, women—who are innately impure, according to *Halacha* (Jewish law)—are necessarily out of the running (see Koren, 2). This theological bias makes for a striking context within which to consider two modernist women poets—both of whom claim Jewishness in complex ways, and fashion their approaches to gender and mysticism. Their forays entail wandering into decidedly Christian territories.

I begin with Mina Loy, who stands out among other modernist poets for her interest not merely in spirituality but also theology. Indeed, unlike some of the other writers I consider who willfully venture into the Jewish Christian borderzone drawn by envy, longing, frustration, or the promise of rich aesthetic possibilities, Loy is born into it. The child of a mixed marriage—her father is a Hungarian Jew, while her British mother is an Evangelical Christian—Loy carves out an interstitial or "third-space," characterized by cultural "impurities," which in this instance entails explicitly violating religious boundaries. As explored extensively in "Anglo-Mongrels and the Rose," Loy's long auto-mythic poem, this space begets a mystical vision, culminating in a radical revisioning of Jesus as a hybridized, cross-religious figure. In this way, the poet makes vivid the religious fissures and differences that reside within presumably inviolate spaces.

Loy's investment in exploring interreligious spaces is clearly grounded in her personal narrative. It is much harder to say what occasions her friend and fellow modernist Gertrude Stein to reach so frequently for religious language, especially terms and phrases belonging to the Catholic lexicon. "Prayer," "Hymn," and "Saints," for example, all appear in various Stein texts to various ends. The turn is perhaps especially curious because she seems to be significantly less interested in considering Judaism—her familial identity/inheritance—either as an aesthetic or a conceptual resource. This steady disinterest notwithstanding, Stein is now routinely included on any list of important Jewish American writers.

What is true, however, is that in *Four Saints in Three Acts*, the libretto for "the most popular and the longest-running American opera in history" (Holbrook, 16), Stein offers an intimate reckoning with one of her "heroines," St. Teresa of Avila (one of the hardest-working mystics around, as we shall see). Offering a powerful counternarrative to the many accounts that focus on Teresa's often eroticized, ecclesiastically sanctioned "ecstasies," Stein's portrait of a decidedly happy and thoroughly grounded Teresa may provide an answer to all the feminist Jewish scholars who have longed to be, or at least be able to read about, a "Jewish nun."[1]

"Divine Irritation": Mina Loy's Take on Gertrude Stein's Spiritual Proclivities

Gertrude Stein is now, of course, a literary celebrity. But at the start of her career, hardly anyone understood what she was up to—hardly anyone, that is, except her fellow avant-gardist Mina Loy. Stein recalled their kinship thus: "Mina Loy . . . was able to understand without the commas. She has always been able to understand" (*Autobiography of Alice B. Toklas*, 124). The two poets met in Italy in 1911 while visiting Mabel Dodge Luhan, the American hostess extraordinaire, and they felt an immediate accord (Burke, *Becoming Modern*, 129–35). On Loy's part, this affinity was grounded not only in a shared interest in linguistic experimentation, in an affection for female saints and religious folk art, but also—at least according to Loy's biographer, Carolyn Burke—in the fact that Stein, unlike others in Loy's social circles, "made no attempt to hide her origins" and "was the first woman Mina had ever met who had the kind of intellect that she associated with being Jewish" (Burke, 130–31).

Burke's basis for this claim is unclear, but we do have "Gertrude Stein," a two-part essay Loy wrote in 1924 for the *transatlantic review* detailing her sense of what makes Stein so extraordinary. Framed as a letter to the journal's editor Ford Madox Ford, Loy begins with a verse epigraph consisting of a precisely drawn word-portrait, likening her subject to "Curie/ of the laboratory / of vocabulary." Invoking the revolutionary female chemist Marie Curie, discoverer of radium, Loy hones in on Stein's singularly innovative, sometimes violent, linguistic prowess. Some readers are drawn particularly to how this identification speaks to Stein's deep interest in science, while others note how Loy's portrait represents Curie as a "hardworking, outsider, celebrity-genius, as a way of highlighting Stein's own marginality" (Meyer; Goody, 139). Both accounts are true; but few readers have much to say about the distinctly Christological turn this poem takes at the end, as Loy celebrates Stein's drive "to extract a radium of the word." With that definite article, the notion of "Logos," as stated in John's Gospel, comes into play: "In the beginning was the Word, and the Word was with God, and the Word was God."

This fundamental linking between the human and the Divine by way of the embodied Word saturates Loy's essay—an essay which is interesting for what it says not only about Stein, but also about Loy's own aesthetic aspirations. After a quick nod to the metaphysician Henri Bergson as a potential way into Stein's processes of "disintegration and reintegration," Loy jettisons the contemporary for the classic, invoking the Bible to convey the enormous scope of Stein's project:

> Gertrude Stein possesses a power of evocation that gives the same lasting substance to her work that is found in *The Book of Job*.
>
> Take the colossal verse
>
> "He spreadeth the north over the empty-place, and hangeth the earth upon nothing."
>
> (*Last Lunar Baedeker*, 296)

It is an uncanny choice, for Job, like Genesis, is a cosmological tale—a work that relays how the world came into being. But the two texts are importantly different. In Genesis, humanity is given a starring role in the creation story; we are represented as God's sacred partners and are accorded special privileges denied to other sentient beings. In Job's world, however, humanity is but one among many of God's splendid accomplishments—and not an especially remarkable one, compared to the "vaults of snow" or "the expanses of the earth" that God has summoned into being. Moreover, unlike Genesis where human language contributes modestly but serviceably to God's creation (Adam names the animals, thus securing their identity), Job compels us to recognize our linguistic limits. All of Job's long-winded complaints are snuffed out by God's torrential response filled with soaring flourishes of rhetoric and arabesques of metaphor. Human beings just cannot compete with divine eloquence. Impressed with how happily Stein wore her "prodigious" bulk, Loy playfully cites Job ("Am I a sea or a whale?") as an "obvious" analogy to her subject (Burke, 129). But this biblical allusion does more than gesture toward Stein's corporeal presence, for Loy understands that Stein's project is singularly original: she is not interested in supplementing or enhancing someone else's cosmology. Instead, Stein is committed to using language as the essential site of world-making.

As the essay nears to a close, Loy takes modernism to task for not locating and activating sites of what she calls "divine irritation"—nodes of spiritual excitation—a failure she attributes to the "bankruptcy of mysticism." In the interest of celebrating Stein as a spectacular example of this sort of "irritation," Loy offers her own freewheeling reading of a line from a short piece by Stein, "A Sweet Tail (Gypsies)": "This is the sun in. This is the lamb of chalk." Deploying a reading strategy generated "by a dual army of associated ideas, her [Stein's] associations and one's own," Loy offers this gloss: "Of sun worship. Lamb worship. Lamb of, light of, the world. (Identical in Christian symbolism.) Shepherd carries lantern. The lantern = lamb's eyes, Chalk white of lamb. Lantern sunshine in chalk pit = absolution of whiteness = pascal lamb = chalk easter toy for peasants" (259). Yet even as both poets were drawn to Christian tropes and shared an affection for religious knickknacks, this gloss speaks more to Loy's interest in Christian concepts about divine materiality than to Stein's own procedures. Loy herself suggests as much, backing off with "apologies to Gertrude Stein, who may have intended the description for . . . a daisy. The sun as a center, chalk as petal white, and the lamb an indication of the season of the year." Indeed, for all of its various insights into Stein's linguistic prowess, the essay also reflects powerfully on some of what, five years earlier, might have inspired Loy to write "Anglo-Mongrels and the Rose"—a long lyric sequence (sometimes described as an "auto-mythography") detailing the psychosocial challenges and theo-poetic opportunities afforded by her mixed religious lineage. Featuring, among other events, a transformative mystical visitation and a recounting of the poet's own birth, the poem answers Loy's call for works of art that "track intellection to the embryo," to thought's preconceptual genesis.

"Anglo-Mongrels and the Rose"

By 1921, when Loy began writing her long poem, she was forty years old and had lived in at least six different cities, some of them more than once, on two continents. Perhaps this nomadism underwrites her affinity for her father, described early on as a "wondering" (rather than a "wandering") Jew—one of many examples of how Loy tweaks and twists anti-Semitic slurs/stereotypes in the interest of crafting her own hybrid theology (excavating a space for her own hybrid, bi-religious identity). Indeed, hybridity is immediately at issue when pressed to simply describe this eccentric and singular achievement. Some opt for a "lyric sequence," and some call it a "mythic-biography in verse," while others prefer "auto-mythology"—even though the entire poem is presented in the third person (Tuma, 187). No matter the term, however, each designation is tentative—since ultimately the poem, like the poet who is also its primary subject, doesn't fit neatly into most operative categories, either aesthetic or religious.

The poem consists of three parts, each featuring a different family member. "Exodus" (aka Sigmund Lowy, the poet's father) starts things off. Without any sort of preamble, we are plunged into the story of this borderzone habitué, who, at eighteen, has spent the night "under an oak tree/bordering on Buda Pest," having been shunned by his "sinister foster parents." From the outset, Loy's linguistic prowess is on extravagant display. Prior to "Anglo-Mongrels," Loy's style tended toward a striking mix of passionate but highly wrought archaisms and cool abstractions; so the avalanche now of clumsy stanzas, alliterative composite constructions ("man-mountain," "cardiac cataracts"), clanging rhymes ("gluttony/humanity"), and groan-worthy puns ("Jewish/juvenile," "Jew/lieu," "circumcised/circumspect")—which has been usefully described as a "mongrel poetics"—suggests that she is indeed up to something new (see Frost, Perloff). One way to understand this high-wire linguistic performance is by returning to Julia Kristeva's account of the "foreigner" and his linguistic proclivities: "Lacking the reins of the maternal tongue, the foreigner who learns a new language is capable of the most unforeseen audacities when using it—intellectual daring and obscenities as well" (31). Loy's description of her father, who, upon emigrating to England, becomes a high-end tailor, resonates uncannily. Known for "speaking fluently 'business English' / to the sartorial world," Exodus's capacity for "jabbering . . . conundrums of finance" is a widely shared skill to which "unlettered immigrants are instantly initiate" (115; again trading in a Jewish stereotype).

One wonders if the cadences of these "jabbering," "unlettered" outsiders unleashed Loy's striking turn toward freewheeling linguistic innovation. More pointedly, we might ask if Yiddish, a polylingual construction, is part of the mix. Of course, her Hungarian Jewish father would have at least had more than a passing knowledge of the *mame loshen*. And we know that just before starting to draft "Anglo-Mongrels," she spent a year in New York—Greenwich Village, to be exact—where she would have discovered what Ariel Resnikoff describes as "the massive civilization of New York Yiddishland," an epicenter of Yiddish arts and culture during the first part of the twentieth century (Resnikoff, "Home Tongue," 103). Alas, there is no hard evidence that Yiddish is an active ingredient—but this absence doesn't deter Resnikoff from proposing, albeit speculatively, that we read Loy as a "crypto-Yiddish modernist," one of a host of poets whose poly-glossic innovations are colored by Yiddish soundings (103).

Resnikoff's move is wonderfully expansive, inviting us to consider what long-standing accounts of the avant-garde might look like if Jewishness were to be made more central. Such recalibrating is clearly in order when it comes to addressing Loy's turn toward Jewishness—a shift that some readers have found, curiously enough, rather bewildering.[2] They wonder what piques her interest since, prior to 1921, she seemed largely occupied with sorting out a relationship to Futurism and other emerging strains of the avant-garde. But, as I see it, this interest is easily attributed to several events and experiences. To start, we should note that, following custom, Loy's formal religious education fell to her mother, Julia Bryan Lowy—a devout Evangelical. Nonetheless, her father never disavowed his Jewish heritage—even though a mixed marriage between an English middle-class woman and a Hungarian Jewish refugee would have been highly unusual, and he was no doubt subjected to all kinds of pressure to convert (Burke, 16). His resolve is especially striking in light of his own exilic narrative. At the start of "Anglo," we learn that Sigmund/Exodus did not flee violent persecution; rather, he was drummed out of town by his own family who saw him as an economic drain. This was despite the fact that his grandfather, Isaac Lowy, "a great and a just man" (117), was a major player in the Hungarian Jewish community. A bit of research reveals that Isaac Lowy, Loy's great-grandfather, helped establish and build the Neolog Dohany Street Synagogue, now the largest synagogue in Europe, home of Neolog Judaism—a precursor of Conservative Judaism. In other words, Loy came from Hungarian Jewish aristocracy; she always knew, to some extent, that she wasn't a full-fledged member of the British middle class to which her mother so desperately sought access—an aspiration that required a certain amount of formulaic anti-Semitism, as evidenced in the episode "Jews and Ragamuffins of Kilburn," in which Loy recalls being afraid of the Jews "who killed Jesus/and are bound for Hades . . . crawling up her socks."

All of this seems to get stirred up when Loy's life becomes especially peripatetic. After spending a year in New York Loy moves to Berlin where, as Cristanne Miller explains, Jews dominated the cultural scene. Indeed, one of the city's foremost literary and political journals was simply called *Der Jude—The Jew*. Moreover, Miller suggests that Loy's live-in boyfriend, simply identified by her biographer as a poor "young Russian poet," was Jewish (Miller, 168). Ultimately, her turn toward Jewishness seems overdetermined, the result of a confluence of events. It may be that she was getting fed up with Italian Futurism—which had been an important aesthetic stimulant but increasingly was becoming embroiled with Fascism. Claiming Jewishness offered her a clear way out of this troubling affiliation. The lure of an exotic countercultural identity may have also been a factor, for Loy was always drawn to the margins. But neither of these scenarios really accounts for the decidedly *religious* tenor of her interest in Judaism; indeed as I understand it, Jewishness becomes a way of her renegotiating a relationship to Christianity, that constrictive maternal legacy horribly bound up with genteel expectations and bourgeois restrictions. Christ, however, aka "Gentle Jesus," is kind, forgiving, and exceptionally accessible—and well worth redeeming. And as young "Ova" (Loy's pseudonym) is pleased to learn, he even eats with his fingers! "He dipped his hand in the sauce-tureen/and allowed his disciples to do the same" (149). With realignment on her mind, the poet seeks to reclaim the "rose"—with all of its saccharine linkings to "Lipton teas," "English rose," and everything else tinged with "pink paralysis"—recasting it instead as a symbol belonging to what she imagines as a "composite" mystical tradition:

> the rose
> that grows
> from the red flowing
> from the flank of Christ
> thorned with the computations
> of the old
> Jehovah's gender
> Where Jesus of Nazareth
> Becomes one-piece
> With Judas Iscariot
> In this composite Anglo-Israelite. (132)

Drawing perhaps on iconography found in such medieval texts as those by Albertus Magnus (Saint Albert the Great), who reads the red rose bush as an earthly manifestation of the passion of Jesus, Loy sutures together her Jewish and Anglo-Christian heritage, presenting herself as "this composite Anglo-Israelite" and highlighting the role played by Judas Iscariot—the twelfth apostle who infamously betrayed Jesus, thereby helping the latter realize his divine mission. It is a linking that lasts a lifetime. Twenty years later, while living in New York's Bowery, she offers a much drier version of this sort of interfaith alliance, writing: "When the gentile world falls over its self it is usual for the

Jews to come to the rescue. When it required a savior they nailed up a Christ" ("Notes on Religion," 15).

But Loy is after more than religious transgression, so often a largely destructive impulse fueled by a desire to shock or disable. Her flair for crossing religious boundaries is central to her own wholly distinctive crafting of what one scholar (Plate) calls her "religious aesthetic"—a world of meaning grounded in material experiences and memories. To make this world vivid, she assembles or "composes" new constructions out of bits and pieces of old mythologies, symbols, and narratives (Plate). Even as these craftings are deeply compelling, she isn't interested in demarcating a fixed space for a third religion, a new Jewish-Christian hybrid, to be formally practiced. (That effort will be left to Paul Levertoff, who is featured in Chapter 5.) Instead, she seems more interested in the *process* of making, rather than in the final product; in the art of mythologizing, rather than in the well-polished myth. These predispositions go some way in explaining why she made so little effort to actually publish her work, leaving her readers to plumb the chaotic sets of fragmented files housed at Yale's Beinecke Rare Book and Manuscript Library, hoping to piece together usable versions of poems, novels, or essays.

That said, when it came to formal religious affiliations, Christian Science seemed to suit her best. Interestingly enough—especially for purposes of this discussion—the movement is itself a fascinating example of a full-blown borderzone religious culture. For during the first few decades of the twentieth century, Christian Science emerged as an attractive alternative for American Jews who found their own tradition stultifying, spiritually as well as socially. Moreover, as Ellen Umansky explains, "Jews who began attending Christian Science meetings were repeatedly told that one did not have to abandon Judaism to receive the blessings of Christian Science and that joining Christian Science would in fact make one a better Jew" ("Ray Frank," 15). In other words, one could improve one's lot—socially, spiritually, and conceivably physically too (since Christian Science promised relief from all kinds of ailments)—without betraying the tribe or having to sever familial ties.

To be sure, as a product of a mixed religious union, Loy didn't necessarily need the sort of escape route that Christian Science provided to so many Jewish others. But its stance on gender might have held special appeal. Founded by Mary Baker Eddy, Christian Science represented a real alternative to both nineteenth-century Judaism and even to normative Christianity, which was/is decidedly ambivalent about women claiming religious expertise. Moreover, Christian Science is keenly focused on questions of the relation between the body and the spirit, one of Loy's central preoccupations. Unlike her mother's version of Christian doctrine, which regards the body as an impediment to spiritual fulfillment, Christian Science maintains that although the "Spirit is sovereign," the body must not be negated.[3] For the body is "the ground where the spirit must be proved" (Armstrong, "Loy and Cornell," 210). In other words, corporeality is the site or the means by which the invisible (the Spirit) is made visible. With this caveat in mind, "Anglo-Mongrels" registers as a sort of spiritual diary or journal—something perhaps along the lines of St. Ignatius Loyola's journal, Augustine's *Confessions*, or St. Teresa's *The Life of Teresa of Jesus*—as Loy maps her childhood onto the story of Jesus, offering an idiosyncratic variation on *Imitatio Christi*. For example, in a section called "Illumination," we read how, after being betrayed by her father (aka Judas Iscariot, who tricks her into prematurely opening a gift, thereby violating established social boundaries), she flees to the garden (an English suburban variation on Gethsemane) where she is gifted with a divine vision: "This saint's prize" that promises a way of enduring "the long nightmare" stretching well into her future, including years of suffering through a bad marriage and decades of battling social restraint. At this turn, Ova/Loy clearly identifies with Christ, whom she "accepts . . . as the sacrificial prototype" (Loy, 167).

The difference, of course, is that Loy never reaches an epiphanic moment, nor is the journey linear. Above all, she is a seeker, restlessly sorting out the various alternatives, resisting dogma at every turn. To leave it here might suggest that Loy commits herself wholly to Christianity (albeit one of its quirkier strains) despite its flaws, oversights, or theological challenges. But Loy is anything but a follower or a routine believer. So even as Christian Science affords some spiritual ballast, it is only a partial solution, particularly limited in light of its rigid account of the body as subordinate to the Spirit. For Loy, as numerous critics have noted, meaning lies in the concrete details, in the material moments that constitute a singular existence. This focus, central to her status as a habitué of the Jewish Christian borderzone, is most fully at play in "Ova Begins to Take Notice"—one of the most evocative and dynamic episodes constituting "Anglo-Mongrels." The section defies prosaic summary, since so much of the pleasure and the meaning depend upon Loy's linguistic skill. So here is just a sketch: on the cusp of her second birthday, Ova acquires a deeper kind of consciousness through a series of key events. These events are quite ordinary, typical of most childhoods, but Loy assigns to them extraordinary significance. First, while playing outside she loses sight of a "crimson ball" when it rolls under a clump of ivy. This ball, which turns out to be a reel of red thread, is an early iteration of the rose, an important symbol in Loy's sacred lexicon. But at this stage of imaginative unfolding, her focus is on "red-/ness" itself—sheer color without fixed meaning. This attunement to color is, as Walter Benjamin suggests, uniquely known by young children who experience it as wonderfully unfixed; color is "the basis for creating the interrelated totality of the world of imagination," a world charged with spiritual valences (Benjamin, "A Child's View of Color," 50–51).

Experienced as pure sensation, "redness," as Ova knows it, has yet to be corralled into service of symbolic meanings and is thus "inadequate to the becoming of a rose" (Loy, 137). This pre-verbal space is rich with spiritual potential, for the sorts of distinctions informing most religious doctrines have yet to take hold. The spiritual/theological implications of this radical openness are wittily played out when Ova, just on the cusp of language, "find[ing] nothing objective new / and only words / mysterious," overhears her mother and her nurse talking about her baby sister's digestive problems. Ever on the lookout for a new word, Ova watches as "iarrhea" 'materializes' before her, and then she hears "It is / quite green." Green diarrhea: the perfect "divine irritant," for the concept, seeded by "an obsessional / colour-fetish," sets off an avalanche of (semantic) associations as the green excrement gives way to the "souvenir" of the ball that disappeared into the (green) ivy, which then brings into focus a "cat's eye" (chrysoberyl) brooch pinned to a caregiver's "bended bust":

And instantly
This fragmentary
Simultaneity
Of ideas

Embodies
The word

Within these nursery walls, all sorts of binaries get disabled: the differences between the sacred and the profane, the esoteric and the exoteric—and perhaps even Jewish and Christian doctrine—are suspended, positions which conventionally depend upon distinguishing between maintaining either that the flesh is made word or that the word is flesh. With this move, Loy wades into the deep waters of nondenominational mysticism—a space that Elliot Wolfson, a renowned scholar of Kabbalah, has increasingly made central to his work, as he explores the interstices between Christian and Jewish mysticism. In "Judaism and Incarnation: The Imaginal Body of God," an essay written expressly to advance interfaith relations, Wolfson takes on one of the most formidable sites of Jewish Christian difference, that of incarnation: "the belief that for the salvation of the world, the Son of God, while remaining fully divine, became truly and fully human" (O'Collins, 103). He argues that, while there is nothing in Judaism precisely equivalent to the idea that the human and the divine are united in the body of Jesus, that doesn't mean that Judaism wholly dismisses the idea of an embodied or incarnate God. Taking a historical approach, Wolfson tracks a Docetic strain in Jewish thought advancing the claim that the physical representation of the divine is not in itself "real," but rather the expression of something "real" in the spiritual plane (Wolfson, 241). As the argument progresses, it becomes clear that there are grounds for something like a Jewish incarnational theology. But as Wolfson works to explain the "secret of incarnation in Judaism, a mystery of transcendence that the imagination alone is capable of considering immanent," his sentences begin, necessarily, to fold in upon themselves, making for increasingly convoluted formulations. Finally, he concludes: "In the end, the Christological doctrine of incarnation is not, as Paul surmised, a stumbling block particularly to the Jews, but rather to anyone whose religious sensibility has not been properly nourished by the well spring of poetic imagination." Citing the French philosopher Gaston Bachelard, Wolfson adds: "To enter into the domain of the superlative, we must leave the positive [i.e., the concrete, the real] for the imaginary. We must listen to the poets" (254). In other words, if you don't understand the concept, it is not because you are Jewish, but because of a failure of imagination; the answer lies in poetry.

So we return to Loy and the final installment of "Anglo-Mongrels and the Rose" to find perhaps not clarity, but certainly insight into the metaphysics of incarnational imaginings, religious fashionings crafted in the Jewish Christian borderzone. She begins with a macro-view of religion, which has long rigidly insisted that the body, "the aboriginal/muscle pattern," be distinguished from the spirit, the fallout of "its ominously/cruciform completion." Yet this binary is defied by the very shape of the body, crafted in "the image and likeness of Deity" (Loy, 172). Loy then takes aim at those who promote such systemic hierarchies, by sharply twisting "transubstantiation" (the doctrine underwriting the Eucharistic ritual whereby bread and wine embody God's true presence) into "dissubstantiation"—a purposely clumsy coinage suggesting a process by which the body becomes purely symbolic—pure Logos, without a shred of flesh in sight:

Theological tinkers
And serious thinkers
Attacked the problem
Of dissubstantiation

Yet these clunky, terribly conspicuous rhymes, which underscore the inescapable materiality of human existence, belie the efforts of "Spiritual drapers/Popes and fakirs and shakers" who "let it [the body] appear to disappear." For it seems that despite all such efforts, people (of "a happy-go-lucky vulgarity") insist on keeping "the unprintable word" (that is, God) in circulation. Then without explanation, we read how amidst this religious mayhem "there arose another/greater than Jehovah/The Tailor"—a kinder incarnation of her own father, who ends up resembling something like a "Jewish Jesus."[4] "Despised" and "ostracized," perhaps for choosing an "occupation all too feminine" (thus activating an old Jewish stereotype), Exodus is superbly gifted with being able to make God's presence manifest in "creasings . . . the latest things in trouserings" (175).

At this point, my readers may be scratching their heads, asking how this all sorts out. If Loy/Ova is a Christ figure, betrayed by her Jewish father, how can the latter also embody Christ? Although this may not suffice, I can only say that Loy, as a religious artist, is more interested in revealing spiritual truths than in promoting rigid identifications or allegories that depend upon and perpetuate firm religious boundaries. Twenty years later, this mystical strain becomes quite urgent when she moves back to New York and she devotes herself to celebrating those homeless and impoverished denizens of the Bowery in poetry and art. These are her "angel bums"—wholly embodied, divine emissaries whose wisdom is all but buried under so much urban grime. Even as such attunement certainly owes something to Christian Science, it is hardly an orthodox rehearsal of Mrs. Eddy's teachings. Instead, it reflects Loy's own idiosyncratic but compelling focus on the interstitial spaces between the real and imagined, the body and the spirit, the revealed and the concealed—for this is where incarnational meaning is to be found.

Here, then, is "Chiffon Velour," one of my favorite poems, a luminous example of Loy's vision:

She is sere.

Her features
Verging on a shriek
Reviling age,

Flee from death in odd direction
Somehow retained by a web of wrinkles.

The site of vanished breasts
Is marked by a safety-pin.

Rigid
At rest against the corner-stone
Of a department store.

Hers alone to model
The last creation,

Original design
Of destitution.

Clothed in memorial scraps
Skimpy even for a skeleton.

Trimmed with one sudden burst
Of flowery cotton
Half her black skirt
Glows as a soiled mirror;
Reflects the gutter—
A yard of chiffon velours. (186)

In addition to being a poet, a painter, and a collage artist, Loy was also known as a high-end dress designer. A clipping from the *Pittsburgh Press* (April 3, 1921) declares that the latest designs from "Madame Mina Loy," including a frock stitched together out of real horse hair and lace, would surely appeal to those who "seek to be different" (https://www.newspapers.com/clip/15430648/mina-loy-fashion-designs/). These eccentric creations, which so often entailed weaving together the coarse and the fine, register yet another expression of her ongoing effort to make manifest the relation between the body and the spirit, the material and the transcendent. It is no wonder, then, that a decrepit woman decked out in assorted scraps catches her eye. For Loy, this is what the sacred looks like. Part diaphanous, part opaque, the poem's title speaks to Loy's long interest in the region of the mystical—the space between the revealed and the concealed. Spare but syntactically complete (unlike the fractured lines of earlier works), the poem accords its subject full respect, while avoiding sentimentality. She is simply "sere"—a lexical choice that allows for "seer" to surface and flicker. Walking the runway between life and death, this divine incarnation is beyond sexuality, in the most conventional sense, yet fully embodied. An incarnation of the divine, she embodies the absence that is presence: "the site of vanished breasts/Is marked by a safety-pin." Unlike so many female saints and mystics who are often portrayed as ripe and fetchingly virginal, Loy represents a vagrant wearing a splendidly outrageous set of rags as the perfect "model," both in the sense of a dressmaker's form and that of a divine ideal. The daughter of "The Tailor," who "achieves/the unachievable Act of the Apostles" by clothing the human body, thus making "the cruciform scourge disappear," goes her Jewish father one better, giving us a glimpse of body and the spirit made whole. Presence on the precipice of transcendence, utterly unconstrained by religious boundaries: a black skirt glowing like a "soiled mirror," and "a yard of chiffon velour."⁵

In 1911, while both were traveling in Italy, Mina Loy and Gertrude Stein became friends. To be sure, the two artists were wildly different. Stein was large and squarish, while Loy was lithe and lean. Stein had just met Alice B. Toklas, and was at the start of a lifelong relationship; Loy's marriage to her first husband was fraying, and she was soon to embark on a life filled with various romantic entanglements. Stein was beginning a writing career that would amount to an impressive body of work. Assisted by Alice, Stein made sure that her work was well-produced and carefully preserved. Loy, by contrast, was busy painting, writing, trying her hand at various forms of material art, but rather indifferent to the business of publication or distribution. As a result, her work all but disappeared for many years, and some of her most compelling work—including "Anglo-Mongrels and the Rose"—is still out of print. Finally, Stein was staunchly secular. Born into a highly assimilated Jewish American family, she never formally belonged (at least as an adult) to any sort of religious organization. By contrast, Loy was an actively identified religious seeker. What drew them together, however, was not only an interest in linguistic experimentation, but a devotion to Catholic saints, and a passion for religious artifacts. That said, Loy was drawn to Stein, according to Burke, precisely because Stein "was the first woman Mina had ever met who had the kind of intellect that she associated with being Jewish"; moreover, "Gertrude didn't hide her Jewish origins (unlike others in their circle)" (Burke, 131).

Therefore, it is perhaps surprising to learn that comparatively little has been said about Stein's interest in religion, especially Catholicism, even though the words "Prayer," "Hymn," and of course "Saints"—all appear in various texts and to various ends. Ulla Dydo, among Stein's strongest readers, suggests, without elaborating further, that liturgical rhythms course throughout: "Her work, though it is not religious, recalls the formula of prayer" (22). But this observation is all but drowned out by the enormous amount of critical attention produced in the interest of sorting out her position as a secular Jew.

Gertrude Stein and Jewishness

Routinely included on virtually every list of "Jewish Writers" (such as the "Jewish Women's Archive" and others), Stein is widely recognized as an important

Jewish American writer. Moreover, poets and critics alike have worked hard to make a case for her contributions to Jewish aesthetics. The contemporary poet Jerome Rothenberg, for example, includes an excerpt from her 1927 piece "Patriarchal Poetry," to illustrate his larger argument about the antinomian function of Jewish verse. Other readers such as Maria Damon understand Stein as a distant relation to other "crypto Yiddishists" (including Zukofsky), in search of ways to unmoor language from cultural and syntactic constraints (218). More recently, Amy Feinstein has approached the question of what Jewishness means for Stein's work, by demonstrating the range of ways the poet puts the word "Jew" into play, including this wonderfully disruptive bit from "A Sonatina Followed by Another" (1921):

> I took a piece of pork and I stuck it on a fork and I gave it to a curly headed jew jew jew.
> I want my little jew to be round like a pork, a young round pork with a cork for his tail. (Cited in Feinstein, 155)

At once subversive and conservative, Stein not only upends Jewish dietary laws, but takes back the word "Jew" at a moment when anti-Semitic slurs are *de rigueur*, using it as a term of affection (addressed perhaps to Alice, whom elsewhere she refers to as "my little Hebrew")—even as she plays into certain normative expectations about domesticity and romance (Feinstein, 156–57).[6]

But Judaism as a religion—a source of ritual and spiritual meaning—is not part of the mix. Stein's family of origin were upper-class German Jews who warmly and profitably embraced America as the proverbial land of opportunity. After a sojourn in Baltimore, followed by a year in Vienna—so that the Stein children could expand their cultural horizons—the family moved to Oakland, California, a locale Brenda Wineapple calls "a frontier suburb" (20). While the family was anything but religious, they did join the First Hebrew Congregation of Oakland and enrolled Gertrude in "Sabbath School." While we have no record of her actually attending the school (it seems that young Gertrude spent much of her time hiking around the California foothills), it is interesting to think a bit more about what this institutional affiliation might have meant for her. "First Hebrew" (as it was known) was an "über-Reform" congregation, which is to say that its leaders advanced a vision of Judaism as a universal, ethical, and highly rational system of belief grounded in historical experience. Practically speaking, the congregation eschewed Hebrew and had little use for those archaic, ritualistic trappings such as dietary restrictions or traditional prayer garb. Moreover, they were remarkably inclusive, at least when it came to gender—for First Hebrew is credited with hiring Rachel ("Ray") Frank, known as America's first woman "rabbi." Although never formally ordained, Frank was a lead teacher in the Sabbath School and was a highly regarded speaker in the larger Oakland community (https://jwa.org/encyclopedia/article/frank-ray). Again, we have no record as to whether or not the Stein family ever attended services, lectures, or classes at the Temple to which they paid dues; such casual indifference would hardly set them apart from so many other American Jewish families. (But it is exciting to think that Gertrude might have at least met this iconoclastic Jewish woman.)

Stein's sturdy secularity informs her essay "The Modern Jew Who Has Given Up the Faith of His Fathers Can Reasonably and Consistently Believe in Isolation" (1896). Writing at age twenty-two, Stein takes a remarkably measured approach to her subject. She argues that the "modern Jew" has little to do with the "faith of his fathers"; "religious practice is not only impractical in this bustling nineteenth century life," but "has become a hard-shell of formalism with all the soul fled and the living substance gone" (424). That said, Jewishness remains for Stein a necessary and irrefutable category of identity. Drawing on the language of scientific racism that was the mode of the times, Stein writes: "the Jew's loyalty to Judaism is not that of obedience to any temporal power, nor to a formation of any kind of government. It is a race-feeling, an enlargement of the family tie" (426). Recognizing the need for free social and economic intercourse with the non-Jewish world, Stein advocated a strong injunction against intermarriage: "The Jew shall only marry the Jew . . . in the sacred precincts of the home, in the close union of family and kinsfolk, he must be a Jew with Jews; the Gentile has no place there" (423). She departs thus from the Anglo-American writer Israel Zangwill, who was a neighbor when Stein first moved to London. For, as famously celebrated in his 1909 play *The Melting Pot*, Zangwill advocated for no-holds-barred assimilation, including interfaith unions. Stein, however, is less accommodating. Indeed, this rigidity may seem out of keeping in light of Stein's radical approach to language and writing. But she is staunchly nonconformist, even when it comes to the expectations of the avant-garde.

So what does Stein contribute to our understanding of the Jewish Christian border crossing and its aesthetic possibilities? Unlike some of the other writers I consider, she doesn't seem to find her Jewish identity particularly burdensome or at odds with her aesthetic ambitions (as with Zukofsky). Nor is her interest in the religious Other fueled by any strong religious or spiritual longings (e.g., Levertov or Loy), or feelings of lack or shame (Shapiro). If anything, she is remarkably indifferent to the American Protestantism that characterized her world until she moved to Europe in 1901, writing, "After all one is brought up not a Christian but in Christian thinking . . . " (*Everybody's Autobiography*, 243). But when she travels to Spain for the first time in 1912 with her new lover Alice B. Toklas, something happens. Many years later, when asked about her creative process, Stein explains, "I wander around. I come home and I write" (Dydo, 26). During that first spring of their travels, she and Alice lose themselves to wandering, developing a special interest in visiting cathedrals. Writing in *The Autobiography of Alice B. Toklas*, Stein recalls their adventures thus:

> In these days Gertrude Stein wore a brown corduroy suit, jacket and skirt, a small straw cap, always crocheted for her by a woman in Fiesole, sandals, and she often carried a cane.... This costume was ideal for Spain, they all thought of her belonging to some religious order and we were always treated with the absolute most respect. (109)

The description begs a question: Might we suspect Stein of playing the part of a religious tourist—a curious interloper who enters into sacred spaces, such as churches or cathedrals, treating them like museums or performance halls? To be sure, she had a taste for religious artifacts: take a look at any one of Man Ray's famous portraits depicting the artist at home in her salon, and note just how many crucifixes—some of them quite large—are prominently displayed. But as contemporary writer Navid Kermani demonstrates, not all travelers are alike. In *Wonder Beyond Belief: On Christianity*, Kermani—an actively identified Muslim—offers an extraordinary example of how one can admire and learn from the religious Other, without negating either distance or difference. Moreover, the distance can afford real advantages, allowing for new meanings and interpretations to make themselves known. In a series of what he calls "meditations" on a specific set of Christian visual images, many of which adorn the walls of some of Europe's greatest Cathedrals, Kermani eloquently wrestles with the attachments and estrangements they provoke. Drawn, for example, to Guido Reni's "Crucifixion," he admits to struggling with the "zest that Catholic art has for Jesus' suffering," tracing his distaste to Shia's celebration of martyrdom. This self-knowing enables Kermani to identify and treasure what is unique about Reni's decision not to fetishize Christ's broken body, and instead to focus on the moment as one of divine transformation; Christ's pain is not human, rather it is transcendent. That is, as an outsider, he helps make vivid an aspect of Christian doctrine that may be completely normalized for most insiders.

Stein's opera, *Four Saints in Three Acts* (1929), operates, I would suggest, in a somewhat similar vein. Taking up the well-known figure, Stein re-sees St. Teresa in a new light. For even as its form is spectacularly public, the opera is the site of an important personal reckoning. Stein turns to St. Teresa of Avila's story to steady her own inquiries into questions of belonging, and of how to negotiate a relation between individual and collective identities. More pointedly, the opera affords an opportunity to consider the field of emotions characterizing the Jewish Christian borderzone from yet another angle. Pursuing a line of thought initiated by her teacher, the philosopher William James, "the most important person in Gertrude Stein's Radcliffe life" (*AABT*), Stein introduces happiness into the mix. As James understands it, religion is not merely a source of comfort or release from life's daily tedium, but is the font of genuine happiness. And, as he understands it, no one is happier than a saint.

"Prepare for Saints"

> A real saint never does anything, a martyr does something but a really good saint does nothing. . . . and I wrote *Four Saints in Three Acts* and they did nothing and that was everything.
>
> (EA, 109)

For Gertrude Stein, 1934 was a great year. *The Autobiography of Alice B. Toklas* (1933) had become a best seller; and in the fall of 1934, she found herself touring America, delivering a set of lectures to packed houses eager to hear (or, really, to see) the expansive genius who socialized regularly with the likes of Picasso and Cézanne. Then on February 20, 1934, *Four Saints in Three Acts* opened on Broadway to great acclaim. With its cast of African American singers and actors decked out in cellophane and rock crystal, *Four Saints* was celebrated as exceptionally "joyous" and "refreshing," becoming the longest-running opera in North America (Holbrook, 16). But all this hoopla must be tempered with a more measured story beginning at least a decade or so before this glorious homecoming (Stein had lived abroad for the previous thirty-one years). The story begins in 1926, when a younger composer named Virgil Thomson approaches the poet about collaborating on an opera. The period leading up to this conversation had been at once enormously productive and challenging. The year 1914 had seen the publication of *Tender Buttons*—a breakthrough achievement on a number of fronts, including its trans-religious foray into Catholic ritual. For, as I will argue elsewhere, ecclesiastical acts serve as a frame for discovering and deploying some of the emerging principles central to her radical aesthetic vision.[7] That is, the Eucharist, otherwise known as the sacrament of the altar, holds great interest for a poet who queries thus: "How can a language alter. It does not it is an altar" (*Useful Knowledge*, 108). But with its unsettling grammar and disorienting tumble of words, the poem was largely dismissed as being either silly or just too difficult/opaque for most readers. Next comes *Geography and Plays* (1922), a collection of stories, word portraits, and short plays (none of which were ever produced, at least not professionally). But the bigger effort belongs to the epic novel *The Making of Americans* (1925): written almost fifteen years before its publication, the task of getting this thousand-page novel to press was formidable. Writing in *The Autobiography of Alice B. Toklas*, Stein describes a long summer spent struggling "with the errors of French compositors. Proof had to be corrected most of it four times and I finally broke my glasses, my eyes gave out and Gertrude Stein finished alone." Ultimately the novel is published by Robert McAlmon, but subsequent plans to publish a second expanded (!) edition go awry when Stein and McAlmon have a permanent falling out (*AABT*, 212).

All the while, Stein is busy writing "portraits": her signature effort to "render anyone's personality" by "making a continuous succession of the statement of what that person was until I had not many things but one thing" (*Portraits and Prayers*, 175–76). A "portrait," as Stein understands it, is nothing like a description, a selective assemblage of physical attributes or defining characteristics; rather, it is a highly concentrated expression born out of a deep knowing of an Other. She explains:

> what I mean by a portrait is this. When I know anybody well they are all something to me each one is. That is natural but then there has to come a moment when I know all I can know about anyone and I know it all at once and then I try to put it down on paper all that I know of anyone. . . and to do it all at once. . . . (*Paris Review*, 90)

Stein offers this account just as *Prayers and Portraits* (her twenty-third book in twenty years!) is about to be published. The volume comprises a wide array of portraits devoted to "everybody" Stein knew, or at least knew well enough, to necessitate a portrait. Entries range from such famous figures as Pablo Picasso and Juan Gris to the all-but-anonymous figure known simply as "The Brazilian Admiral's Son." But the volume, despite its title, seems to offer us nothing in the way of "prayers"—no hymns, laments, or doxologies. In the absence of the obvious, we wonder: Perhaps to Stein portraits *are* prayers? Indeed, each word portrait is much more than a record of Stein's impressions of her subject; actually, it is something closer to an exorcism, a way of expelling the presence of someone who has come to inhabit one's innermost being. Stein explains: "after anyone has become very well known to me I have tried to make a portrait of them well I might almost say *in order to get rid of them inside of me*. Otherwise I would have got too full up inside me with what I had inside me of anyone" (*Paris Review*, 90; emphasis mine).

At this point, a turn to St. Teresa of Avila, one of Stein's "heroines" (*AABT*, 109), is illuminating. For in the course of her massive spiritual autobiography, Teresa recounts her theory of "mental prayer": the articulation of a "special friendship" with a divine Other whose presence enters the very being of the self

(*Life*, 216). Like Stein, Teresa was highly disciplined and deeply enamored of habit. Although known for her ecstatic visions, she was mostly occupied with the hard work of cultivating a soul and building a network of convents. Large swathes of her autobiography are devoted to describing the "mechanics" of prayer—a highly focused process best likened to the precise workings of a water wheel as a mode of generating energy. The connections between Stein's intense interpersonal reckonings, as made manifest in her many portraits, and Teresa's intimate but focused encounters with the divine, are especially relevant when it comes to understanding not only the depth of Stein's aesthetic objectives, but the personal, indeed spiritually charged, nature of her attachment to this Catholic luminary: "mental prayer" and "portrait" were, for both, an intense interpersonal and spiritual encounter.

This affinity may help explain why, in 1927, Stein takes Thomson up on his invitation and plunges into writing a libretto featuring the saint herself. The turn to collaboration seems perplexing. To begin, fiercely independent-minded, Stein is known for insisting on her exceptionalism. At one point, she provocatively ranks herself along with Jesus and Spinoza as one of three Jewish "originative geniuses" (hardly a collaborative predisposition). Furthermore, she eschews most theater, objecting to how the genre denies one the ability to control the experience, since a given viewer must follow the action onstage regardless if one is emotionally and cognitively ready to move on (*Lectures in America*, 94). Nonetheless, she accepts the offer. In the absence of hard answers, we can only wonder if she agreed to partner with Thomson in order to mitigate some of the fatigue incurred by working alone, with little in the way of public recognition. Writing in her preface to Stein's 1926 lecture "Composition as Explanation," Ulla Dydo describes how Stein, worn down by rejection, wanted an audience "desperately" (*Stein Reader*, 493). That is, does opera, in all its spectacular publicness and polyvocality, offer the opportunity to engage some of the demons—external as well as internal—besetting her during this formative but challenging time? As is often the case with Stein, the answers are necessarily speculative and open-ended.

What we can say, however, is that while Thomson proposed the genre, Stein chose the subject. Upon meeting to discuss the project, Thomson explains that the opera must be epic in scope, of mythic import. Initially, Stein suggests that the American Revolution would make for a fine setting (it seems that she identified with George Washington). But Thomson rejects the idea, claiming that all those wigs would make all the actors look alike—a staging nightmare, to be sure. Stein then fastens on saints—specifically Spanish saints—as the focus. Later, Thomson treats the choice somewhat dismissively, claiming that they were both actually interested in depicting the lives of "working artists" as represented by saints. Stein herself, however, has little interest in metaphors or resemblances; to this end, she insists emphatically that saints *are* her subject—figures defined by their fully realized presence, that they simply *are*: "Saints do not have anything to do they are very busy but they do not have anything to do.... So I wrote *Four Saints in Three Acts* and when it was played it was a success" (*EA*, 110).

From a certain vantage, Stein's investment in saints is rather remarkable. As noted at the outset of this discussion, Judaism is most certainly not a resource. Again, of all the three major Western religions, only Judaism can claim the dubious distinction of lacking a single female mystic. Hemmed in by a worldview that depended upon consigning women to a state of innate impurity, the very prospect of a woman being able to access the divine realm, a region defined as unquestionably pure and intact, was simply impossible. A lack to be sure. That said, Stein never let Jewishness limit her; on the contrary, she regarded herself as a by-product not of "Christianity" as such, but certainly of "Christian thinking" (*EA*, 243). Like many assimilated Jews for whom Jewishness functioned largely as a sociocultural premise of being, Stein grew up in a world where culture (*kultur*) overrode most fixed categories of identity or belonging. That is, there was little to deter her from cultivating a strong affinity for a powerful female figure known for her restless energy, remarkable writing skills, and privileged relationship with seats of power (including that of the divine). In this regard, she occupies a unique position vis-à-vis the Jewish Christian borderzone. She certainly never claims an interest in Christianity as a faith position, nor does she apologize for or otherwise defend her interest in its concepts and iconography.[8] Wholly unrestrained by the usual religious dictates, Stein takes up the story of a revered Christian saint and, without refuting or questioning Teresa's divine status, celebrates her as an extraordinary human being: "to know to know to love her so." Indeed, it may well be that Stein's outlier/outsider perspective licenses this rendering.

Having lived much of her life in France and having traveled to Italy and Spain on numerous occasions, Stein, we can assume, was familiar with both Bernini's famous sculpture (in Rome) depicting "The Ecstasy of St. Teresa," as well as Rubens's portraits of the saint. In light of her special affection for Avila, and of course for Teresa, perhaps Stein sought out these images especially. But her interest extends well beyond visiting museums and cathedrals. According to Dydo, the poet was well versed in the details of St. Teresa's life and writings, as well as the broader aspects of the world in which she lived. Copies of both *The Life of St. Teresa of Jesus* (translated into English in 1916) and E. Allison Peers's classic work *Studies of the Spanish Mystics* (1924)—which includes detailed accounts not only of Teresa but also of St. Ignatius of Loyola (another of Stein's beloved saints)—may be found in Stein's extensive library. Each volume contains evidence of having been not merely owned, but read. Moreover, Stein was good friends with Georgiana Goddard King, an art historian with expertise in Spanish Gothic architecture, who provided Stein and Toklas with authoritative guidance during their travels to Spain (*AABT*, 109).

Even more to the point, Stein probably knew (and maybe even heard) lectures by her teacher William James, including those on "Saintliness" and "The Value of Saintliness," which eventually appeared as part of *The Varieties of Religious Experience* (1902). Explicitly uninterested in how religion functions as a public institution, James devotes himself to investigating how religion serves individual needs—intellectually, psychologically, and spiritually. After establishing that happiness and "enthusiastic gladness" dominate the religious temperament, James turns to consider the "passionate happiness of Christian saints." Even as their biographies detail lives filled with poverty, acute physical pain, and suffering, James understands them to be persons who embody "the ripe fruits of religion." They experience "a feeling of being in a wider life than that of this world's *selfish* little interests" (my emphasis). Furthermore, saints are uniquely "sensible of . . . the existence of an Ideal Power"—a purposively vague term, since, as James understands it, this status does not depend necessarily on directing oneself toward God, as there are all kinds of power sources, including abstract moral, civic, and aesthetic ideals (230). This inclusive approach suits Stein, who is a-religious, but completely driven by her aesthetic ideals—so much so that even after nearly twenty years of rejection and ridicule, she remains firmly committed to her vision and principles.

Such pure resolve may be chief among the reasons Stein is drawn to St. Teresa—even as it is a quality that James finds off-putting. Altogether, his take on the Carmelite nun is rather measured. He begins with high praise, recognizing her as "one of the ablest women, in many respects, of whose life we have the record." He then expands: "She had a powerful intellect of the practical order. She wrote admirable descriptive psychology, possessed a will equal to any emergency, great talent for politics and business, a buoyant disposition, and a first-rate literary style. She was tenaciously aspiring, and put her whole life at the service of her religious ideals" (292). But his portrait then takes on darker hues, as we read on: "Yet so paltry were these [achievements], according to our present way of thinking that . . . I confess that my only feeling in reading her has been pity that so much vitality of soul should have found such poor employment." That is, compared perhaps to St. Ignatius, that other famous Spanish saint, Teresa's accomplishments—which included not only a lifetime spent praying, teaching, and writing, but also reforming a flagging ministry as well as establishing over sixteen convents—just didn't measure up! More pointedly, James maintains that Teresa's "voluble egotism" was "typical of shrewdom"—his term for someone whose highly charged emotional responses are disproportionate relative to the given occasion or experience. In other words, without putting too fine a spin on it, James views Teresa as a bit of a hysteric—as did so many others at the turn of the century. Indeed, Freud's mentor Josef Breuer, writing in 1895, dubbed Teresa "the patron saint of hysteria" (Medwick, *Teresa of Avila*, xv). This account is clearly on Stein's mind when she sits down to write her libretto, where she works hard to counter this misogynistic reading of Teresa. In *The Autobiography*, we read how "she used to explain to Virgil, the Catholic Church makes a very sharp distinction between a hysteric and a saint" (*AABT*, 215). This distinction clearly informs her own decisive rendering of *Saint* Teresa.

The Libretto

Operas typically begin with an overture, an orchestral introduction that sets the mood and anticipates the themes to follow. Usually, this component is strictly orchestral, serving to set the tone musically. Stein, however, is hardly ever typical—and her opera is no exception. Once she and Thomson agreed on a subject, each worked separately on their own piece of the project, leaving Stein to her own devices. For this reason, I focus here solely on the published libretto, leaving aside whatever questions Thomson's score may engender. The 1927 text opens with a tumble of words, a long discursive meditation, as the poet finds her way into the project, beginning with a quatrain:

> To know to know to love her so.
> Four saints prepare for saints
> It makes it well fish
>
> Four saints it makes it well fish. (581)

At once opaque and comparatively simple, this passage names Stein's central objective—for what follows is a valentine to St. Teresa, a showcase for the saint in all her complexities, including her capacity for intense self-absorption, a quality that James dismisses as "voluble egotism." Exercising her propensity for linguistic slippage ("selfish" becomes "well fish"), Stein hones in on Teresa's paradoxical nature. On the one hand, intent on establishing an intimate relationship with the divine, Teresa became sharply attuned to the shifts in her own emotional and spiritual development, and chronicled them in great detail—a move garnering her reputation for being selfish and extravagantly egotistical. On the other hand, she understood these writings as being wholly of a piece with her other very public, charitable efforts, which included establishing a new convent—a move mightily opposed by Church authorities (Medwick, 116). At this point, it becomes clear why Stein proclaims Teresa to be "her favorite," since the two have much in common: separated by centuries and religious dispositions, the two women are both exceptionally courageous and single-minded when it comes to realizing their respective callings; moreover, they are both ambitious and acutely vulnerable. With this rendition, Stein pointedly complicates James's focus on sainthood as defined by egoless-ness, for in Stein's account, "selfishness" is requisite to saintly well-being—as St. Teresa, and her cohort, declare.

Indeed, *Four Saints* stands out as one of Stein's most intimate pieces. To be sure, other explicitly autobiographical works such as *The Autobiography of Alice B. Toklas* (1933), *Everybody's Autobiography* (1933), and *Wars I Have Seen* (1945) provide all kinds of insights into the panoramic sweep of friends, places, and sensibilities that made for an exceptionally fascinating life. However, it is *Four Saints* to which we must turn for a sense of Stein's interior life—especially during those early years when success was still a ways off. The gentle ironies here are quite wonderful and in keeping with Stein's disregard for generic convention. For surely, an opera—a sprawling, public display—would be the least likely space for private musings; but then, Gertrude Stein always lives large.

Moving deeper into the prelude qua overture, we find ourselves wading through a highly disjunctive text. Lines pile up without much in the way of connective tissue—save Stein's signature use of repetition, which helps the reader keep somewhat afloat. It is as if we are looking at a set of pages belonging to an artist's sketchbook or journal, filled with musings and fragments of thought as the work takes shape. Some lines such as "Imagine four benches separately" or "Large pigeons in small trees" register as stage directions—while others, such as "Acts three acts," seem to refer to the opera's structure. And then spliced in among these more prosaic remarks, there are lines which bristle with feeling as the poet maps out the sweep of emotions that lie ahead. We read of Teresa's/Stein's fear and uncertainty, "Come panic come / Come close." Jubilation follows quickly, "Rejoice saints," topped off exuberantly with exaltation, "My country 'tis of thee sweet land of liberty of thee I sing" (Stein's Americanness is just under the opera's surface—an element which Thomson's score plays up by weaving in bits and pieces of American folk music, along with a healthy dose of church music). The prelude ends in a rush of sheer giddiness as Stein offers up a litany of saints, starting with Teresa and Ignatius (who also appears in the libretto proper)—but then takes a comic turn by summoning a whole new host of invented saints, including "Saint Electra," "Saint Wilhelmina," "Saint Paul Seize," "Saint Plan," and "Saint Settlement."

To be sure, humor is central to this sprawling enterprise. Known for her own "beefsteak" of a laugh, Stein was more interested in having people enjoy the opera than understand it ("A Radio Interview," 89; http://brbl-archive.library.yale.edu/exhibitions/awia/gallery/stein.html). Yet with such an emotionally turbulent beginning, one wonders if, good intentions notwithstanding, Stein is setting us up for yet another rendition of Teresa as hysteric par excellence. As the opera unfolds, however, we find something altogether different; unlike those static representations of Teresa in arrested states of ecstasy à la Bernini, Stein's Teresa is highly mobile and very much in the process of becoming and being. Early on, we read "Teresa about to be" demarcating a liminal position that becomes part of the opera's leitmotif, for repeatedly we read, "Teresa half in doors and half out of doors." This interpolated stage direction speaks exquisitely to Teresa's complexity: she cultivated an intense capacity for inwardness; but she was also known as a community activist with a strong public presence. Indeed, Saints "Plan" and "Settlement" (as mentioned above) may figure as pet names for Teresa herself, who took a leading role in planning and establishing numerous new religious "settlements" (aka convents). For Stein was passionate about nicknames, another expression perhaps of her deep interest in knowing people in singularly intimate ways.

Four Saints thus comes into focus as itself a liminal text, a borderzone work by a non-Christian outsider. Even as she is recognized as a full-blown saint, Teresa, as Stein would have it, is absorbed by the human business of being. Based on the libretto, it seems that our protagonist rarely has the stage to herself; a strategic choice perhaps designed to counter James's critique of Teresa's "voluble egotism." Indeed the relative lack of arias, *de rigueur* for most operas, is one of the many reasons why *Four Saints* is now rarely performed. Instead, Stein's saint is constantly in the company of, and in concert with, others. More pointedly, Stein constantly draws our attention to the full-blown humanity, and the materiality, of Teresa's world. For example, as Dydo notes, the famous passage beginning with "How many nails in it" may reach back to Teresa's vision of her betrothal to Christ, as relayed in her *Spiritual Relation*, where Jesus proclaims: "Behold this nail. It is a sign that from today onward thou shalt be my bride" (Dydo, 191). But with the next line, Stein firmly redirects our attention earthward, continuing thus: "Hard shoe nails and silver nails," leaving us to think less about Christ's divine status and more about the hard and dirty business of the Crucifixion itself (with Christ nailed to the cross), as we begin to ponder just how many different kinds of nails there are. This sturdy emphasis on the material world, a concern that she shares with Loy, similarly informs an extended exchange involving Saints "Chavez" and "Placide," as well as Teresa, who gather to ponder: "How many doors how many floors how many windows are there in it. . . . How many doors how many floors and how many doors are there in it" (603)—questions possibly prompted by one of Teresa's many construction projects.

But nowhere perhaps is Stein's investment in the ordinary, the embodied, so clearly on display as when engaged with all things avian. Two kinds of birds figure large in the opera: magpies and pigeons.

> Pigeons on the grass alas.
> Pigeons on the grass alas . . .
> If they were not pigeons what were they.
> If they were not pigeons on the grass what were they. . . . If a magpie in the sky on the sky can not cry if the pigeon on the grass alas can alas. . . . (605)

Almost a decade after completing the libretto, in a lecture devoted to "Plays," Stein comments in passing how magpies, part of the landscape of Avila, look exactly like the birds in the Annunciation pictures which represent the Holy Ghost. Pigeons, however, remain a bit of a mystery even as they dominate the scene. That is, until an interviewer asks her bluntly: "Will you explain the passage from *Four Saints* about the pigeons on the grass?" Instead of deflecting or circumventing the question, as is often her wont, Stein responds quite directly:

> That is simple. I was walking in the gardens of Luxembourg in Paris it was the end of summer the grass was yellow I was sorry that it was the end of summer and I saw the big fat pigeons in the yellow grass and I said to myself pigeons on the yellow grass, alas, and I kept on writing pigeons on the grass, alas, . . . and I kept on writing until I had emptied myself of the emotion.

That is, while magpies belong to the divine (again, she links them to the Annunciation—a divine emanation central to a certain iteration of St. Teresa's life), Stein herself identifies more closely with, and is more interested in, the everyday aspects of her being and the emotional vicissitudes attendant upon the ordinary travails of human existence (beloved friends die; time passes; seasons change): "Pigeons on the yellow grass, alas."[9]

"Happiness," "joy," or "love" are not part of Stein's writerly lexicon. Just as she rewires our understanding of nouns, so she takes on our understanding of the language of affect. As a student of William James, Stein understands that feelings are indelibly bound up with cognition. To understand something is to enjoy it, and to enjoy something is to understand it (Meyers, *Irresistible Dictation*, 28). Furthermore, emotion is a matter of bodily experience. To paraphrase James, who launches his argument in the 1884 essay "What Is Emotion?": we are sad not because something causes us grief, but because we cry; similarly, we are happy because we smile or laugh. That is, instead of understanding a bodily expression as a manifestation or a symptom of an emotion, James maintains that it is the site of the emotion itself.

Gertrude Stein's forays into the Jewish Christian borderzone make for a singular contribution when it comes to understanding what this in-between space may yield. Unlike so many of the other writers represented in this study, Stein bypasses the web of partisan polemics altogether—for she neither advocates for Christianity nor criticizes it. Although she lives in a predominantly Christian world, she is not limited by what Shaul Magid calls the "Christian gaze"—his term for the cultural mechanism by which Christianity influences textual production, Jewish and Christian alike. But Stein has little patience for or interest in such institutional distinctions. Fueled by her own aesthetic principles, she draws boldly, some might say shamelessly, on Catholic concepts and figurations to realize her vision.[10]

3
Hiding in Plain Sight
Louis Zukofsky, Shame, and the Sorrows of Yiddish

Jewish literary production has always been a multilingual enterprise. For some native English writers, this has been a cause for concern—an obstacle to be confronted, if not resolved. For unlike those who write in "authentically" Jewish languages—such as Hebrew or Yiddish—the English writer is doomed to traffic in the language of what writer Cynthia Ozick many years ago called the "Gentile Other" (27). At least twenty years after Ozick struck this mournful stance, another well-known American literary figure, John Hollander, grievously noted that the English writer seeking to make Jewishness central to his or her creative project must contend with that weighty presence known as the "English"—or King James—Bible, "a polemically Protestant translation of an orthodox Christian book called the 'Old Testament'" (Hollander, "Question of American Jewish Poetry," 44)—and not the Hebrew Bible. The point here is that Christianity is a perpetual problem for the writer who would be Jewish.[1]

Now surely, you say, these claims are out of date. After all, our own literary moment is singularly diverse—ethnically, racially, and religiously. And yet, just ten years ago poet-critic Rachel Blau DuPlessis noted that "modern literary culture for more than thirty years (covertly and overtly) embodied a Christianizing structure of feeling *that still needs careful consideration*" ("Midrashic Sensibilities," 202; emphasis mine). Indeed, one way to understand the rise of a certain strain of contemporary (postmodern) avant-garde writing is as a kind of counterresponse, an act of linguistic resistance, a casting off of what was understood to be the coercive shackles of Christian ideology and expectations. Charles Bernstein, one of the most accomplished and playful proponents of this stance, makes this target explicit—posing as a "Jewish Jesus" for the cover of his latest book: "crucified," it would seem, for the "sins" of prior

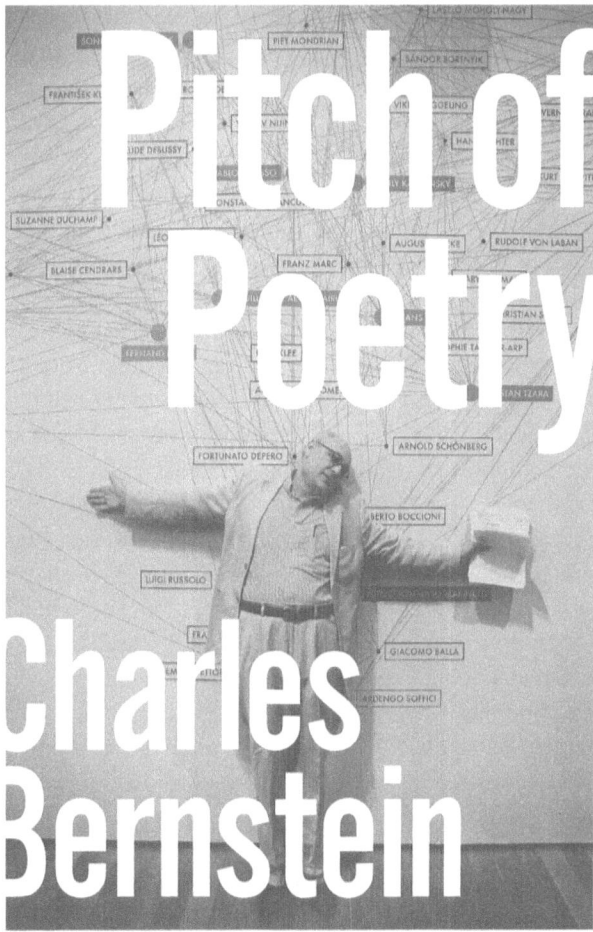

literary movements (depicted in the background of the image[2]) that spawned his achievements.

It is a wonderfully ironic image: a late stop, as it were, on the long train of secular Jewish writers who take up this image as a means of negotiating a relationship to the larger culture which they are at once part of and apart from (Hoffman, *Modern Jewish Culture*, 9).

Like a number of scholars,[3] I believe that Louis Zukofsky is central to any investigation focused on discovering what Jewish Christian interactions may mean for poetic production, and what poetry may teach us about such encounters. But as I understand it, the story he tells is much muddier, darker, and more painful than most critical analyses have conceded. Even as so much of the work bristles with defiance, he also risks real anxiety, even shame—as he confronts his genuine desire for the Christian Other. By speaking of desire, I don't mean—in his case—a "want" or a "need," an objective, concrete lack to be definitively filled. Instead, as Zukofsky plays it out, especially in his early work, "desire" here is something closer to what the French psychotherapist Jacques Lacan has in mind when he identifies an unconscious engine thus: "Desire is desire of/for the other" (Seminar XI, 235). That is, desire takes the form not only of a desire to be in the place of the other, but also it means a desire for a kind of otherness—a desire to be other than oneself. Paradoxically, this sort of longing makes one acutely aware of one's own otherness, one's status as a perpetual outsider—someone who Julia Kristeva might describe as a "foreigner" (*Strangers to Ourselves*); it is an identity position to which I will return later in this discussion. So to my readers well versed in modernist poetry, I offer this discussion in the interest of tempering those tendencies to celebrate Zukofsky in a narrowly heroic vein, a one-dimensional figure in the pantheon of Jewish modernism. And to my readers interested in religious studies, I offer this narrative as a kind of cautionary tale to those who might somewhat naïvely embrace cross-religious dialogue as a purely restorative solution. For in making himself so acutely vulnerable to the real psychic demands attendant upon such encounters—and then chronicling the fallout—Zukofsky gives us another occasion to think hard about just what theologian Krister Stendahl had in mind when asserting that understanding the religious Other depends upon discovering genuine feelings of lack and of spiritual deprivation—feelings which engender what he enigmatically called " holy envy." Finally, with his own intense interests in Yiddish, a language known for exceptionally fluid lexical boundaries—and in translation, a practice that necessarily entails crossing over into alien territory—Zukofsky gives us an opportunity to think about the role language plays in constructing religious difference, which for Zukofsky, as we will see, really means cultural difference.

    Louis Zukofsky grew up in what some might call a "good" Jewish home, a home where Orthodox religious Jewish practice was the norm. His father, Reb Pinchos Zukofsky, left Lithuania in 1898 and resettled in New York, where he found work on the Lower East Side in the garment industry. There he labored six days a week until he was eighty-one. But, as his son later recalls, Reb Pinchos maintained that his primary job "[i]s to keep Sabbath" ("A" 12, 152)—which he did faithfully and joyfully. His wife, Chana, devoted herself to her family, especially her sons Morris and Louis, the youngest child, born in 1909. Both boys went to *cheder* (Talmud Torah school), which in America functioned as a supplementary school program, where they learned some Hebrew, Bible, Talmud, and received Bar Mitzvah training.

The child of European Jewish immigrants, Zukofsky spoke Yiddish as his first language. Curiously, however, his biographer Marc Scroggins downplays the role Yiddish plays in the poet's formative years. Taking a notably offhand approach to the question, Scroggins quickly dismisses Yiddish as a "preschool tongue"—a linguistic inheritance that Zukofsky promptly abandoned upon entering the Lower East Side's P.S. 7, where presumably his "real" education began. Commenting on Zukofsky's signature attunement to the pleasures and possibilities of linguistic play, Scroggins simply notes that at the turn of the century, the streets of the Lower East Side were awash in multiple languages, suggesting that Yiddish was but one influence among many (Scroggins, *Biography*, 19). As Scroggins's narrative unfolds, however, it becomes clear that Yiddish played a central role in Zukofsky's earliest negotiations with the non-Jewish world. That is, from his earliest years the would-be poet was exposed to the vagaries of language, an attunement informing his singular approach to the pleasures and possibilities of linguistic play—with Yiddish, itself already a polylingual construction (German, Russian, French, Hebrew, etc.), occupying a special place in a multilingual world. At the same time, it is also true that Yiddish mediated Zukofsky's earliest encounters with the world of "high culture" that he came to revere.

Escorted by his older brother Morris, young Louis attended all kinds of Yiddish-language theatrical productions of plays by non-Jewish playwrights. Citing Zukofsky's *Autobiography*, Scroggins notes how "by the age of nine he [the poet] had seen a good deal of Shakespeare, Ibsen, Strindberg, and Tolstoy performed—all in Yiddish" (18). Moreover, at Morris's urging, Louis memorized large swathes of Yiddish verse, including much of Longfellow's *Hiawatha*—as rendered into Yiddish by the poet Solomon Bloomgarden, better known as "Yehoash." Armed thus, he would recite this Yiddish classic to keep from being harassed by gangs of Italian-American schoolboys by entertaining them with his recitations and thus encouraging them to throw pennies instead of insults or punches (21). It is a prescient strategy, for as we will see, long after Zukofsky moves out of the Lower East Side, leaving most of the vestiges of traditional Jewish life behind, Yehoash continues to figure large in the poet's aesthetic arsenal as he sets about crafting a relationship to the Christian culture that is wholly part of the literature and art he so loves. In this respect, he is importantly different from other modernist writers known for making Yiddish central to their aesthetic. Henry Roth, for example, works to make his readers achingly aware of Yiddish as the absent source language, that which must be inevitably lost, by representing English as an alien tongue (Wirth-Nesher, *Jewish American Literature*, 80–81). Zukofsky, however, takes a counterintuitive approach treating the *mame loshen* (the mother tongue) as a portal to world cultures, larding his English verse with long renderings of well-known Yiddish texts, often without attribution.

Zukofsky was hardly the only one interested in exploring how Yiddish could contribute to the avant-garde. Around the same time, he was drafting the poems that would launch his reputation, a vital new school of modern American Yiddish poetry was taking root. Known as "The Introspectivists," these poets—most of whom were immigrants—embraced many of the aesthetic principles characteristic of avant-garde American poetics, including a penchant for fractured lines and a disdain for conventional lyric flourishes. But Zukofsky was American-born and, as Scroggins puts it, "From the moment he began school, Zukofsky's main intent was to render himself a consummate master of English, the official language of the nation in which he had been born" (Scroggins, 19). As we will see, this desire to belong, matched simultaneously by a desire to be recognized as a distinct Other, drives much of the early work. Had he gone to New York University (NYU) (like Jacob Glatstein, a founding member of The Introspectivists), he might have fallen in with other Jewish literati and tried his hand at Yiddish verse. But with his sights set on "high" Western culture, Zukofsky eschews the comforts of the known for the chilly halls of Columbia University, where "Great Books" reigned supreme—accompanied by the subtle wafts of anti-Semitism. There, alongside such WASP blue bloods as Clifton Fadiman and Whittaker Chambers, Zukofsky immerses himself in the study of English literature, learning to appreciate the language of the New Testament and acquiring an affection for a wide array of Christian images and figures which fill his earliest poems (52).

Zukofsky attends Columbia for four years, which includes putting in time with Professor John Erskine, best known for designing the university's signature "Course on General Study" (i.e., the "Great Books"). As Lionel Trilling, Columbia's first Jewish professor, puts it, this program was a supreme instance of social engineering "directed to show young men how they might escape from the limitations of their middle-class or lower-middle-class upbringings by putting before them great models of thought, feeling and imagination" (Freedman, *Temple of Culture*, 193). Needless to say, these "models" are thoroughly grounded in Christian thought. Zukofsky, however, resists wholesale indoctrination. Instead, working to navigate a space between cultures, between worlds, he seeks neither to wholly "escape" his lowly origins nor to completely refute the mainstays of traditional high culture central to Columbia's ideology. On the contrary, many of the "Great Books" and other works of art that he first encountered while in school become part of an aesthetic wellspring to which he returns throughout his career. More pointedly, some of these pieces, which are decidedly Christian, ignite—as we will see—a gripping passion that never really dissipates.

At the same time, however, he was beginning to define his aesthetic commitment to making poems that attend to specific differences, "particulars—historic and contemporary" rather than universals—a claim that has real implications for those of us who are interested in conducting ongoing conversations with those of different faiths (Zukofsky, "Program: 'Objectivists' 1931," 189). All too often, such exchanges are hijacked by an anxious need to arrive at a "universal" truth, preempting the opportunity for real differences to emerge. To be sure, Zukofsky is influenced by his contemporaries, somewhat older poets—such as Ezra Pound, who was breaking new ground writing poems "containing history," and William Carlos Williams, who was working to narrow the gap between ordinary, real-time conversation and poetic speech. But this commitment also reflects Zukfosky's own distinctive polylingual inheritance, especially his immersive experiences with Yiddish. Known as a compound language, Yiddish is highly mobile, with various dialects that vary from region to region. Perhaps even more to the point, Yiddish, unlike so many other languages, was primarily a spoken language, the stuff of conversation—and therefore singularly resonant for an artist who believes that poems as "phrases of utterance"[4] depend on the cadences of human speech (Harshav, 99; Quatermain, 99). Finally, as a language of conversation, specific meanings and valences in Yiddish can vary depending on particular contexts and occasions. So when Zukofsky sets about negotiating his relationship with Christian culture and ideals, he turns to Yiddish as an aesthetic resource. The effort absorbs him for more than a decade, dominating his first long poem, "Poem Beginning 'The'"— as well as the first third of an epic achievement, a poem known simply as "A" (short for "a poem of a life"). These are the poems that will occupy our attention in the pages that follow.

"I might as well look Shagetz just as much as Jew"

Brash, arrogant, even a little manic, "Poem Beginning 'The'" is the work of a young poet eager to claim a place in the literary world, but also more than a little anxious. Right off, he aims his sights at T. S. Eliot, explaining as much in a letter to Pound: "[I] . . . intended to tell him why, spiritually speaking, a wimpus was still possible and might even bear the fruit of another generation" (*Pound/Zukofsky*, 79). With a portmanteau word combining "wimpy" with "whimper," Zukofsky takes aim at Eliot's "The Hollow Men," which has the world ending "not with a bang, but a whimper"—for in "The" the young poet sets out to topple, or at least destabilize, the apocalyptic Christianizing narrative underwriting modernism, as exemplified by Eliot's precedent-setting apocalyptic poem *The Waste Land*, and to make space for a distinctively Jewish presence.[5] From the get-go, Zukofsky comes out swinging—with Christianity clearly in his sight line, as the poem opens thus:

> The
> Voice of Jesus I. Rush singing
>   In the wilderness
> A boy's best friend is his mother
> It's your mother all the time.
> Residue of Oedipus-faced wrecks
> Creating out of the dead (9)

Juxtaposing a cheeky rendition of Jesus wandering in the desert (Matthew 4:1–7) with a popular song ("A boy's best friend . . ."), Zukofsky links Christianity's maternal fetishizing to modernism's obsessive grieving for the past. But this is just a warm-up for what turns out to be a full-fledged attack on Western/ Christian literary culture. Working hard to slough off the weighty legacy of Columbia Professor John Erskine's signature "Great Books" course—dubbed elsewhere in the poem as "Askforaclassic Inc"—Zukofsky takes on a whole host of august writers including Christopher Marlowe, Robert Herrick, Henry James, Virginia Woolf, and, of course, T. S. Eliot.

His mood, however, is hardly constant. After mounting a steady attack for nearly fifty lines, the poet is beset by doubt, haunted by a version of those well-known, quasi-rabbinic/mythic prohibitions facing the Jewish would-be artist:

> Let me be
> Not by art have we lived,
> Not by graven images forbidden to us
> Not by letters I fancy. . . .

With these lines, Zukofsky offers an especially dour take on the Jewish constraints limiting creative production, rooted in the Second Commandment's prohibition against graven images (Exodus 20:4–5).

Historical particulars, however, help him regain emotional equilibrium, as he quickly continues: "Do we dare say / With Spinoza grinding lenses, Rabbaisai . . . ?" The gloom lifts as Zukofsky sturdies himself by invoking the Portuguese-born Baruch Spinoza, a philosopher (known for his critique of the perils of emotions) who was formally excommunicated by the Jewish community and feared as a dangerous atheist by the Christians. Memorably dubbed by critic Stephen Fredman as "the patron saint of betweenness," Spinoza not only quells Zukofsky's anxieties about alienating both Jews and Christians alike but helps him identify a linguistic strategy for managing his desire for a relationship with the non-Jewish culture, without sacrificing his difference. The strategy is coded here in the word "Rabbaisai"—as in "gentlemen"—or, in this instance, a term used to gesture ironically toward the Yiddish literati who celebrated the seventeenth-century philosopher as the harbinger of Jewish secularity (Berger, Sholomo). Quite pointedly untranslated, "Rabbaisai" is the first time that readers of "The" encounter a Yiddish word. But it is hardly the last. Instead, it is a tip-off—a sly invitation to be on the lookout for this "Jewish tongue" that is often construed as the bedrock of "authentic" Jewishness. As if anticipating that trend in Jewish Studies that now finds scholars busy picking through layers of acquired languages to discover nuggets of Yiddish buried underneath the crust of other languages, Zukofsky dangles Yiddish before his readers, daring us to wonder if there is more to it than a single slip of the tongue.[6]

The notion of a secret or "hidden language" may also bring to mind that nefarious anti-Semitic trope representing Jews as an essentially duplicitous people, guilty of using language to deceitful ends. As cultural historian Sander Gilman explains, Jewish discourse has a long history of being cast as the language of the Other—"hidden, dark, magical, dangerous, private" (Gilman, *Jewish Self-Hatred*, 16). Such associations become especially acute during the seventeenth century when Yiddish is widely figured as a language of thieves, known for "stealing" from "such pure" tongues as German, "mutilating" words, and perverting the integrity of this source language (Gilman, 71). In this account, Yiddish occupies an adversarial stance vis-à-vis the dominant Christian culture. Interestingly enough, Ezra Pound—a notorious anti-Semite and one of Zukofsky's early mentors—suggests that this is effectively what the young poet is up to, writing: "Capital idea that the next wave of literature is jewish . . . also lack of prose in German due to all idiomatic energy being drawn off into yiddish" (*Pound/Zukofsky*, 26). It is a curious and backhanded sort of compliment. Even as the modernist elder seems to celebrate his protégé's efforts, he also represents Yiddish as a kind of parasite or vampire, a linguistic cowbird, as it were.

From this vantage, Yiddish seems to serve as one of Zukofsky's most effective weapons in his war on the dominant culture—a battle whose lines are drawn tight, pitting Jews against Christians, outsiders against insiders. But, as we shall see, Zukofsky is far more ambivalent about his position (an ambivalence informing his varied approach to Yiddish). In the fifth movement we encounter a little ditty that speaks to this complexity: "Assimilation is not hard, / And once the Faith's askew / I might as well look Shagetz just as much / as Jew." To read *Shagetz*, a markedly brutal and disparaging term for a non-Jewish male, derived from the Hebrew *shekez* or "detestable," in such a context might well set those in the know (aka Yiddish readers) back on their heels. It is a paradigmatic example of what sociolinguist Max Weinreich identifies as the function of Yiddish as a *lehavdel loshen*—or "differentiation language"—a strain of vocabulary setting "insiders" apart from "outsiders" (193–95). Typically the word "shagetz" appears exclusively in intra-Jewish contexts. So, by boldly using the word in a broader, more inclusive context, Zukofsky moves to dismantle Yiddish's function as a "differentiation language." Rather than perpetuating the idea of Yiddish as a secret code accessible to some but not to others, he deploys the *mame loshen* in the service of dissolving the boundaries between "insiders" and "outsiders," between the Jewish self and the non-Jewish Other. As we will see, the move is hardly isolated. Instead, it belongs to a broader effort that finds Zukofsky counterintuitively using Yiddish not to set himself apart, but to use as a cross-cultural/dialogic strategy—a means of crafting a relation with the Western/Christian culture he finds so very compelling.

Yehoash (in translation)

Zukofsky, however, is not always so transparent when it comes to deploying Yiddish in the service of his larger aesthetic objectives. As it turns out, almost 20 percent of "The" is composed of Yiddish material (mostly folk songs and poetry) translated into English but without any sort of identification or attribution (Schimmel, 560). In other words, Yiddish is a covert presence—everywhere and yet only occasionally detectable, functioning in a capacity akin to what French philosopher Jacques Derrida calls a "trace": his term for "the always already absent present," the sign that is left by the thing that is now absent, after it has left the scene of its former presence (Derrida, "Scene of Writing," 230). Zukofsky's tactical range invites us to consider, albeit briefly, the complex role translation plays in the making of religious identities/narratives.[7]

Historically, for example, translation has been weaponized, serving as a means of helping one religion to claim sovereignty over another. One classic example of this function may be found in William Barnstone's discussion exploring how early scribes of Christian Scriptures used mistranslation to thoroughly scrub away any hint of Jesus's Jewishness (62–81). Following Barnstone's lead, Naomi Seidman shows how, through a long process of serial "mistranslations" or "misrememberings," a passage in the Book of Isaiah (part of the Hebrew Bible) becomes a Christian proof text authorizing Matthew's account of the miraculous birth of a divinely conceived child (*JANT*, 699). These examples make for an interesting backdrop against which to consider Zukofsky's deft approach to translation—especially when it comes to making space for his favorite Yiddish poet, Solomon Bloomgarden (aka "Yehoash").

Before, however, turning to the passages themselves, I want to ask: Why Yehoash? After all, in the early part of the twentieth century, all kinds of poets were making interesting contributions to Yiddish letters. But Yehoash brought something unique to this already lively scene. A skilled linguist, he translated hundreds of works from numerous languages, including Russian, French, English, German, and Arabic. Yehoash was thus responsible for expanding the world of Yiddish readers, providing access to such "exotic" works as Byron's "Hebrew Melodies," Merezhkovsky's "Sakya Muni," Longfellow's "Hiawatha" (the very poem which the young Zukofsky once used to fend off street gangs), and Omar Khayyam's *Rubaiyat*. This last text is of particular interest because "The" takes as its epigraph an untranslated, calligraphed bit of this Persian poem—Zukofsky's way, perhaps, of obliquely gesturing toward the Yiddish (also written in non-Roman letters) suffusing the work to follow. Yehoash was notably prolific and ambitious; his translation of the complete Hebrew Bible is widely recognized as "one of the richest books of Yiddish literature," and his dictionary of Hebrew, Aramaic, and Arabic words used in Yiddish speaks to his deep interest in showing how the language was served by its penchant for linguistic borrowings and culturally dissonant lexical encounters (Harshav, *The Meaning of Yiddish*, 71–72; Harshav, *Sing, Stranger*, 80). As even this briefest of biosketches suggests, there was much about Yehoash that a young Zukofsky, perched on the edge of the Anglo-Yiddish world and preparing to write an epic, or what he would call a "life-poem," might find compelling and resonant.

Out of sixty lines translated from Yiddish in "The," most belong to Yehoash. These are largely freewheeling renderings that some might call "mistranslations," and others might read as extensions of a long tradition of Yiddish translations that routinely "improve" the original to suit various purposes. For his part, Zukofsky is interested in using translation as a way of staging dialogic encounters, conversations between poets and between traditions. The section called "Autobiography," for example, features a long swath from "Chesvan" (the name of the Hebrew month which Benjamin Harshav translates as "October"). Following upon Zukofsky's tribute to his mother's exilic journey, the autumnal scene is well suited to a melancholic pose. But his version differs significantly from Yehoash's original, or at least in Harshav's translation. Not only are the sections reshuffled, but other sorts of liberties are also at work. Yehoash, for example, imagines an innocent pastoral scene with a boy "swishing" his staff, "standing in soft mud" (Harshav, *Sing, Stranger*, 101). Zukofsky's version, however, takes a much darker route, representing the boy as "striding in the mire: / Swishing indifferently a peeled branch" at a flock originally described simply as "weary," but now specified as "jaded."

The strongest example of this dialogic strategy occurs early in the poem where Zukofsky juxtaposes his lament for "Ricky" Chambers (the younger brother of his college chum Whittaker), who died by suicide—with another long rendering of Yehoash. In this instance, the interreligious stakes are clear. Lovingly addressed as "Lion-heart, frate mio," Ricky—like Richard the Lion-hearted, who gave himself over to the Crusades—is cast as a victim of Christian apocalyptic fictions. Seeking "revenge" for Ricky's untimely death, Zukofsky counters with Yehoash's *"Bakhr Esh-Shaytan"*—a long poem celebrating a princely Bedouin prince who vanquishes "the Desert-Night / Big his heart and young with life." Serving as a displaced incarnation of a proto-Semitic hero, the prince swoops in to take back the narrative hijacked by Christianity—which Zukofsky blames for the loss of his beloved friend. That is, Zukofsky commandeers a Yiddish poem about exotic Semitic royalty and, by way of translation, counters the Christian narrative, promoting an alternate hero—and an alternate outcome. The move makes vivid how translation can function as an interreligious power grab—a drive that continues through to the end of the poem. Zukofsky gives Yehoash the last word, bringing "The" to a rousing conclusion with an extended bit from "On the Ruins": "By the wrack we shall sing our Sun-Song . . . / We shall open our arms wide / Call out of pure might— / Sun, you great Sun, our Comrade." With a grand flourish, Zukofsky overrides the Christian narrative which so much of the poem is pitted against, brazenly replacing the "Son," as the right object of devotion, with the gloriously ecumenical "Sun"—a term, which, according to the poem's notes, signifies the triumphant reign of temporality ("the power of past, present, future") at the expense of Christianity's apocalyptic disregard for history.

"If horses could but sing Bach"

In "The," Yiddish plays a strategic role as the young poet seeks to find his aesthetic footing. Taking explicit aim at a certain strain of high modernist writing informed by Christian ideologies, as exemplified by T. S. Eliot's seismic work *The Waste Land*, Zukofsky claims victory, audaciously asserting that Yiddish poetry can hold its own against canonical heavyweights like Shakespeare and Chaucer. Yet even as (in his view) the battle may have been won, the war is far from over. While working through his adversarial relationship with a particular literary orientation, he discovers that the contest is considerably more complicated—since his feelings actually run much deeper than mere disdain for another poet and for the culture to which he belongs. After another long rendering from Yehoash, which Zukofsky dedicates to his mother and her experiences in Czarist Russia, he breaks off wistfully: "If horses could but sing Bach, mother,— / Now I kiss you who can never sing Bach." To new readers of Zukofsky, the sentiment may register as a complete non sequitur, an inscrutable aside irrelevant to the project's scope. Only by wading deeper into the work do we come to understand that both "horses" and "Bach" loom large in his private cosmology as sublime examples of aesthetic perfection. And while it may be relatively easy to take on Eliot, Bach is a whole different matter. Whereas the former is merely irritating, the latter rouses a desire, incites a passion that demands sustained reckoning. More pointedly, this desire, which, as we will see, is specifically linked to Bach's sacred masterpiece "St. Matthew Passion," leads to a profound encounter with the Christian Other.

Of course, Zukofsky is hardly the first Jewish poet to be smitten with a Christian artist. Consider, for example, Jacob Glatstein's "Mozart"—a Yiddish language poem that speaks both to the kind of emotional challenge Christian art can pose for the Jewish artist seeking a place in a broader cultural arena and to the important role language plays in this negotiation. Glatstein's position is especially fraught because, as he understands it, Christianity is thoroughly bound up with the horrors of the Holocaust (see Chapter 1). Dated 1946, just barely after the war has ended, the poem finds Glatstein—taking perhaps a page from Chagall's "White Crucifixion"—depicting a "crucified Mozart" ignored by all "Save the Jews who saw the God in the man that died / And kept his memory sanctified." Framed as a dream and written in a Jewish language, Glatstein's poem dissociates a beloved composer—known for both his sacred and secular compositions—from Christianity, claiming him instead as a true "King of the Jews":

> The Sermon on the Mount:
> How stingy, indigent
> Next to the bounty
> Of Mozart's testament . . .
>
> (Trans. A. Z. Forman)

Audacious and smart, the poem displays qualities that theoretically resonate with Zukofsky's sensibilities. But Glatstein's position is simply not available to the American-born poet. A Polish-born Jew (whose family never emigrates), Glatstein moves to America and helps found an avant-garde movement known as Introspectivism—a collective that fervently believes in Yiddish as an aesthetic powerhouse, a real contender in the world of modernist poetics. The difference informs their respective aesthetic choices.[8] Zukofsky's cultural inheritance differs significantly. For him, Yiddish (as a sort of concealed aesthetic weapon) is a means to an end, not an end in itself. The difference is rooted in their respective aesthetic choices. As my readers may recall, Glatstein went to NYU where half of the students were Jewish—and where it was relatively easy to dip into the dominant culture while maintaining one's own religious/cultural boundaries. Zukofsky, however, only eight years younger than Glatstein, went off to Columbia, an institution known not only for promoting a hegemonic cultural agenda (the "Great Books"), but for an atmosphere characterized by "unspoken anti-Semitism" (Klingenstein, *Jews in the American Academy*, 99). This decision speaks to a life devoted to Anglo-American literary achievement—a life to be lived in English.

"It was also Passover"

It is also, at least during these early years, a life to be lived in the Jewish Christian borderzone—as mapped out in the first seven sections of his magnum opus, an epic called "A." In 1928, the same year "The" is published, Zukofsky starts on a long project, a poem that he often described as "a poem of a life." Occupying his attention off and on for nearly forty-seven years and comprising twenty-four parts (one for each hour of the day), "A" is an absorbing achievement. The first seven movements ("A" 1–"A" 7), rapidly drafted in just two years, find Zukofsky especially absorbed by his desire for the Christian Other, an outsize embodiment of aesthetic perfection. In the course of exploring his liminal status, as one who lives in between cultural and religious domains, Zukofsky suggests how we might think about the Jewish Christian borderzone as a generative domain where desire is a two-way street—an effect that flows in at least two directions. The project is well suited for a poet who approaches his art as an occasion to put concepts and words into dynamic interplay (Zukofsky, "Program: 'Objectivists' 1931," 22). So, rather than seeing Passover and Easter as discrete, contrasting rituals belonging to wholly separable groups, he sets out to make visible the points of connection, of contiguity. Working one's way through these early movements means discovering not only why the Jew may be drawn to Christianity, but also what Christianity may find alluring about the Jewish other. Zukofsky thus anticipates what is later made explicit when a group of Jewish theologians preface their guide to Jewish Christian dialogue by insisting on its bilateral nature. As they see it, such dialogue must recognize that "the greatest temptation for a Jew is Christianity, and the greatest temptation for a Christian is Judaism" (Novak, *Jewish-Christian Dialogue*, 5).

Zukofsky's own interfaith encounter begins with him locating his poem specifically in both time and space: Carnegie Hall, "St. Matthew Passion" as performed on April 5, 1928. In this way, he eschews the general (a province perhaps of Christianity's universalizing proclivities) in favor of "historic and contemporary particulars." He starts by splicing lines from the libretto in between snapshots of the audience in attendance while keeping a firm eye on Jesus's corporeal presence:

> Round of fiddles playing Bach.
> *Come, ye daughters, share my anguish –*
> Bare arms, black dresses,
> *See Him! Whom?* . . .
> His legs blue, tendons bleeding ("A" 1: 1–7)

"St. Matthew Passion" is an iconic piece of sacred music featuring the story of Christ's crucifixion as told in the Gospel of Matthew. And while not nearly as problematic as the version told in Bach's other great sacred work, "St. John Passion," "Matthew" still gives us a "chorus" of Jews rallying to what has been notoriously called "the blood cry": "Let us crucify him!"—a line that has done serious damage to Jewish Christian relations historically. Yet known also as one of the most "exalted" pieces of music in the Western canon as well as being a work of "deep devotion," "the Passion" is a formidable presence, aesthetically and spiritually ("Holy Dread," *New Yorker*, 2017). It makes sense then to find Zukofsky, at the concert's end, at once fixated by "Desire longing for perfection" ("A" 1: 2) and fumbling to find his way out of the performance hall. In an earlier version of the poem, he names himself explicitly as the target of an usher's harsh rebuke: "No suh / Not past that exit, Zukofsky!" ("A" 1: 2). Even as the scene is literal, figurative readings are just under the surface. In these early movements, Zukofsky's position brings to mind theorist Julia Kristeva's account of the prototypical "foreigner"—"one who belongs to nothing." On the one hand, the foreigner is often bewildered by the unspoken rules dictating social expectations; on the other hand, because he is an outsider, he is poised to indulge with "extravagant ease" in "the art of innovation" (Kristeva, *Strangers to Ourselves*, 31–32). In this instance, innovation means exercising a gift for making connections between words, places, and cultural regions of meaning.

This skill is clearly on display as the concert hall gives way to the street, with Zukofsky now honing in on one of the many conversations swirling around him:

> And on one side street near an elevated
> Lamenting,
> Foreheads wrinkled with injunctions:
> "The Pennsylvania miners are again on the lockout,
> We must send relief to the wives and children—

What's your next editorial about, Carat,
We need propaganda, the thing's
becoming a mass movement"
It was also Passover. ("A" 1: 3)

Reading Zukofsky means trying to connect the dots; so let's begin. The "elevated": Well into the 1940s (and even now in some locations), New Yorkers traveled by way of elevated subway trains commonly known as "the el." "Elevated/Lamenting": this linking invokes one of the most famous laments in the Western tradition: *"Eli, Eli lama sabachtani?*, that is, 'My God, My God, why hast thou forsaken me?'" (Matthew 27:46), Jesus's anguished cry on the cross. Comprising both Hebrew (the Jewish holy tongue) and Aramaic (Jesus's vernacular), the line is among the few traces of Jesus's Jewish origins that managed to escape erasure. Interestingly enough, the line itself includes an act of translation, alerting us thus to the linguistic operation responsible for this sort of excision. As previously noted, major Scriptural figures—including Christ—were widely scrubbed clean of their Jewish heritage through careful editing and deft acts of translation (23). Only the Gospel of Matthew, recognized by Daniel Boyarin as one of the most "Torah-friendly" books of the New Testament and which may have been written for a Jewish-Christian community, retains the traces of a linguistic Other (Boyarin, *Gospels*, 179).

Now Zukofsky is anything but a Messianic Jew (a Jew who believes in Jesus as the Jewish messiah). As we will see, he is "the foreigner" incarnate—keeping a steady distance from all institutions, even those committed to exploring Jewishness as a cultural, rather than a religious identity. Nonetheless, our initial impression of Christianity as the site of unequivocal sublimity (exemplified by Bach's "Passion") dims somewhat as we are made to note how it can also be woefully indifferent to social inequities—an argument achieved by showcasing the idea of Jesus as a social activist within a decidedly secular Jewish context. After gesturing toward an image of Christ on the Cross, one which foregrounds his Jewish lineage, Zukofsky now offers a scrap of an overheard conversation, which is at once insistently Jewish (albeit decidedly secular), but which also helps bridge the religious divide. As cited above, the exchange begins thus: "The Pennsylvania miners are again on the lockout, / We must send relief to the wives and children." The subject here is the 1927–28 coal miners' strike that ravaged the community of Rossiter, Pennsylvania, and other nearby towns. Described in the *New York Daily News* as "Hell-in Pennsylvania," "hundreds of destitute families" were left to starve as a result of a "system of despotic tyranny reminiscent of Czarist-Siberia at its worst." Marking the defeat of one of the nation's largest labor unions, the tragedy garnered outrage particularly among the liberal left, including Mike Gold (who went by the nickname "Carat")—known primarily for his proletarian novel, *Jews Without Money*, and for his frequent editorials in the pages of the socialist journal *The New Masses* (coded here by way of a light pun: "the thing's becoming a mass movement"). After all, like the Jewish socialist Gold ("Carat"), Jesus also was a social activist. By juxtaposing Jesus's lament with the plight of the Pennsylvania miners, Zukofsky helps make a real case for the value of interfaith exchange: by encountering the Other, the Self (in this instance, the dominant religious culture) can rediscover qualities and values that have been lost or forgotten.

All of this is more or less clear. But then Zukofsky—ever on the lookout for new meanings, new connections—takes us in an utterly new direction. Activated perhaps by the ecclesiastical meaning of "mass," he finishes off the scene by pointedly observing that "It was also Passover." And indeed it was. That year Sunday, April 8, 1928, was both Easter and the fourth day of Passover (traditionally a weeklong holiday). With this densely packed passage, Zukofsky plunges us into one of the most charged sites of contiguity and difference in the story of Jewish Christian engagement. Indeed, with the rising popularity of interfaith dialogic encounters, it has now become all the rage for Christian communities to host Passover Seders—an often well-meaning effort that begins with openhearted, celebratory claims about "the Last Supper" actually being a "Passover Seder." This is itself a complicated assertion because the "Seder," as we have come to know it, didn't exist during Jesus's lifetime. Good intentions notwithstanding, these efforts sometimes end up in a muddied space marked by cultural distortions and appropriations. Anyone who has attended such an event might wonder about what larger issues might be at stake.

As Israel Yuval, a medieval Jewish historian scholar explains, Passover long served as a narrative battle zone, as Jews and Christians struggled over dominant meanings. For Jews, the holiday was an occasion to retell the story of national liberation; for Christians, "Easter" (an English word of uncertain origin)—known in both Latin and Greek as *Pascha*—focused on the deliverance of Jesus as a divine savior and his ultimate resurrection. Different stories indeed. At first, the two events happened at the same time, the fourteenth day of the Hebrew month of Nisan. But as tensions between the two groups intensified, some Christian factions (belonging to the Western Church) began celebrating Easter on "the first Sunday after the middle of the lunar month following the spring equinox" (*Two Nations*, 61). According to Yuval, this temporal modification was part of a concerted effort to obscure the Jewish origins of Easter. By the fourth century, the wedge was firmly in place; Easter was to be that first Sunday, regardless of when Passover was to be celebrated.

Read against this historical background, "It was also Passover" shows how much work a single line can do. Exercising his penchant for making connections—across time as well as with words and concepts—Zukofsky puts together what has long been set apart. What needs to be stressed, however, is that he is not interested in anything like "syncretism"—the sort of religious or cultural mash-up that is sometimes the outcome of benevolent interfaith exchange.[9] Quite the contrary, Zukofsky's vision depends upon attending to particular, concrete differences. Recognizing the proximities linking Passover to Easter leads him not to mute the differences between the two traditions, but to invite readers to consider how such encounters might complicate and expand preexisting institutional boundaries.

"When It comes to Taking on Bach, Yiddish Bests Hebrew"

This space, however, is necessarily fragile and hard to maintain; religious boundaries, it seems, have a way of reasserting themselves. A few months later, Zukofsky returns to the old opposition, pitting Jewish aesthetic resources against those engendered by Christianity. But this time he takes an alternative approach, differentiating between traditional (religious) Jewishness and its secular alternative. Whereas in "The" Zukofsky deploys Yiddish in service of his attack on high modernism, in "A" 4 the stakes are higher. In this movement, Zukofsky makes one of his strongest cases for Yiddish (the vernacular of the "ordinary," the secular) as a viable response to the lure of Christian aesthetics.

"A" 4 opens with the spectacular "Festa del Rendentore"—the annual Venetian celebration commemorating the end of the plague (1577) and the subsequent construction of the marvelous cathedral. The scene stirs admiration and desire as the poet offers a set of softly rhyming couplets devoted to the fabulous shower of fireworks: "Giant sparkler / Lights of the river" ("A" 4: 12). But appreciation quickly gives way to dark comparisons, shot through with envy, as the poet—ventriloquizing an unspecified group of cranky Jewish elders—reflects gloomily upon their own considerably darker Diasporic inheritance (a shift marked poetically, as sonorous couplets give way to blank verse, a metrical form closer to ordinary speech):

> Wherever we put our hats is our home
> Our aged heads are our homes,
> Eyes wink to their own phosphorescence,
> No feast lights of Venice or Last Supper light. ("A" 4: 12)

Compared to the aesthetic wonders sponsored by Christianity, Jewish resources fall short. In these lines Zukofsky voices the kind of self-pitying resignation that, twenty-five years later, another poet, Karl Shapiro, will give himself over to wholly (as we will see). Even the ancient covenantal promise is of little comfort, as the elders dourly continue: "His Stars of Deuteronomy are with us, / Always with us" ("A" 4: 12). Of all the many occasions when the "children of Israel" are divinely guaranteed a legacy of robust growth, Zukofsky seizes upon the one iteration when this blessing registers as something of a curse; for the biblical book of Deuteronomy finds Moses grumbling to his charges: "I cannot bear the burden of you myself. The Lord your God has multiplied you until you are today as numerous as the stars in the sky" (Deuteronomy 1:9–10). Complaints proliferate, as these malcontents (again, ventriloquized by Zukofsky) continue: "We had a Speech, our children have evolved a jargon." Pitting "speech" (aka Hebrew or *lashon hakodesh*, the holy tongue) against "jargon" (a notoriously derogatory term for Yiddish as a "mongrel" construction), Zukofsky revisits an old linguistic battle that had raged during the latter half of the nineteenth century—which had Yiddish fighting to be recognized as a legitimate language, suited to high literary production. The matter is resolved in 1908 at the "Czernowitz Conference" where the word "jargon" or "zhargon" had been officially abolished by a celebrated gathering of Yiddish writers, announcing that their native tongue, a true "Jewish national language," was not only equal to Hebrew, but culturally superior (Harshav, 86). Zukofsky, however, upends this "official" position by celebrating "jargon" with all of its transgressive associations as the language of the new generation.

Zukofsky prefaces his own celebratory take on Yiddish's aesthetic possibilities with a portrait of Diasporic despair, comprised of what we might call (after Eliot) a "broken heap"—a patchwork of images and verses culled mostly from the Psalms. Among them, reworked shards of Psalm 24 ("O gates lift up your heads! Up high, you everlasting doors, so that the King of glory may enter") stand out: "We prayed, Open God. Gate of Psalmody that our Psalms may reach. . . . " This particular Psalm, petitioning God's arrival, is traditionally said as part of the Jewish morning service on Sunday—the very day when the Christian world celebrates His full-blown presence. This dismal state deepens with a protracted lament, again a composite construction: first, Zukofsky gestures elliptically toward that bizarre moment in Samuel 2 when the oxen transporting the "Ark of God" stumble and Uzzah (an Israelite bystander) is struck down "on the spot" by God upon reaching out to prevent its fall; the line from "A" 4 reads, "Fierce Ark . . . / Split cedar chest harboring our Law." Then, things go from bad to worse, as Zukofsky splices in talismanic images evoking the destruction of the Temple, the prototypical site of cosmic Jewish/Orthodox despair: "Dead love stones of our Temple walls / Ripped up pebble-stones of our tessellation." In a subsequent canto, he returns to the scene, emphatically linking this chronic grief to the antiquated world of the religious orthodox who desperately cling to Hebrew "Speech bewailing a Wall" ("A" 5: 18).[10] The "Wall" here, of course, refers to what is widely known as the Wailing Wall—the western retaining wall which is all that remains of the Second Temple.[11]

The poet then calls on Bach to deliver the final blow. Following upon this scene of national/religious destruction, we read: "Hear / He calleth for Elias" (13), a line from Bach's libretto. Nearly undone by this promise of imminent Christian redemption, the elders respond rather pitifully as they pray: "Deafen us, God, to their music, / Our own children have passed over to the ostracized. . . . And have mouthed a jargon" ("A" 4: 13). With a sly pun on "Passover," Zukofsky overrides this worn-out resistance to what the elders dismissively refer to as "jargon" (again, a derogatory term highlighting what is perceived as Yiddish's grating sounds) with a generous rendering from the work of his favorite Yiddish poet, Yehoash. Indeed, nothing could be farther from the Yiddish-speaking "snarling monsters" who drive those pious elders to despair, than Yehoash's delicately wrought take on Japonaiserie poetics:

> Rain blows, light on quiet water
> I watch the rings spread and travel
> Shimaunu-San, Samurai,
> When will you come home?
> Shimaunu-San, my clear-star. (13)

Most readers interested in understanding Zukofsky's investment in Yiddish focus on how the language works as a source of creative vitality, inspiring his own penchant for linguistic play.[12] In the example cited above, however, Zukofsky doesn't seem as interested in showcasing Yiddish's hybridity as much as he wishes to make a case for its lyricism: as Sarah Ponichtera demonstrates, Zukofsky's translation purposefully intensifies the Japanese-like elements of the poem by streamlining Yehoash's original, which is considerably wordier. That is, Zukofsky turns to Yehoash (whose name is repeated almost talismanically, conspicuously incorporated into the poem itself) as an aesthetic counterresponse to the lure of Bach and the Christian culture he embodies. Skillfully deploying the art of juxtaposition, the correspondence between the modern Yiddish poet—who made his reputation as a polyglot with a penchant for wandering deep into the world of "Gentile" writing—and the seventeenth-century Bach is made explicit. First, Zukofsky establishes his own link to Yehoash ("Yehoash / Song's kinship, / The roots we strike . . . Yehoash, / The courses we tide from" [14–15]). Then he turns immediately to another origin story, that of the Baroque composer: "Tree of the Bach family / Compiled by Sebastian himself." One sort of tree is matched by another as Zukofsky's fanciful account of "Veit Bach" (the composer's great-great-grandfather) teaching his son to play the lute gives way to another long swath of Yehoash, this one from a long, soaring lyric spoken by a poet, wandering "Among the Trees."

On this occasion, Zukofsky's rendering is especially telling. Although both versions depict the allures of a pastoral retreat, which affords plenty of opportunities for picking wildflowers ("red anemones, daisies"), Yehoash's speaker longs to escape a world of empty ambitions or "false thrones"—whereas Zukofsky's speaker seeks to forget every unhappy encounter or "hostile see" (that is, hostile "confrontation"). It is a poignant and revelatory modification, speaking perhaps to an early history colored both by a deep desire for the religious Other as a paragon of aesthetic achievement and a deeply traumatic encounter with his own kind. Sometime during 1928, at the start of his career, Zukofsky sent off a sample of his translation of the Yiddish writer Sholem Asch's novel, *Die Mutter*, to *The Menorah Journal*, only to receive a "printed rejection slip." Bad enough to be excluded by America's premier English-language journal devoted to Jewish literature and thought, but to have one's Yiddish renderings rejected as a "poor piece of translation" at a moment when such efforts are central to one's poetics: that is nearly unbearable. True to his feisty nature, Zukofsky goes on the offensive. In an earlier version of "A" 4 (published in 1932 as part of *An "Objectivist's" Anthology*), Zukofsky includes bits of "The Editor's" rejection, including a critique of the "pale" poet with a "painfully inarticulate soul," as well as an ironic "apology" to Yehoash for (mis)using his "jargon" version, sandwiched between long renderings of Yehoash's work (126). Happily, this cranky digression is excised from a later version. But Zukofsky's peevish recounting of the event remains very much part of the public record. In a letter to Pound dated Jan 12, 1930, he explains—rather disingenuously—that he was never really interested in placing any of his work in *Menorah*: "I've always avoided them, wished to avoid them and things seem to be turning out the way I wanted them to" (*Pound/Zukofsky*, 32). The pain is palpable; not only does rejection come at a moment when he is economically struggling, but to target his Yiddish translations means attacking one of the cornerstones of his aesthetic enterprise.

Shame/Space: On the Dumps / In the Dumps

"A" is a singularly restive poem characterized by rapid shifts in perspective and wild mood swings. There is one striking moment when the dust settles and Zukofsky disentangles himself from the throes of desire for the Christian

Other—and considers the fundamental aesthetic issue, asking simply and dispassionately:

> *Can*
> The design
> Of the fugue
> Be transferred
> To poetry? ("A" 6: 3)

But such equanimity sinks under the affective weight generated by his investment in Yiddish and the response it engenders. His faith in Yiddish (and in his renderings or translations) as a worthy response to Bach's formidable achievement (including fugues)—and what it represents—is undermined not by his non-Jewish readers, but by members of his own tribe. Like Spinoza, who was ostracized by both Jews and Christians alike, Zukofsky feels doubly exiled. He cannot claim full access to Christian culture. Nor is he wholly accepted by the Jewish literary elite. So when he comes to "A" 7—that movement that turns out to be the last installment in this first block of his long poem—he finds himself in what I would describe as a "no-man's-land," isolated and beset by a host of difficult feelings: disappointment, frustration—and perhaps even more darkly—*shame*. At least this is one way to think about what drives the explosive performance that is "A" 7.

Space plays a crucial role in these early movements. As we saw, "A" begins with the poet inside Carnegie Hall, absorbed by a passion for the Christian Other, even as he is fumbling for the exit. The next six movements find him moving in and out of "sacred" spaces, trying to make connections between cultures, religions, and languages. Again, his position is akin to Kristeva's "foreigner"—one who is constantly in motion, whose otherness confronts us with our insiderness and with the prospect of becoming Other ourselves. It is an inhospitable space that may explain why, after spending nearly a decade negotiating a range of social differences, Zukofsky has had enough, writing in "A" 6: "Everyone tired of trying to see differences; crosses or uncrossed" (22). (Indeed, interfaith encounters *can* be exhausting.) At this point, Zukofsky seems resigned to taking up his post as perpetual outsider. "A" 7 finds him not merely outside the bulwarks of High Culture, but in a construction zone—an in-between space that brings to mind the work of the Russian philosopher and literary critic Mikhail Bakhtin, who focuses on places where social interactions are in flux. At their best, Zukofsky's poetic spaces aspire to be something like Bakhtin's "marketplace"—a socially indeterminate arena where persons (and their voices) who belong to different social groups (including those of class, gender, religion, ethnicity, and race) come into contact. These are fast-moving, chaotic spaces where the usual assumptions about absolute, reliable difference begin to fray—and where different and transgressive, as well as transformative, connections come into being.

But there are also other sorts of in-between spaces, where the social fallout is more complicated. Consider another one of Bakhtin's sites of interest, the "carnival" (from *Rabelais and His World*). On the one hand, such public revelries (often marked by outrageous linguistic displays) can work to liberating ends, inviting participants to imagine alternatives to the usual structures of power and dominance. On the other hand, insofar as such gatherings are often licensed by the Church or the State, they actually work in the service of sustaining the sanctioning institutions. That is, even as such spaces license a certain amount of socially subversive play, they are a circumscribed outlet that ultimately shores up the very boundaries that are ostensibly being tested. Or to put it another way, Mardi Gras indulgences are but a prequel to Lent with all its restrictions.

Turning back to the final installment in Zukofsky's extended forays into the spaces where Jewishness and Christianity touch (the Jewish Christian borderzone)—an effort undertaken in the interest of identifying sites of cultural/ religious contiguities and reciprocities and perhaps even in redefining boundaries—we discover him occupying a space more like a carnival than a marketplace. Perched "on a stoop to sit here tho no one / Asked me," the poet lets loose with an explosive display of scatology and linguistic play, some of it quite awful, braying: "what month's rent in arrear?? . . . butt butt." Bathroom humor abounds as the poet makes much of digestive disorders, including one bald visual pun that he finds so appealing as to repeat it twice: "A sign creaks— LAUNDRY TO-LET / (creaked—wind)." Then there is an avalanche of bald-faced puns and jokes targeting Christian iconography and precepts, as we stumble our way through a pile of lines about broken rose windows, dead "wood" and "wooden" words, including a wicked jab aimed at both the Gospel according to John and the Book of Exodus: "I- Are Logs"—a mash-up of "In the beginning was the word" (*logos*) and "I am that I am."

Once again Yiddish courses underneath this all—not so much as an explicit linguistic or aesthetic resource (there isn't a single "real" Yiddish word in the entire sequence) but as a hidden, or as Ariel Resnikoff calls it, a "submerged structure" (Resnikoff, 85). With this evocative locution, Resnikoff suggests that Yehoash is merely the tip of the iceberg, the most visible expression of an aesthetic inheritance that runs deep, providing much more than specific literary resources. Rather, Yiddish is a "writing process" (89)—an aesthetic model for bringing multiple cultural registers into dialogue with one another. The importance and role of Yiddish in Zukofsky's work has been a topic of evolving critical debate.[13]

Zukofsky approaches Yiddish as something like a linguistic cauldron, a hyper-intense space characterized by what Ezra Pound might call *melopoeia*, a kind of verse-making in which sound patterns dominate and sometimes even preempt lexical meanings. Here is one striking example of what this approach engenders:

> (Whose clavicembalo? bum? bum? te-hum . . .)
> Not in the say but in the sound's hey-hey-
> The way to-day, Die, die, die, die tap, slow,
> Die, wake up, up up! O Saviour, to day!
> Choose Jews' shoes or whose: anyway Choose! Go! ("A" 7: 41)

"Not in the say but in the sound's hey-hey": offering his variation on a Hasidic *niggun*—a ubiquitous musical form in Ashkenazic culture, a wordless tune characterized by varying melodic phrases and endless phonetic repetitions (like "Die, die, die, die")—Zukofsky not only dismantles that most sacred of scenes, the Crucifixion ("wood," "wooden," "Logs"), but also upends that other sacred association linking Jews to chosenness, rendering them all into a carnival of pure sound. Even Bach (represented metonymically by way of his "clavicembalo") becomes part of the Yiddish song. Like Kristeva's foreigner, Zukofsky becomes an unfettered "dauntless speaker," ferreting out possibilities in a language not wholly his own (32). It is fun stuff, to be sure, but there is also a dark undertow to these lines—which I read as a manifestation of what Jacques Derrida calls "the trace," the full erasure of presence. That is, Zukofsky's renderings retain the sonic qualities but evacuate the possibility of meaning, sounds "signifying nothing" ("Scene of Writing," 230). Even as it performs presence, Yiddish is all but absent.

Writing out of a space that is at once playful, transgressive, and melancholy, Zukofsky reaches for a formal poetic constraint to stage his attack. Unlike the prior movements, which are pretty freewheeling, "A" 7 comprises seven Petrarchan sonnets, dedicated to "horses"—a favorite figure signifying sublime perfection. But any decorous associations that may come to mind when thinking of sonnets—including those comprising Dante's *La Vita Nuova*—scatter to the winds when we realize that these "horses" "have no manes, . . . for their legs are wood" (39). Indeed, it is safe to say that, for Zukofsky, sonnets are the stuff out of which bad poetry is made. As he explains to Pound: "The intention of A7 is to justify an attack on the sonneteers in A1" (a term—"sonneteers"—he uses to describe the likes of Robert Frost and Yvor Winters who reigned supreme among "conservative"—as opposed to avant-garde—modernists) (80). Not even his beloved Bach remains unscathed, as slivers of the Mass find their way into the mix: "The Son / Of Man . . . he found them sleeping . . . Against wood his body close"; that is, the sacred cross is overwritten by a sawhorse.

But Zukofsky is hardly jubilant. After spending a good ten years or so exploring the aesthetic possibilities of Yiddish, Zukofsky ends up in a place memorably described (many years later) by Cynthia Ozick in her classic tragicomedy, "Envy: Or Yiddish in America." Writing on the precipice of Yiddish's extinction, Heschel Edelstein (a beleaguered Yiddish writer desperate to have his work translated into English) bemoans untraversable gaps between his mother tongue and English: "Mameloshen doesn't produce Wastelands" (50). The dilemma seems to speak directly to Zukofsky's poetic breakthrough "Poem Beginning 'The,'" which—as readers will remember—deploys translations of Yiddish poetry in service of a wholesale attack on Eliot's iconic text (*The Waste Land*). Ozick's account of the obstacles facing Yiddish writers seeking to find a place in the American literary landscape becomes even more relevant when Edelstein complains: "The gait, the prance, the hobble of Yiddish is not the same as the gait of English" (49). The image takes us straight to the heart of "A" 7—a movement featuring a pair of "saw horses" which inspires a grand display of the rhythms, the clotted densities of soundings and rude associations linked to Yiddish as "zhargon"—a vulgar, impure, construction. These creatures are a far cry from (and a distorted incarnation of) the glorious steed belonging to Yehoash's Bedouin prince who rode in to reclaim a narrative hijacked by Christianity—or from any of the other equestrian figures of aesthetic sublimity that Zukofsky loves so well. It is tempting to read the entire volcanic sequence as an example of what critic Naomi Seidman has in mind when she describes how a "Jewish" language can go underground working to disrupt or jam the dominant culture—which in this case means mounting an assault on Christianity, the seat of aesthetic wonder (Seidman, 7). Nonetheless, I am reluctant to read Zukofsky in a purely celebratory vein. Instead, I wonder if the poet means to target not only Christian culture, but also his own tribe, who treated him so shabbily. That is, at the risk of sounding like a killjoy, I want to ask if what we hear coursing underneath all the scatology and crude puns comprising "A" 7 is not so much triumph as shame?

Now, as has been frequently pointed out, Yiddish is far from dead. Scholars such as Merle Bachman and Jeffrey Shandler have carefully shown how Yiddish as a "postvernacular" tongue continues to serve an important cultural function—an ongoing source of new music, new literature, not to mention a steadily popular subject for academic as well as communal classes and workshops. These arguments bear out when, turning to the popular press, we discover such testimonies as "Hot Yiddish" and "How I Fell in Love with Yiddish": just two of the recent pieces published in the online Jewish magazine *Tablet*, attesting to a renewed passion for the *mame loshen*. Generally speaking, such pieces, even as they may help foster interest in the language, also lean heavily toward nostalgia. For her part, Seidman offers a more nuanced account in a recent interview pointedly called "Confronting Yiddish Shame." Fearless when it comes to asking hard questions about Jewish culture, Seidman discusses the range of strong emotions provoked by Yiddish, not all of them positive. In the course of the discussion she confesses how, having grown up in a Yiddish-speaking household, she hated her linguistic inheritance. Her given name "Shayndle": "uncool." Only upon discovering that this background could be successfully parlayed into an academic career did she immerse herself in its literature, allowing herself "to fall in love." But such affections do not derail her interest in probing the darker valences of Yiddish as the locus of *shame*, "something to be kept under wraps." Long associated with the feminine, Yiddish was also considered to be coarse, backward, and generally ill-suited to high culture. As but one example of many stories attesting to Yiddish as shame-inducing, Seidman recounts how the acclaimed Yiddish writer known popularly as "Mendele the Book Peddler" would regularly hide whatever Yiddish volume he happened to be reading at the time under a *tallit* (a prayer shawl, a garment linked metonymically to *lashon Hakodesh*—Hebrew, the sacred and hence superior tongue), lest he run into a friend or colleague and risk public embarrassment (https://www.judaismunbound.com/podcast/episode-204-naomi-seidman).

This image invites us to see Zukofsky's stealthy engagement with Yiddish from multiple vantages. To be sure, he views Yiddish as a rich aesthetic resource, a way of enlivening English verse; but he is also acutely aware of its long-marginalized status in the world to which he seeks access—a position at least partially confirmed by his painful encounters with the Jewish American literary establishment, who seemed to have harbored their own biases against the Jewish vernacular. That is, his decision to lard his work with Yiddish either by interpolating unattributed passages of translations or by drawing on its rhythms—while largely concealing its presence—may speak as much to the shame he experiences as to his literary cunning. A profoundly social emotion, shame has been described as a "tribal" response precipitated by the sense of falling short of others' expectations (Solomon, 95), an emotion viscerally manifest in bodily expressions (see Probyn, *Faces of Shame*, 75). Shame foregrounds our intense longing for affirming connections with others, which paradoxically leads to a condition of acute self-awareness (Probyn, 14). In the grips of shame, after being rebuffed by his tribe, Zukofsky produces a highly contrived set of verses, conspicuously calling attention to himself as their maker. It isn't hard to imagine how, after more than a decade spent deploying Yiddish in service of both interfaith and intrafaith dialogue, he finds himself utterly depleted. In a burst of frustration, he gives in to what he has known all along—that Yiddish is horribly, terribly embarrassing—an irredeemably embodied language best suited for fart jokes and other modes of corporeal expression. And thus it is perfectly suited to discharging shame which is, after all, itself a profoundly embodied feeling.

This is a hard place—for me—to end. But a kind of redemptive reading may be had by way of an essay written by James Baldwin in 1953 called "Stranger in the Village." In these pages, Baldwin recounts how, in search of a cheap, quiet place to write, he ends up living in a tiny, isolated Swiss village high in the Alps. Most of the inhabitants are Catholic and have never seen anyone of African descent. Even as they are friendly, they also regard him as a bit of a freak—marveling at his hair, his skin, which they frequently touch—acting, Baldwin speculates, out of a combination of wonder, disbelief, and horror. His feelings of alienation deepen upon realizing that, despite his intimate knowledge of Western high culture, each of these villagers, even "the most illiterate among them, is related in a way that I [Baldwin] am not, to Dante, Shakespeare, Michelangelo, Aeschylus, Da Vinci, Rembrandt, and Racine; the cathedral at Chartres says something to them it cannot say to me" (Baldwin, *Collected Essays*, 44). With this painful knowledge in hand, Baldwin comes into a new kind of self-knowing; renouncing the desire to be other than himself (the affect initially underwriting his approach), he comes into a new sort of self-recognition. He continues: "The cathedral at Chartres . . . says something to the people of this village which it cannot say to me; but it is important to understand that this cathedral says something to me which it cannot say to them." While they experience awe, he experiences terror; for as a man of African descent, he is "identified with the devil." Once acknowledged, the dominant account of his Otherness potentially becomes less powerful, as "I must accept the status which myth, if nothing else, gives me in the West before I can hope to change the myth."

Baldwin's words perhaps help us understand Zukofsky's shame: for "A" 7 finds Zukofsky playing up both the "myth" of Yiddish and the myth of Jewishness as constructed by the Christian Other—as he sets out to find the exit door, a way out of interfaith encounters . . . and a desire to be anything other than himself.

4
Unholy Envy
Karl Shapiro and the Problem of "Judeo-Christianity"

In 1990, Karl Shapiro—then in his seventies—petulantly returned to a wound from which he never fully recovered. He called it his "Jewish problem," writing:

> I once published a book called Poems of a Jew
> To get rid of my Jewish Problem,
> It only made it worse. (*Coda*, 59)

Darkly, provocatively, Shapiro reaches for a term—the "Jewish Problem"—indelibly linked to the horrific event known as the "Final Solution," prodding his reader to ask: Well, what exactly *was* his problem? And, in what ways did writing about Jewishness exacerbate rather than assuage this ache?

This gloomy turn seems surprising, given Shapiro's illustrious start. When he was just thirty years old, his first book, *Person, Place, and Thing* (1942), appeared to wide acclaim. Two years later, he won a Pulitzer Prize for *V-Letter and Other Poems*, a volume composed while serving in the US Army. Upon discharge, Shapiro catapulted to literary stardom, becoming the poetry consultant for the Library of Congress—a position now known as the "United States Poet Laureate." After completing that stint, he took a position at Johns Hopkins University, joining the faculty as an associate professor in creative writing (despite lacking a graduate degree) and becoming the second Jewish professor to ever receive tenure at that august institution. Around the same time, the "problem" makes itself known—or, to put it more precisely, becomes a matter of national attention. I refer here to that literary and politically charged event known as "the Bollingen affair": a fascinating episode in the annals of twentieth-century literary history in which questions of racism, anti-Semitism, and aesthetics converged, making for a roiling mess—especially for Shapiro. Although the incident is well documented and has been told and retold, the details bear repeating. A year into the job at Hopkins, Shapiro is invited to help select the winner of a newly established award to be given to the best book of verse published within the last two years. The rest of the prize committee was a virtual "Who's Who" in American letters, including W. H. Auden, Allen Tate, Katherine Anne Porter, Robert Lowell, and T. S. Eliot. The contest ended up pitting William Carlos Williams's *Paterson* against Ezra Pound's *Pisan Cantos*. Initially, the committee voted unanimously for Pound—who, at the time of these deliberations, was confined to St. Elizabeth's Hospital for the Criminally Insane after being arrested for supporting the Axis powers with his pro-Fascist radio broadcasts. But the day after the vote, Shapiro changed his mind, deciding that Jewishness trumped aesthetics and that he could not endorse an anti-Semite, no matter how luminous or compelling the verse. Many years after the episode, he recalls: "I was suddenly forced into a conscious decision to stand up and be counted as a Jew" (*Paris Review*, 199). The ensuing controversy, memorably described as a "small scale poetic Dreyfus case," had *The Saturday Review of Literature* leading a pack of journalists seeking out various committee members to solicit more information about the conversations leading up to the incendiary decision (Rubin, 112). Although most of the participants, including Shapiro and Eliot, shunned the press, the incident—which was initially cast in terms of anti-Semitism—quickly devolved into a debate between those who favored "high" literary works, such as those of Pound, and those who advocated for a more "middlebrow" aesthetics, as practiced by Williams. In his brief account of the episode, Anthony Julius pointedly rebukes Eliot for evading the challenge of anti-Semitism first by claiming simply to be "thoroughly discomforted by the affair," and then shifting the attention away from the particulars by complaining about "the degree of terrorization men of letters appear to suffer" (Julius, 208). Shapiro, however, finds the episode much more searing, and with lasting consequences. Somewhat melodramatically, he recalls feeling "with the innate sadness of the Jew that from then on the door of their Establishment would be closed, or half-closed to him, in the same way he would never be invited to their Club where things were decided once and for all and that from then on he would be considered just another refuser" (Rubin, 113–14).

Drama notwithstanding, both the Bollingen affair and Shapiro's response are strikingly prescient, for together they speak to a much larger and messier cultural phenomenon: even more than in Zukofsky's earlier decades, the Christianizing narrative underwriting American literary culture now flourishes in the mid-1950s. In the course of mapping how the tensions between the push and pull of assimilation and anti-Semitism shaped twentieth-century Anglo-American literary culture, Jonathan Freedman focuses on the power wielded by the New Critics, such as Cleanth Brooks and W. K. Wimsatt, and by that poem central to their enterprise, T. S. Eliot's *The Waste Land*. As noted in the preceding chapter, Eliot's epic, written in the early '20s, had a long reach. During the '50s the poem figured large in high school and college curricula. And more often than not, it was taught as a "quest to rescue a specifically Christian faith" from a sterile modernity (Freedman, 179–81). This is the worldview beginning to take root when Shapiro, who as early as 1945 dismissively calls Eliot's poem "our world-weary masterpiece," joins the Department of English at Johns Hopkins University (*Essay on Rime*, 17). From 1947 to 1950, he uneasily plays the part of poet-in-residence. Of those years at Hopkins, a former student recalls how Shapiro dwelled in a kind of self-imposed exile—dramatized by his decision to work in a "garret," in the building's cupola, rather than occupying an office on the fourth floor with the rest of the English faculty (Rubin, 108).

Depleted by the Bollingen "business," and longing to get away from both academia and the Baltimore area, Shapiro jumps at an invitation to move to Chicago and take on the editorship of *Poetry*, the illustrious literary magazine that had fallen on hard times (Rubin, 114). For the next six years, he demonstrates a remarkable talent for soliciting work from such canonical figures as Williams, Marianne Moore, Wallace Stevens, and, yes, even Ezra Pound and T. S. Eliot—as well as cultivating new talent. Adrienne Rich, Frank O'Hara, James Merrill, and Allen Ginsberg were among those whose reputations grew under Shapiro's tutelage. But it seems that Shapiro may have been just biding his time, holding his breath until he felt free to speak his mind. After a successful run at *Poetry*, he reenters the academic world, taking a position at the University of Nebraska. While there, he writes an essay for the *American Scholar*, attacking the high "priests" of modern verse—Yeats, Pound, and Eliot—for crafting a religion of culture that now dominates the academy as "every sophomore is dismally aware" ("Modern Poetry as Religion," 289). Although Shapiro has it out for all the modernists, he saves his harshest words for Eliot. He questions the depth of the poet's commitment to Anglicanism, suggesting that it is but a "dismal crutch for a society he detests," and that what Eliot really wants is to preside over a religion of culture where he plays not merely priest but God himself. A year later, Shapiro refines his attack, at once questioning the radical originality of Eliot's "world-weary masterpiece" and explicitly targeting its Christianizing aesthetic: "Every major doctrine of Eliot's can be found in Hulme's *Speculations*, the most basic one that relates fundamental Christian doctrine to a theory of society and a theory of poetics" (Shapiro, *The Poetry Wreck*, 22).

Surveying Shapiro's career, scholars seem to fasten upon the Bollingen episode as the defining moment when the poet was obliged to acknowledge his Jewishness and to take up arms against the modernist cabal so deeply implicated in a Christianized aesthetic.[1] To be sure, the event was traumatic and had a profound effect on the young poet. But it is also true that Shapiro had been chafing against certain religious undercurrents long before this seismic occasion. As it turns out, nearly a third of the poems constituting the bluntly titled *Poems of a Jew* had initially appeared already in *V-Letter and Other Poems*, a volume composed in the Pacific Theater where Shapiro served during World War II. That is, Shapiro comes of age, at least poetically, during what has been described as the "triumphant" establishment of "Tri-Faith America," a cultural construct designed to dismantle and replace the Protestant hegemony with a counterimage of Catholic, Jewish, and Protestant ecumenical coexistence founded upon a shared commitment to religious, social, political, and civic equality and reciprocal tolerance. This development is fueled by multiple events and concerns, including and perhaps most especially by America's involvement in World War II, which played a major role in the nation's collective investment in the idea of a "Judeo-Christian" tradition. Historian Deborah Dash Moore identifies this link—in the course of exploring the role that military service had in transforming the idea of American Jewishness—as a provincial category of ethnic/religious belonging, to a more capacious and "progressive" model of faith-based identity. While the term "Judeo-Christianity" doesn't become popular until the 1950s, experientially it is woven into the life of American soldiers—who participated regularly in ecumenical services in which a Jewish chaplain might preside over a Sunday morning service comprising readings from the New Testament (read by Protestant and Catholic soldiers) and deliver a sermon that preached against the perils of Nazism by relaying a story about Jewish heroism and the Warsaw ghetto uprising (31–35).

Recently, Kevin Schultz has expanded upon this momentous turn in the history of religion in American life, paying particular attention to the prominent role played by the National Conference of Christian and Jews (NCCJ), which understood the marketability of the "Judeo-Christian tradition" as a way of galvanizing widespread support for the war effort. With great success, the organization sent out "war trios" (representatives from Judaism, Catholicism, and Protestantism) to share their vision of national unity and religious harmony with the troops stationed throughout the European and Pacific Theaters. In addition to mounting programs promoting religious freedom as an indisputably democratic value, the trios distributed "tri-faith prayer cards" so that soldiers would have ready access to the liturgies affirming this vision (43–49). Schultz maintains that the effort was so effective and wide-reaching that "by the end of the war nearly every American soldier had touched a piece of NCCJ literature, watched an NCCJ film, or gone to an NCCJ army base event." And you didn't even have to be enlisted to receive its unifying message. In 1941, Everett Clinchy, president of the NCCJ, warned Americans in a nationwide radio broadcast that they "needed to know that there would be no Judaeo-Christian religion if the Nazis win" (58). In other words, the war was not about racial, religious, or ethnic tolerance; it was about securing a uniquely hybrid American brand of spirituality. To be clear, its founders were absolutely aware of the theological morass with which they were playing. There were the Catholics, "some who had been taught to see other religions as fundamentally wrong and the Jews, some who wondered how Jesus fit into all this"—but by and large NCCJ side-stepped these potential sinkholes by focusing on the larger, shared goal of civic harmony and world peace.

Shapiro, however, is decidedly reluctant to embrace this new, theologically charged brand of democracy flying under the sign of "Judeo-Christianity," explicitly naming his discomfort in two poems, both of which were first presented in *V-Letter* (first celebrated) and then reprinted in *Poems of a Jew* (now reviled). As an ardent formalist, at least during his early years, Shapiro deploys received poetic forms to contain expressions of dissent—but only just barely. In "Sunday: New Guinea" balladically rhymed quatrains, comprising three decasyllabic lines and a fourth bleeding out into twelve or thirteen syllables, make for a weighty, all too earthbound poem. The first two stanzas depict infantrymen dutifully answering the call to religious service as "From every side, singly, in groups, in pairs, / Each to his kind of service come to worship Him." But this careful ritual does little to stave off the encroaching chaos; in the third stanza, religious equanimity doesn't stand a chance in the face of natural and social entropy: "The jungle outmaneuvers creeping war / And crawls within the circle of our sacred rites." With this interruption, collective duty gives way to individual reverie, as the poet-speaker admits that "I long for our disheveled Sundays home, / Breakfast, the comics, news of latest crimes." Unlike Wallace Stevens who, in "Sunday Morning," celebrates such casual rituals as the solitary consumption of "coffee and oranges . . . [which] mingle to dissipate the holy hush of ancient sacrifice," Shapiro isn't interested in making a bid for a secularized spirituality. Rather, his claim is more modest, but profoundly true: for an American Jew, Sunday is not the Sabbath, a day designated for sacred worship; despite the dictates of the US Army or the NCCJ, Sunday is simply a day off—filled with small domestic pleasures, no more and no less.

Wistfulness gives way to something bleaker in "Christmas Eve, Australia." With this Petrarchan sonnet, Shapiro efficiently punctures whatever illusory notions Americans at home may have about GI's enjoying a day of holiday cheer and holy reflection. The octave depicts an ominously unsettled landscape featuring a dark variation on the rising of the eastern star which was said to have heralded Christ's birth: "And there one crystal like a grain of light / Sticks in the crucible of day and cools." Abandoned by the promise of religion as a unifying force, the sestet then finds the poet-speaker turning inward and, in perfect iambic pentameter, indulging in a perfectly ordinary response: "I smoke and read my Bible and chew gum" as he thinks about "Christ and Christmas." And what of Jesus, the figure to whom this day is dedicated? He is but a "serious name," invoked as the soldiers curse the war that has brought them to this place with its strange insects and "foreign birds."

Read within the context of *V-Letter*, such poems register as sober efforts to describe the mindset of American soldiers during the waning days of World War II. But read within the context of *Poems of a Jew*, they register as highly crafted, ill-tempered expressions of a resentful, alienated Jew estranged from the dominant narrative underwriting a collective ethos. Writing in the latter volume's short introduction, Shapiro specifies that as far as he is concerned Judaism is not a religion; and, moreover, when it comes to religion, "the artist's contribution . . . must in the nature of things be heretical" (ix). With this aside, Shapiro briefly revisits his long quarrel with high modernism's distorted investment in the "religion of poetry." He then quickly regains his focus, insisting that Judaism is an indelible, intransigent identity category, sealed by "the Covenant, the intimacy of Jew and God. This intimacy is not sentimental; on the contrary, it is unfriendly" (x).[2] At a moment when this position is at risk of being absorbed by that sprawling construction known as "Judeo-Christianity," Shapiro writes in the service of securing Jewish difference—even as he views this affiliation harshly. Taking a position that he later likens to that of "a guerrilla fighter or sniper," Shapiro makes strategic forays into the Jewish Christian borderzone (Phillips, "Interview," 13). But it is rough going, since the terrain requires navigating some decidedly ugly, ignoble feelings—feelings that make way for some interesting, purposively ugly poems.

A Poetics of Envy

Typically, when it comes to feelings, literary studies tends to privilege such major passions as fury, awe, and grief—feelings that lead to some kind of cathartic reckoning. But now, with the appearance of Sianne Ngai's *Ugly Feelings*, which has taken affect studies in important new directions, we have begun to attend to a range of so-called minor emotions including paranoia, irritation, disgust, and envy—the latter of which saturates *Poems of a Jew*. Rather than being a source of pride or even just cultural/religious affirmation, Jewish difference is an irritant that provokes a state of chronic envy—one among several repugnant feelings that Ngai identifies as "ugly" (11).

As my readers will recall, this is not the first time the word "envy" appears in conjunction with interfaith encounters. At the outset of this study, I discussed Krister Stendahl's evocative claim that effective interfaith dialogue depends upon participants being willing to cultivate a certain mode of psychic vulnerability that he calls "holy envy." This is a decidedly challenging invitation, since it requires one who seeks to engage in interfaith exchange to do more than offer the usual gestures of tolerance, or even the well-meaning murmurings of mild curiosity. Instead, one must be first open to admitting that another religion has something genuinely desirable to offer that is absent from one's own, and then be willing to actively feel longing for this quality or attribute. Once the ache of real lack is experienced, the door swings open wide to admit of envy—at which point dialogue can commence.

What Stendahl has in mind, of course, is a certain kind of elevated envy that will advance cross-religious harmony and mutual understanding, envy of a "holy" kind. He doesn't mean to sanction the kind of embarrassingly meanspirited barbs at religious otherness or outwardly aggressive attacks to which Shapiro's speaker gives voice, for the kind of painful contortions on display in *Poems of a Jew*, as we shall see, cast a real pall on the idealized affect to which Stendahl would have us aspire.

As I understand it, this dark and sometimes cringeworthy volume offers a compelling narrative detailing Shapiro's efforts to work through—or at least know—this exceptionally "ugly feeling." Focusing on a handful of its poems, I want to track how the poet navigates a discrete set of emotive positions, starting with "The Alphabet"—a stern utterance offered in the interest of eliminating all prospects of envy by establishing firm religious boundaries and affirming Jewish triumphalism. Yet upon facing the aesthetic consequences of this difference, his efforts crumble; consumed by envy, the poet is undone. The next suite of texts finds Shapiro—who in some instances speaks as a "lyric I," and sometimes assumes the guise either of an unspecified narrator or a thinly veiled persona—descending deeper into this noxious feeling. The narrative, however, ends on a note of equanimity, as evidenced in a pair of poems which find the poet first exploring sites of religious contiguities—and then, in a poignant turn, imagining what it would mean to do away with religious difference altogether. As we will see, this psychic journey is far from pleasant—and makes for some mean-spirited, rather awful poems. But it affords real insight into the pain that such unvarnished encounters with the religious other can engender.

First, however, I want to give a brief working account of some of the more salient features of this notoriously non-cathartic emotion, beginning with Melanie Klein's concise definition: "Envy is the angry feeling that another person possesses and enjoys something desirable—the envious impulse being to take it away or to spoil it" (181). What clinicians explain, poets make vivid—as in Ovid's lurid account of this monstrous creature:

> Envy's house is filthy with dark decay. Her cave was hidden deep among valleys, sunless and inaccessible to the winds, a melancholy place and filled with a numbing cold. Fire is always absent, and fog always fills it. . . .
> Her sight is skewed, her teeth are livid with decay, her breast is green with bile, and her tongue is suffused with venom. She only smiles at the sight of suffering. She never sleeps, excited by watchful cares. She finds men's successes disagreeable, and pines away at the sight. She gnaws and being gnawed is also her own punishment. (*Metamorphosis*, II, 757–60)

Note especially here how Ovid's representation highlights not only the all-consuming nature of this negative emotion, but also how it impedes one's ability to see an Other clearly or fairly. Recognized by the Catholic tradition as one of the seven "capital" or "cardinal" sins, envy is often named as the primary motive when recounting well-known stories about sibling rivalry, such as the murderous encounter between Cain and Abel, and the all-but-lethal efforts of Joseph's brothers to dispose of their father's favorite son. Not surprisingly, however, it is the psychoanalysts who have attended to envy most thoroughly. In the interest of generating a frame for reading the vagaries of envy coursing through *Poems of a Jew*, I offer below a thumbnail review of the three most salient accounts of this "minor" emotion.

Most psychoanalytic accounts of envy, including that of Klein's, locate this dystopic emotion in childhood. Freud, for example, uses the term to describe an older child's feeling of bitter resentment upon seeing her younger sibling nursing. More famously and provocatively, he also reaches for the term envy to describe what he maintains is the gnawing desire on the part of a girl-child to possess a penis just like her male counterparts (boys, it seems, are exempt from such destructive feelings, since Freud doesn't posit any parallel experience on their part). In a move that might be understood as a pointed corrective to this biased account, Klein locates the genesis of envy at a much earlier stage of development, taking the maternal "breast"—a metonym for the source of the child's sense of well-being—as the object of desire (183–90). As she understands it, envy is triggered once the child perceives that the object which was once experienced solely as a source of comfort and nourishment (the maternal breast) is now also a source of painful deprivation. This recognition sets off intense feelings of frustration and rage that result in an aggressive effort to attack and destroy the desired object. But rather than shoring up a sense of self, these envious outbursts make for an acutely frayed sense of identity. Indeed, the corrosive effects of envy are central to Jacques Lacan's contribution—which importantly introduces the role of a third party, the autonomous Other, into the psychic drama fostering envy. Like Klein, Lacan begins with a primal scene, that of a child looking on as another child is being nursed—based on his reading of Saint Augustine: "I have myself observed a baby to be jealous, though it could not speak; it was livid as it watched bitterly another infant at the breast" (Smith, *Envy*, 278). According to Lacan, what spurs envy here (he dismisses the word "jealousy" as inadequate) is the recognition that the love and attention of the Other (mother) are being bestowed upon another. With this reading, Lacan introduces two points central to understanding the situation in which Shapiro's speaker finds himself. First, Lacan clarifies how the object of envy is distinctly similar to the person experiencing envy; that is, envy is a narcissistic disorder. Second, he demonstrates how envy is triggered by the gaze of the Other—an agent of power and prestige—who bestows favor upon one person instead of another, thus engendering a sense of lack, shame, and chronic inferiority—or, to put it more bluntly, a full-blown identity crisis.

Turning back to Shapiro, we discover a poet in the grips of envy, with no resolution in sight; his distorted and distorting perspective is further aggravated by a whole host of negative feelings that he brings to the very idea of an identity-based poetics. Like others who are drawn to the strange arc of Shapiro's career, Andrew Gross begins his thoroughgoing analysis of how questions of identity and aesthetics impacted Shapiro's poetry with the Bollingen affair. As Gross understands it, the problem was not so much a matter of Shapiro being forced to own up to his Jewishness—for while the poet never enthusiastically embraced this affiliation, he certainly never denied it. Instead, voting against Pound meant that Shapiro had to forgo a strong investment in a modernist poetics of impersonality and of his previously disinterested stance in order to make a concerted claim on behalf of a group identity—that of Jewishness. But the problem doesn't end there. Even as he implicitly refutes the dominant view of art as strictly a matter of individual rather than political expression, thereby alienating the so-called liberal constituency with whom he had been affiliated, he also alienates the Jewish press, who see him as dangerously at odds with the idea of "positive" or "affirmative Jewishness"—an ideology proclaimed loudly from American synagogue pulpits and in Jewish community board rooms in the aftermath of World War II (Glenn, *The Jewish Cold War*, 5–6). Shortly after the publication of *Poems of a Jew*, Irving Feldman, writing in the pages of *Commentary*, finds it profoundly lacking conceptually and aesthetically. Calling the poems "dull and factitious," Feldman declares that "viewed as documents, these poems seem to lack an inner Jewish consciousness; viewed as art, they lack lyric centrality." He then complains that they must be dismissed as symptomatic of a "waning Jewish identity," noting how instead of writing about Jewish holidays and "ceremonies," Shapiro features "Sunday, Christmas, and confirmation." With this observation, Feldman stumbles onto one of the volume's central preoccupations, only to dismiss it as a liability rather than recognizing it as an asset, a subject of real interest. Fifteen years later, Harold Bloom counts Shapiro among those who contribute to "The Sorrows of American Jewish Poetry," contending that the volume offers little other than "a curious mixture of sentimentalism, misinformation about Judaism, and the by now too familiar incongruity of an overtly Jewish stance being rendered in an alien idiom, here that of W. H. Auden and Louis MacNeice" (5). With this last complaint, Bloom reveals, like Feldman before him, a failure to understand what fuels Shapiro's fierce attachment to received English forms and metrical patterns. In 1975, many years after *Poems of a Jew*, when free verse had become *de rigueur*, Shapiro bemoans "the degeneration of intellectual literacy" as evidenced by students in his creative writing classes who champion their right to express their personal feelings without being constrained by the dictates of formal verse. In a telling outburst, he carps that "the only students who know as simple and *universal* a thing as iambic pentameter have gone to Catholic schools. Iambic pentameter is not Catholic; it happens to be the metrical form in which almost all English poetry since Chaucer has been written and is still" (Shapiro, *The Poetry Wreck*, 255; emphasis mine). That is, what Bloom takes as an act of religious or cultural capitulation, Shapiro promotes as an act of resistance, defying the Christianizing narrative underwriting English letters.

Time does not seem to take the edge off things. In 2005, David Kaufmann reviews a new edition of Shapiro's *Selected Poems* in the Arts section of the well-known Jewish newspaper, *The Forward*. Treating the poet as a sad relic of the '50s, Kaufmann calls Shapiro a "defensive and self-contained Jew" who, in the absence of an urgent focus like the Holocaust, offers only an "indeterminate version of Jewishness . . . without a trace of Yiddishkeit" (2). Kaufmann's failure to engage *any* of the poems is itself unfair, maybe even unconscionable; but hastily dismissing Shapiro as nothing more than a cultural artifact also means riding roughshod over a complex and subtle turn in the story of the Jewish Christian borderzone.

Indeed, most readers are so thoroughly distracted by Shapiro's petulant tone and confrontational stance (exemplified by such emphatic claims as "The unbelievable survival of the Jews must be seen against a background of Nothing, a people outside art or literature") that they have little to say about the poems themselves. Furthermore, they overlook this odd, but striking epigraph:

branding instead of beauty

DEAD SEA SCROLLS

With this move, Shapiro gestures toward a fascinating installment in the construction of Jewish Christianity, at least as played out in the American imagination: the discovery of the Dead Sea Scrolls. Although unearthed in 1947, it took nearly a decade for the world to learn of their existence. Writing in 1955, the renowned critic and journalist Edmund Wilson was among the first of the nonacademic press to provide a wonderfully long, detailed account of this historic event for the *New Yorker*, focusing particularly on what the scrolls meant for that nascent construction: "Judeo-Christianity." Given that throughout the '50s this publication frequently included Shapiro's work, it is likely that the poet knew of the essay. Even if there is no direct evidence of his familiarity, the *New Yorker* was certainly part of the world in which he trafficked.

The piece is completely absorbing, as Wilson offers both a wide-angle view of the "monotonous, dreadful wilderness" where the scrolls were first discovered and a telephoto take on the complex and controversial nature of their contents. Drawing extensively on the ancient historical narratives of Josephus, Pliny, and Philo, Wilson reports that the scrolls belonged to the Essenes—a monastic sect whose practices and beliefs "obviously" resemble that of early Christianity. Moreover, unlike the Jews, who conceived of themselves as a "race" into which one must be born, the Essenes, like the Christians, were a volitional community (65). Occupying a space in between Judaism and Christianity, the scrolls are best viewed as a body of "transitional literature." Dwelling in the borderzone, they provoke a "certain nervousness" on both sides of the aisle. Jews resist these documents because they suggest that Judaism could have birthed the "religion of Jesus," while Christians are made unhappy by their suggestion that Christ's ascent "was not strictly a result of a magnanimous act of God to allow the salvation of the human race," but rather an outcome of cultural, religious interaction and mutual transformation (116).[3]

What is it about these scrolls that Shapiro finds so compelling? How do they speak to his larger project? My answer begins by noting how, like the NCCJ, the Dead Sea Scrolls might be construed as a religiously leaky entity—especially as described by Wilson—and thus ideally suited to a cultural moment defined by the rise of "Judeo-Christianity."[4] The very concept sets Shapiro's teeth on edge. And, intent upon clear distinctions, he lands firmly on the side of Jewish severity as opposed to Christian sublimity: "branding instead of beauty" (1). Taking his lead perhaps from what Wilson represents as the Essenian conviction in an identity grounded in discipline, Shapiro makes his allegiances clear with the opening poem, "The Alphabet," which begins: "The letters of the Jews are strict as flames." "Strict" is, indeed, the operative word here. Although it does not conform to any identifiable form, the poem is conspicuously structured: two stanzas, twelve lines, written in iambic pentameter woven tightly by an intricate rhyme scheme—a loose variation, perhaps, on a sestina. Shapiro began his career as a staunch formalist, eschewing free verse—a strategy marshaled as part of an overall resistance to high modernist aesthetics.[5] But in "The Alphabet," like many of the poems in the volume, form plays a polemical, explicitly marked mimetic strategy, dramatizing a "Jewish" commitment to corporeal rigor or embodied discipline, by contrast to a "Christian" affinity for spiritual expansiveness. That is, for Shapiro, formal verse is "Jewish" while free verse is "Christian."[6]

Although he is known and mostly praised for being an "accessible" poet who celebrates the ordinary (auto wrecks, drugstores, and flies as opposed to conceits about fleas à la John Donne), Shapiro turns, in "The Alphabet," to the opaque and the elliptical, as the poem is filled with lip-numbing alliterations and obscure allusions. Furthermore, we are confronted with a tangle of images whereby the alphabetical "letters of the Jews" are variously likened to "barbed wire," "tinder flowers," and "dancing knives," much of which is hard to make sense of—that is, until we recall the opening gesture toward the Dead Sea Scrolls. Read within the context of that seismic discovery, and even more pointedly within Wilson's account of their murky doctrinal status, the poem comes into focus as a fierce claim for Jewishness as an unassimilable entity. Staging an imaginary encounter with the newly discovered scrolls, or another bit of unspecified Hebrew text, the poet-speaker takes its sheer presence as part and parcel of its harsh message: "The chosen letters bristle like barbed wire / That hedge the flesh of man / Twisting and tightening the book that warns. . . ." Unconcerned with specific content, the poet-speaker attends to the text's materiality as hard evidence of the insoluble difference between Jewishness and Christianity: "The letters of the Jews are black and clean / And lie in chain-line over white Christian pages" (3).

According to Wilson, the scrolls are to be understood as proto-Christian documents, and the Qumran monastery where they were found should be celebrated "more than Bethlehem or Nazareth [as] the very cradle of Christianity"—material evidence requisite to securing an argument for theological supersession. That is, the Dead Sea Scrolls dwell in that gray zone known by some as "Judeo-Christianity"—with an emphasis on Christianity. Shapiro obliquely counters this account by suggesting that these ancient parchments speak to a kind of apocalyptic messianism (a more dynamic, selective view of temporality) to disable a problematic historical narrative in which catastrophic anti-Semitism is clumsily bandaged over with sentimental odes to universal brotherhood under the sign of "Judeo-Christianity"—a formulation which again casts Christianity in the starring role. In this way, he uncannily takes on two of the main sources of anxiety afflicting the Jewish American community during the '40s and '50s: anti-Semitism and assimilation (Glenn, *The Jewish Cold War*, 23). But as we know, prophets are rarely thanked for their trouble.

In the first stanza of "The Alphabet," unspecified words are likened to a "burning bush," functioning as searing manifestations of divine presence. These words, fiercely ablaze, consume the dominant Christian narrative: "this flickering pyre / Unsacrifices as the bled son of man," even as "his crown of thorns" are plaited—presumably in anticipation of a "real" messianic arrival. The process gains momentum in the second stanza where the legacy of anti-Semitism, a feature of linear history, gives way to ahistorical, vaguely apocalyptic redemption. Rising from the "still speaking embers of ghettos," "the letters of the Jews" are likened first to "tinder flowers" and then more ominously to "dancing knives":

> These are the letters that all men refuse
> And will refuse until the king arrives
> And will refuse until the death of time
> And all is rolled back in the book of days. (3)

With these lines Shapiro secures the idea of Jewish difference, alienating those who lean toward the more expedient, less antagonistic notion of "Judeo-Christianity" and also fending off those Christian readers who might cherish the idea of supersessionism. The poem, indeed, has a chilling effect on at least one Christian reader—a New Jersey pastor who recently uploaded "The Alphabet" on his blog, commenting that surely the poem "will cause Christian readers to wonder and wince." "Wonder" provoked perhaps by the firm stance taken against the unquestionable appeal of Christian messianism while "wincing" in response to the poet's unflinching account of the role Christianity played in the anti-Semitic scourge that culminated in the Holocaust: "Where go the sisters of the Gothic rose . . . past the almost natural crime. / Past the still speaking embers of the ghettos. . . ."

Such resolve, however, is hard to sustain, especially when Shapiro confronts the stark material difference between the kinds of aesthetic possibilities licensed by each doctrine. At this point, Shapiro's unique status as the poet of "Jewish lack" comes into focus: the result, as chronicled in "The Synagogue," makes for a sober, earthbound reckoning with the aesthetic consequences of religious difference. "The Synagogue" is a singularly stolid piece of work: eleven sestets, composed of doggedly iambic pentameter lines, all dedicated to a dour exercise in comparison and contrast—with Judaism coming up short, at least as far as poetic potential is concerned. The first stanza lays it out deftly, grimly:

> The synagogue dispirits the deep street,
> Shadows the face of the pedestrian,
> It is the adumbration of the Wall,
> The stone survival that laments itself,
> Our old entelechy of stubborn God,
> Our calendar that marks a separate race. (8)

In addition to his use of conspicuous sibilance and alliteration, which makes for a weighty effect, Shapiro's use of archaisms ("adumbration," "entelechy") ensures a strikingly unlovely start. This weightiness becomes all but unbearable when, in the next stanza, we are dazzled by this luminous portrait: "The swift cathedral palpitates the blood / The soul moves upward like a wing to meet / The pinnacles of the saints" (8). The contrast between the gloomy versus the glorious is a tidy example of what Sianne Ngai might call "stupblimity versus sublimity"—the former being a "mutation of the other." "Stupblimity": a purposively off-putting word crafted to describe the numbing or stupefying effects of what Ngai calls the kind of "thick language" that figures widely in the work of such avant-garde poets as Gertrude Stein, Samuel Beckett, and Kenneth Goldsmith, who offer linguistic pileups to disquieting ends. These poets preempt the longing for sublime transport that we typically bring to poetry, mostly by exhausting us with repetition. Instead of the "holy awe" (Ngai's term for the sublime swell) that we may feel when confronted or gifted by a glimpse of the vast and infinite, we find ourselves slogging through pages and pages of the ordinary with little in the way of revelation or relief (248–99).

Now Shapiro, of course, is anything but a poet of the avant-garde. Thoroughly committed to formal verse—except for a brief dalliance with prose poetry—Shapiro is not much of an experimentalist. But in a poem such as "The Synagogue," with its grim complaining lines, the dysphoric nature of the "stupblime" is rather plain, as he offers his litany of lack. First, he mourns the relative paucity of life-affirming rituals when it comes to Jewish funeral rites: "The Jew has no bedecked magnificat / But sits in stricken ashes after death, / Refusing grace; his grave is flowerless. . . ." Never mind that Catholic funerals do not typically include the "magnificat"; it is clear that Jewish tradition simply does not measure up. Complaints pile up as the poet directs his grief toward the chronically androcentric nature of Jewish (read "rabbinic") culture: "Zion womanless refuses grace / To the first woman as to Magdalene." Even as this complaint may register as all too familiar, Shapiro adds something new by suggesting that this patriarchal bias comes at a real theological cost. Eschewing both flowers and the feminine is symptomatic of a greater loss, a loss so grievous that it merits repetition. Wallowing in grief, the Jew "refuses" "grace"—the gift of God's openhanded love that Christians receive upon baptism. Suffering from a condition of perpetual displacement, Jews decidedly get the short end of the stick, impoverished recipients of what, at the poem's close, Shapiro calls "a devious reward / For faith he gave us land and took the land / Thinking us exiles of all humankind." Yet these gripes are minor compared to the real deprivation underwriting these grievances:

> Our wine is wine, our bread is harvest bread
> That feeds the body and is not the body.
> Our blessing is to wine but not the blood
> Nor to the sangreal, the sacred dish. We bless
> The whiteness of the dish and bless the water
> And are not anthropophagous to him. (9)

With its unremarkable repetitions and ugly archaisms, the stanza speaks to an aesthetic firmly grounded in the domain of the material rather than the transcendent. Moreover, with these lines, Shapiro makes the source of this constraint explicit. Setting himself against that subtly coercive construction known as "Judeo-Christianity," Shapiro insists on asserting clear, unassailable differences between the two religious dispositions. This kind of theological discernment, however, comes at a cost. A few years ago, reflecting upon Jewish aesthetics, I noted how, in this poem, Shapiro maintains that this cultural/religious orientation precludes the art of metaphoric transformation: "Our blessing is to wine but not the blood." Indeed, Shapiro declares in the collection's preface that "Jews are an artless people, a people in dread of the graven image" (x). As I commented:

> Specifically, this claim speaks to an anti-iconic strain in Jewish thought. More generally, it calls attention to the problematic status of

the art of representation, which often depends on metaphoric equations. That is, . . . the Jew is at a disadvantage when it comes to practicing the art of metaphoric transformation. Ideologically bound to the literal, the Jew supposedly has a fundamental distrust of the figurative. (Shreiber, *Singing*, 47)

Thus, necessarily, "Our wine is wine, our bread is harvest bread."

Rereading the poem now through the lens of envy, I see the deficit as even more severe. From this perspective, Jewishness precludes access to what Regina Schwartz calls the "sacramental art." Grounded in the Eucharist, the paradigmatic sacrament during which the primary elements of bread and wine are substantively transformed/transubstantiated into Christ's body and his blood, thereby rendering the Savior fully present: this is potent indeed. Underwriting this theopoetic platform is a fundamental belief in a world that is overflowing with potential meanings, for sacramental language swells "toward significance beyond what is strictly signified." As Schwartz explains further, "with its evocation of sounds and images, indeed an entire sensory reservoir, poetry is especially well suited to this surplus of meaning" (6). Such is the world available to the poet writing under the sign of the Eucharist. Thus the poet who consigns himself to what Shapiro views as the comparatively narrow straits of "Jewish" aesthetics forgoes the abundant realms of "sacramental art" and is utterly excluded from such soaring regions. But it is not merely a matter of having diminished access to poetic resources; rather, it means being put at a real aesthetic disadvantage. Kimberly Johnson, in her account of "eucharistic poetics," expanding upon Schwartz's argument, focuses on the sacrament's function as the site of "Real Presence," a means of enabling the worshipper's body to make manifest Christ's full presence—both materially and spiritually (25). That is, the Eucharist realizes what is one of lyric's primary aspirations, to render both the poem and the poem's speaker fully present—or as poet-critic Allen Grossman puts it, to make manifest "the presence of presence." To be barred from this world, which also affords access to the art of metaphoric transformation/transubstantiation, puts the would-be lyric poet at a real disadvantage—or so Shapiro suggests.

Confronting the full weight of deprivation, Shapiro is consumed by envy—a feeling that begets a response much darker and protracted than a mere fit of pique or irritated outburst—a deep ache saturating much of the volume. Now this pain has not gone unnoticed; but interestingly enough, when readers try to name the feelings underwriting *Poems of a Jew*, they choose words like "cranky," "irritable," and "contrary"—instead of loftier terms such as anger, outrage, or fear, or discomforting descriptors such as "envy." In addition to commenting on the peculiarly aggressive, quarrelsome nature of the volume, some readers duly note that Shapiro seems intent on resisting or subverting the prevailing view that somehow Christianity has a lock on universal human experience. But the connections between theme, motive, aesthetics, and effect have gone largely unexplored (Kaufmann, Goldstein). So to begin redressing this oversight, I propose taking my lead from Ngai's work, pursuing the notion of ugliness: for one of the distinguishing features of the poems constituting *Poems of a Jew* is that they are filled with ugly images, ugly words, and ugly feelings.

Ugly Feelings Can Make for Ugly Poems

Consider, to start, Shapiro's choice of a particularly cumbersome and offensive word, "anthropophagous" (as in cannibalism) to describe the Eucharist—a ritual of which Jews most decidedly do not partake: "We bless / The whiteness of the dish and bless the water / And are not anthropophagous to him." Out of all the options available, Shapiro certainly takes one of the more provocative routes. How to understand such a move? Well, at least two possibilities come to mind. The first is rather benign, indeed perhaps too much so. It begins with Anthony Julius's analysis of explicitly anti-Semitic poems such as Eliot's "Bleistein with a Cigar," "Burbank with a Baedeker" and "Dirge"—and how Eliot doesn't merely represent anti-Semitic stereotypes, but is actively implicated in perpetuating the dynamic by confirming his readers' inclination to "recoil in disgust" when encountering the "Jew" as the embodiment of social disorder and disease. Keeping in mind Shapiro's unmitigated hostility toward this modernist giant, it may be that he risks his own poetic reputation by writing ugly poems in order to expose and perhaps disable this toxic phenomenon; that is, Shapiro seeks to disarm or at least neutralize his nemesis by strategically co-opting his aesthetic strategies. But this admittedly generous explanation only goes so far; this reasoning doesn't account for Shapiro's fixation with probing what he understands as Jewish difference, distinct from Christian otherness. Poem after poem finds Shapiro's speaker not just revisiting, but actively picking at and reopening the wounds engendered by the difference upon which, paradoxically, he insists on maintaining. Rather than being a source of pride or even cultural/religious affirmation, this difference is an irritant that provokes a state of chronic envy—one of the repugnant feelings that Ngai identifies as "ugly." It seems then that Shapiro makes ugly aesthetic choices not merely because he is interested in taking on the mechanics of what we might call "anti-Semitic poetics"—but because he is in the throes of envy, the primary emotion underwriting this sometimes embarrassing volume.

Wading deeper into the volume, it is worth remembering what Melanie Klein says about envy as a destructive impulse. More than a passive response to a perceived lack, envy actively drives one to try to take possession of the object of desire—or failing that, "spoil it" so that it is no longer worthy of desire (181). Again Ovid's wretched portrait comes to mind, with its monstrous creature who not only "gnaws" but for whom "being gnawed is also her own punishment." Obsessive, paranoid, destructive, attacking oneself as well as others, Ovid's Envy finds new life in Shapiro's volume—where we find how a poet in the throes of envy may suffer fits of delusion and may be given to vicious assaults that, instead of affording comfort or relief, seem only to exacerbate the wound.

The ache of aesthetic inequity, as detailed in "The Synagogue," gives way to the next installment in a darkening narrative: "The Confirmation," a perverse rendering of the Catholic coming-of-age ceremony, is surely one of Shapiro's nastier poems. The poet shows his claws from the outset: "When mothers weep and fathers richly proud / Worship on Sunday morning their tall son" (25). Making the son, rather than the "Son," the object of their joyful devotion, these good people are unaware that their darling progeny is less worthy than presumed. The ensuing stanzas reveal that the recipient, on the eve of a ritual dedicated to affirming that one is "strong and perfect in faith," engaged in what the Church views a "grave matter": masturbation. Stirred awake by a "photograph still sinning in the drawer" of "An actress naked in the night," the boy submits to desire. What follows is an extravagant display of religious sacrilege, as Shapiro plunders the ecclesiastical lexicon to perverse ends:

> And to confirm his sex, breathless and white
> With benediction self-bestowed he knelt
> Oh tightly married to his childish grip,
>   And unction smooth as holy-oil
>   Fell from the vessel's level lip
>   Upon the altar-cloth;
> Like Easter boys the blood sang in his head
>   And all night long the tallow beads
>   Like tears dried in the bed.

With blasphemous puns on the sacramental (Confirmation, Benediction, Extreme Unction, Easter, and so on), Shapiro reaches flagrantly for the language of Marriage (another sacrament) and then likens the moment of ejaculation to a sacred last rite (Extreme "Unction") complete with "holy-oil" and "tallow beads" (aka sperm) which in turn are likened to "tears"—a metonymic link to Christ on the Cross. Distasteful, to be sure; but since Jewishness is not explicitly marked in any way, one might ask: Why read this as a site of interreligious conflict?

Writing in *The American Poet at the Movies*, Laurence Goldstein helps make the case by showing how, as early as 1944, Shapiro understood Hollywood as a Jewish enterprise, an entity that Goldstein fortuitously calls "the gospel of eroticism" (144). By way of proof, he cites these opening lines from Shapiro's 1944 poem, "Movie Actress": "She is young and lies curved on the velvety floor of her fame.... And her dreams are as black as the Jew who uncovered / her name." A decade later, Shapiro once again draws upon this cultural linking between product and producer. Functioning metonymically, the photograph, a manifestation of Jewish power, is a weapon in a guerilla-style attack on Christianity, deployed in the surreptitious service of sullying a sacred Catholic rite. Not content to leave well enough alone, the poet-speaker turns in the final stanza to the presiding cleric, smugly suggesting that both Confirmation and masturbation constitute "sacred" rites of passage: "Be doubly proud, you priest, / Once for his passion in the rose / Once for his body self-released."

To be sure, the poem marks a singularly low moment in Shapiro's foray into the Jewish Christian borderzone. But the narrative threaded throughout the pages of *Poems of a Jew* doesn't end here. Indeed there are several more installments, as the poet works his way through the vagaries of envy's dark undertow, struggling to negotiate what we might call "the gaze of the Other"—and its shame-inducing effects. "Teasing the Nuns," for example, serves as a kind of counterweight to "The Confirmation," in which we saw the male subject (the Christian Other), aroused by a photo of an actress (a cipher for Jewishness by virtue of association), masturbate—thus committing an act of religious sacrilege. The scene may be understood as a variation on what bell hooks calls "the oppositional gaze," whereby the object—in this case, the woman in the photograph—acquires agency. It is a smart move, but of only limited success. Envy is a particularly intractable emotion, as evidenced in "Teasing the Nuns," in which the poet-speaker finds himself caught up in the gaze of the Other to disturbing ends.

As Shapiro relays in an endnote, the poem is based on a personal experience. While teaching at Chicago's Loyola University, he took a brief but traumatic elevator ride with a group of nuns. The explanatory note is at once blunt and utterly opaque: "The theme of the poem is the essential inability of the Jew to speak to the nuns" (70). Fluency is indeed at issue from the outset, as the poet seems uncertain as to how to best describe this sisterhood. Likened first to "a cage of undomestic ducks... Gay in captivity," and then to "a flirtatious flock / Of waterfowl tipped with black" with their "unclipped hats"—an odd detail that becomes more readable when placed within context of the volume's singular preoccupation with circumcision ("clipped" as opposed to "unclipped") and other variations on castration—these nuns are an unsettling presence. So much so that the poet finds himself stuttering as consonants tumble out, one on top of the other: flirtatious, flock, waterfowl, turning, twisting, higher, hauled, hair, heaven, split, strands.

How to regain equilibrium? Once again, ugly language and off-putting images are the poet's first line of defense. An elevator ride with nuns? Conceivably a perfect opportunity for soaring images and metaphoric renditions of heavenly ascents. But gripped by envy, the poet chooses otherwise, reaching for the clumsy and weird, as he recalls being in the car "Hauled on by rosaries and split strands of hair . . . / Yanked into heaven by a hairy Roc." Taking the part of Sinbad, from the Arabic-Islamic masterpiece *The Thousand and One Nights*, our hero sails upward in the clutches of another avian species: the mythic Roc, a giant bird. The journey ends in a "towery cell / Where holy cross was splayed upon the wall / In taxidermy of the eternal." At this point, all vestiges of equanimity dissipate, as the poet-speaker sharpens his own talons, offering readers an especially noxious rendering of a crucifix. Yet even as he seems poised for further attack, he gets no further. A staring (or gazing) contest ensues, as the poet tries to intercept their devotional turn toward their Savior, and the nuns "fixed their gaze on mine that floated out / Between them and their poised hawk"—launching another blasphemous image designed to bait and torment: it is as if Gerard Manley Hopkins's glorious "Windhover," a symbol for Christ ("in taxidermy of the eternal"), is recast as a predatory "hawk." The quasi-heroic subject (aka "Sinbad") becomes a silent other—all body, no voice, as the poem sputters to its conclusion: "'Sisters,' I said.—And then I stopped." At its worst, envy is a hopeless, all-consuming affect—a traumatizing, pre-conscious, maybe even pre-linguistic, experience.

There is, however, a way out; redemption can be had: envy can be resolved, and one can recover a measure of affability or social grace. But the process is excruciating—for once the gaze of the Other makes itself felt, shame follows. Here is how phenomenologist Thomas Fuchs describes the experience, in a passage that serves as a useful frame for the next stage of my discussion:

> I [the one who is shamed] am torn out of the centrality of my lived-body and become an object inside another world. The other's gaze decentralizes my world. This is why every time two people catch sight of each other a subtle fight of gazes for impact, power and rank begins. My face above all is exposed to the other's gaze, bare and unprotected. To withstand his gaze is like struggling against a torrent. This flooding, then, is also expressed by the face's blushing in shame. (226)

Fuchs's melodramatic, urgent account finds its poetic correlative in Shapiro's own overblown text, "The First Time." Unlike "Teasing the Nuns" with its stuttering lines, "The First Time" is hyperfluent: five pentameter sestets, crafted out of such dull rhymes as shame/flame, door/floor, and wall/all. Often rhymes are a source of sonic pleasure or semantic surprise; but such experiences are hardly to be had by reading "The First Time." Instead, in this instance, Shapiro deploys rhyme to establish "aesthetic distance"—a requisite strategy for poetically managing an emotionally charged subject or occasion. As he explains in his manifesto, *A Prosody Handbook*:

> Rhyme can help a poet get the aesthetic distance he needs in order to write at all of a subject in which he is intimately involved, and which threatens to overwhelm him with paralyzing emotion as he contemplates it and tries to write of it in the most straightforward way. The necessity of constructing rhyme may in some cases force the poet to move the original experience just far enough to the rear of the immediate feelings involved that he will be able to write about it. (104)

That is, for Shapiro the rigors of rhyme can help corral unruly feelings, making poetic representation possible. As it turns out, rhyme also serves the reader, especially when it comes to encountering that which Shapiro himself calls "ugly." Later in the passage cited above, he continues: "Ugliness must be made attractive and endurable—as Rouault [a French expressionist] often made his prostitutes and degenerates endurable by the luminosity and delicious coolness of his color. The more a poem deals in *guts and gutters*, the more we appreciate the aesthetic distance of rhymes and iambs" (105; emphasis mine). Best intentions notwithstanding, not to mention sturdy iambs and predictable rhymes, "The First Time" is a bluntly unlovely poem, depicting shame precipitated by sexual vulnerability—with a bit of anti-Semitism thrown in for good measure; truly the stuff of "guts and gutters."

This grim portrait opens with a "boy, who is no more than seventeen" entering a brothel and stripping down to wait "as one might in a doctor's anteroom," perfumed with "iodine and rose" giving off whiffs of a "medicinal bloom." Caught in a "cross-draft of fear and shame," the poor thing ejaculates prematurely—"a candle swimming down to nothingness / Put out by its own wetted gusts of flame." Such images make it pretty clear why male critics, especially the Jewish ones, savaged this volume; and the worst is yet to come. As the poem unfolds, Shapiro lays bare a tangle of emotions, honing in on the feelings of inadequacy and shame so often bound up with envy, attending particularly to the intensely embodied nature of this affect. Shame, that feeling of acute physical displacement, is made so vivid that readers may wince, squirm, and be tempted to look away or stop reading altogether (Kaufmann, 45). Those, however, who do continue discover that beyond the dispiriting waiting room or entry hall of what seems to be a brothel, the boy sees "the great bed drugged with its own perfume / Spread[ing] its carnivorous flower-mouth for all." A *vagina dentata*, vagina-with-teeth, one of the more nakedly misogynistic myths around: born out of a free-floating fear of the unknown, a fear of the feminine Other who, in Shapiro's poem, is unappealingly described as wearing a "black thing" while "rak[ing] her hair." Although short on glamor, the prostitute is not any less powerful, as "the female gaze" once again comes into play. The penultimate stanza finds the prostitute studying herself in the mirror, an action affording a blissful moment of youthful certainty (à la Lacan) and perhaps a glimpse of illusory wholeness. Inverting the usual formula, Shapiro gives us an active female who gazes upon the passive male; for although "she is sitting with her back to him," she sees his image reflected in the mirror. Matters get even more complicated in the last stanza, where, after casting a Medusa-like gaze upon the "boy" and "transfixing him in space like some grotesque," she turns around, gives his naked body the once-over, and—fixing upon his circumcised penis—asks "almost gently," in a tone I hear as more cutting than curious: "*Are you a Jew?*" This is how the poem ends, with Shapiro taking one more jab by rhyming "untrue" with "Jew." With this cutting end-rhyme, the poet descends even further into an emotional netherworld, exposing the connective tissue binding envy—a soul-crushing experience of deep, irremediable lack—to shame, an excruciatingly disaggregated state that can leave one feeling utterly unmoored.

This is a dark place indeed. But as it turns out, shame, nourished by envy, need not always be a dead end; sometimes it can be a portal, a way out. As cultural theorist Elspeth Probyn has argued, shame is an intensely embodied affect, often manifesting itself as a feeling of not belonging, of displacement—exemplified above by the boy who is physically undone by the prospect of entering the prostitute's lair. On occasion, however, Probyn suggests that this feeling can precipitate a psychic reorientation, making one more open to possibilities, engendering a desire to productively engage with the person or place that has provoked such an acute sense of lack (Probyn, *Faces of Shame*, 75). Such is the dynamic played out in *Poems of a Jew*. As we shall see, instead of stifling those feelings of mournful lack and envious rage aroused by the Christian Other, Shapiro gives them full rein—and subsequently discovers a desire to connect with this entity who has provoked such acute feelings of lack. Read within the narrative proposed here, "The First Time" serves as more than a prurient example of envy's aesthetic fallout; instead, it contributes substantively, albeit provocatively, to our understanding of just how emotionally messy and complex the Jewish Christian borderzone can be. And curiously enough, the same figure—that of the circumcised penis, which serves in one instance as a site of alienating Jewish difference—can also serve as the site of Jewish Christian contiguity, as instanced by "The Leg."

Loss and Gain

First published in *V-Letter*, "The Leg" chronicles an amputee (presumably a wounded soldier) working through his loss. By contrast to "The First Time," with its intermittent rhyme scheme designed to cushion its "ugly" content, "The Leg" is comprised of five unrhymed septets in a profoundly "ordinary," embodied kind of poetic speech (almost blank verse). Metrically, it is a perfect choice for a poem devoted to exploring the psychic fallout from a life-changing physical trauma. Struggling through a post-operative haze, the patient "Peers in the middle distance where a pain, / Ghost of a nurse, hazily moves, and day / Her blinding presence pressing in his eyes . . ." Groggily he asks, "*What have I lost?*" This is the question guiding the poem's unfolding. But before turning fully to this vital matter, Shapiro quips à la Henny Youngman: "He wants to get up"—giving readers a bit of ironic reprieve from the grim dysfunctionality of "The First Time," and signaling a very different mood and mode of affect.

In a note written especially for *Poems of a Jew*, Shapiro explains that "The Leg" is about "the wholeness even of the mutilated." Within the context of *V-Letters*, mutilation means battle wounds. But new contexts make for new meanings. For in this same note, he links "The Leg" to Freud's infamous view that "every Jew" suffers from the trauma of "violent defloration": "mutilation, circumcision, and the 'fear of being eaten' are all one" (70). Like "The First Time," "The Leg" represents circumcision as a blight, a mark of profound lack. The former poem, however, simply concludes with this stark knowledge—while the latter artfully rereads the loss transforming a mark of absence into a scene of meaningful presence: with this rereading, Jewish Christian difference becomes less certain, less absolute.

Never known for his subtleties, Shapiro outdoes himself depicting the patient's response as he begins to regain consciousness:

He will be thinking, *When will I look at it?*
And pain, still in the middle distance, will reply,
At what? and he will know it's gone,
O where! and begin to tremble and cry.

He will begin to cry as a child cries
Whose puppy is mangled under a screaming wheel.

Penned by the poet who made his reputation with an ode to a Buick, extravagant, self-consciously poetic gestures directed toward a severed limb aren't much of a surprise. Nonetheless, this is an exceptionally histrionic stanza, even for Shapiro. Working to represent the patient's loss in all its emotional depth, he reaches for a remarkably melodramatic image, likening the patient's sodden grief to that of a child who begins to wail upon witnessing the grisly death of his puppy, "mangled under a screaming wheel." The image is so over-the-top, so shamelessly gruesome, that we may find ourselves thinking less about the patient and more about the poet's own investment in his subject. To put it another way, we begin to wonder if the wail belongs to the poet who is grieving his own perceived lack, and hence his limited agency. Even as they are disconcerting, these sobs mark a crucial turn in the narrative.

For much of this discussion, I have been tracking the poet's ongoing struggle with envy, a devastating experience of lack coupled with an absence of self-consciousness. In risking embarrassment by offering such an off-putting image in such a highly poeticized manner, the poet awkwardly moves toward self-awareness. In other words, we are looking at something like a breakthrough on the part of a poet beset by envy—an emotion that, as we have seen, consolidates around the wound of circumcision, the mark of Jewish difference. But as the poem unfolds, inchoate grief gives way to a deft rereading of loss as gain—for in the next stanza we read: "The amputation becomes an acquisition." Absence becomes presence; a scene of irremediable loss (be it a limb or a foreskin) becomes one of rebirth. Moreover, this shift has important implications for Shapiro, with his deeply engrained animosities toward Christianity; what was once a fixed sign of absolute difference becomes the site of religious contiguity.

My account of this shift begins by suggesting that we hear the amputee's cry as an iteration of another kind of outburst, this one belonging to the circumcised infant; this sonic overlap brings us to a crossroads, a place where Jewishness and Christianity meet—or at least it is heard as such by the sixteenth-century essayist Michel de Montaigne who, upon attending a circumcision, posits an affinity between Jewish and Christian rituals by noting that "the infant's cry is like of ours when they are baptized" (Shaye Cohen, *Why Aren't Jewish Women Circumcised?*, 4). For all of its studied informality, Montaigne's observations are quite radical in light of early Christianity's insistence on setting these two rituals firmly apart. Paul, for example, views the Jewish ritual as little more than a flesh wound, spiritually lacking when compared to "true circumcision" which is of the heart (Cohen, 69). Not only is circumcision spiritually inferior, but it is divisive, setting persons apart, rather than bringing them together. Baptism, however, "the basic sacrament of 'rebirth,'" is accessible to all, regardless of gender or religious affiliation (O'Collins, 23). Pitting flesh against spirit, we hear echoes of that static binary that causes Shapiro to grieve: "Our wine is wine, our bread is harvest bread / That feeds the body and is not the body" (Shapiro, 9).

But in "The Leg," these ideological/theological boundaries begin to erode, as the poet (ventriloquizing the patient) declares: "all is not lost." Once his tears have dried, the patient begins to probe in a more nuanced vein, displaying a peculiar sort of empathy for the severed limb, discovering a sense of self as separate from the lost object, reflecting thus: "he has a duty to the leg. . . . He must cultivate the mind for the leg / Pray for the part that is missing, pray for peace / In the image of man, pray, pray for its safety. . . ." At first, it is hard not to hear little more than a bald pun—"peace" as in "piece"—that is, the amputated leg. But then other possible meanings surface as the line continues: "peace / In the image of a man," bringing to mind the prophet Isaiah's ecstatic invocation of Christ as "The Prince of Peace" (Isaiah 9:6). With this liturgical turn, which seems quite heartfelt, the speaker/patient accomplishes what the contemporary philosopher Jacques Derrida memorably grieves as impossible: for it is as if the speaker is present at his own *bris*, his own circumcision. Instead of just being what Derrida calls a "hostage to heritage," an involuntary participant in a "rite of initiation into a self-enclosed Jewish community" (61), the speaker actively embraces the loss as an aperture, a spiritual opportunity.[7] And as Shapiro begins to put his demons to rest, the boundary between Jewishness and Christianity that he once defended so fiercely begins to crumble. Fissures appear in the form of an odd locution: "pray . . . in the image of man." Tweaking one of the most perplexing verses in the Hebrew Bible, in which God proclaims "Let us make man in our image" (Genesis 1:26), the poet opens the door toward Christian doctrine which maintains, at least according to Pauline doctrine, that it is Jesus (a man) who is the image of the invisible God (Altmann, *Journal of Religion*, 1968). One prayer gives way to another; after laying the phantom limb to rest, the speaker turns his attention fully to God, the ultimate Other: "The body, what is it, Father, but a sign / To love the force that grows us. . . ." With this iteration, the distance and difference between baptism and circumcision begin to dissolve; the wound becomes a sign of connection to the divine Other and the site of spiritual transformation. The shift is of real consequence—since now metaphoric transformation, so long beyond reach, can be accessed. No longer hampered by the kind of aesthetic limits described in "The Synagogue," in which the poet complains that "our bread is harvest bread / That feeds the body and is not the body," the poet of "The Leg" joyfully and exuberantly tries his hand at "sacramental art," capitalizing on the mystery of transubstantiation by petitioning God thus: "Knead, knead the substance of our understanding / which must be beautiful in flesh to walk. . . ." In a move tantamount poetically to doing a backward summersault or flip, the poet giddily reverses the founding metaphor—as the body, that was once the "substance" of bread prior to its Eucharistic/Christological transformation, is restored to its doughy state, thus laying bare the metaphoric scaffolding upon which this mystery of transubstantiation depends. Triumphantly, Shapiro arrives at a "both /and" moment—for it is bread *and* it is the body! Stopping short, therefore, of giving in fully to the steady undertow of "Judeo-Christianity," Shapiro claims that it is at once possible to have a firm grasp on materiality (the bread) *and* to participate in the art of figurative transformation (which is the Body).

"The artist's contribution to religion must in the nature of things be heretical"

"The Leg" is a high-wire act: urgent, theologically complex, and exhausting. By its conclusion, the poet-speaker finds himself deep into that rough terrain known as the Jewish Christian borderzone. But as my next chapter will demonstrate, this space is ill-suited to long sojourns, much less permanent residence. Indeed, the narrative I have pieced together out of the poems constituting Shapiro's angst-ridden volume ends with this recognition. For this last poem, "The Crucifix in the Filing Cabinet," written especially for *Poems of a Jew*,[8] finds the poet fancifully doing away with religious difference altogether.

This time there is no mask, no persona. Making public what has long been private, this is as close as Shapiro gets to the confessional mode. As if working to dispel the toxic fumes of envy and shame permeating so much of the narrative, emotions fueled by secrecy, the poet takes us into his office—the inner sanctum—to reveal the contents of a filing cabinet. In addition to drawers filled with the "letters, bills / Manuscripts, contracts" and assorted "trash of praise," there is another "drawer that rolls on hidden wheels." Until this moment, ugly shame-inducing secrets have been relegated to exclusive spaces such as bedrooms or hospital chambers. Now it seems that revelation may be at hand—heralded by the vaguely apocalyptic soundings of "hidden wheels," bringing to mind perhaps Ezekiel's psychedelic vision with its own version of secret wheels (Ezekiel 1:16). Out of this drawer, the speaker takes a rosary: "Still new and frightened looking and absurd"—not so much ridiculous as out of place, and fragile in contrast to the rigid antiquities of Jewishness. Cupping the rosary in his hand so that the beads pool and "form a small mountain of stones," he reconstructs the crucifixion in miniature, describing a tree with "Some ancient teacher hanging by his hands." Pointedly avoiding calling "Jesus" by name, the poet at once diminishes Christ's iconic power, and re-Judaicizes this figure, inviting us to see him as a "teacher," a "Rabbi." While the tone is hardly reverential, it is not malicious or confrontational (as with so many of the other poems leading up to this moment).

But the ritual is not yet complete. Like a magician dipping deeper into his bag of tricks, the poet again reaches into the drawer, this time finding "a velvet bag sewn by the Jews / For holy shawls and frontlets and soft thongs / That bind the arm at morning for great wrongs / Done in Pharaoh's time. . . ." Readers familiar with the ritual might immediately start to protest: after all, the daily obligation to don *tefillin* (phylacteries), two small boxes containing Biblical verses—one bound to the forehead with black leather straps, the second to the left forearm—has nothing to do with expressing guilt or doing penance. At least not explicitly. Rather, it signifies commitment. While winding the strap around the middle finger of the left hand, one chants this verse from Hosea: "I will betroth you to Me forever," verbally affirming participation in a sacred, intimate contract between God and Israel. But like so many rituals, the meaning of *tefillin* changes over time. Each box contains a different set of verses, one from the Book of Exodus and the second from Deuteronomy, both of which include the obligation to wear *tefillin*. But in one instance the obligation serves as a reminder of divine redemption (Exodus), while the second names the ritual as a precondition for remaining in the Promised Land: "If, then, you keep all this Instruction that I command you, . . . Every spot on which your foot treads shall be yours" (Deuteronomy 11:22, 24). Upon noting that the Jews were already in exile by the time these verses had been redacted, liturgy scholar Jeremy Schonfield suggests that wearing *tefillin* became, implicitly, an expression of anxiety—a dramatic enactment of a longing to return. Or, as he memorably puts it, "binding is an act of desperation" (98).

In light of Shapiro's ongoing struggle with anxiety, precipitated by feelings of lack and chronic inferiority, Schonfield's gloss is especially resonant. "The Crucifix" ends with a new ritual, a nonsectarian sacrament, an act of conjury, conducted in the service of unraveling these constraints and the differences upon which they depend and perpetuate. Opening the *tefillin* bag wide, the poet-speaker picks up the crucifix, drop[ping] it "down in the darkness of this pouch," offering up a chant and intoning thus:

Thought tangled with thought and chain with chain,
Till time untie the dark with greedy look,
Crumble the cross and bleed the leathery vein.

Comprising five quatrains with regular iambs, "The Crucifix" is a tidy poem; only the rhyme scheme is noticeably idiosyncratic (*abcc deff ghih jkkl mene*). Unlike "The First Time," where predictable rhymes buffer the impact of nasty sentiments, the technique here initially registers as mostly just a source of sonic pleasure and interest—experiences that until now have been in short supply. But Shapiro is after more than a short reprieve from the dark forays into a psychic underworld inhabited by envy and shame; he wants something to happen, to change. And so he composes a kind of charm, a form of poetic utterance which rarely uses full end-rhymes, but depends heavily on internal soundings such as assonance, repetition, and alliteration (thought, tangled, thought, chain, chain, till, time, untie). That is, these last lines find him turning to what his archnemesis, Ezra Pound, has taught us to hear as *melopoeia*—that lyric mode whereby language is charged "over and above their plain meaning with some musical property, which directs the bearing or trend of that meaning." For *melopoeia*, which privileges sound over meaning, is the stuff out of which chants, incantations, and charms are made. As Andrew Welsh explains, "Charms are meant to make things happen, to cause action" (Welsh, *Roots of Lyric*, 144). In Shapiro's world, there isn't much room for thoughtful dialogic exchange with the religious other, since painful revelations occasioned by interfaith encounters dominate the space; and prayer is hopelessly partisan. But, as it turns out, there is the possibility of charm, of magical utterance: a chant to accompany a not-so-ancient ritual conducted in the interest of dissolving religious difference altogether, or at least those aspects of doctrine that would keep us apart.

5
The Certainty of Wings
*Denise Levertov and the Legacy
of Her Hebrew-Christian Father*

When it comes to visual representations of Jewish Christian relations, Marc Chagall's "The White Crucifixion" (1938)—one of at least twenty images of his featuring the "Jewish Jesus"—is surely among the best known. As noted in Chapter 1, Chagall conceives of the image as a way of responding to rising anti-Semitism by reminding his largely Christian audience of their own Jewish lineage. He offers up these images not to test the limits of religious difference or to challenge the boundaries, but to mitigate the lethal relationship between the Christian self and the Jewish other so as to stave off further violence. This, however, may not be Chagall's only foray into the "borderzone"—at least according to poet Denise Levertov. Twenty years before "White Crucifixion," Chagall gives us "Over Vitebsk," an homage to his hometown featuring a Jewish peddler floating high in the sky nearly touching the spires of a nearby cathedral (http://www.chagallpaintings.com/over-vitebsk/). Benjamin Harshav (114) reads the image as a visual rendering of the Yiddish literary trope known as the *leuft mensch* (a man of the air; one who lives in the clouds). Others understand it as the representation of another well-known trope, that of the "Wandering Jew." But Levertov reads the painting rather differently in the ekphrastic poem, "Wings in the Pedlar's Sack" (1989). It begins:

> The certainty of wings; a child's bold heart,
> not, good little *Schul*-boy, Torah or Talmud
> gave it to you, a practical vision
> wings were needed
> why should people
> plod on forever on foot, not glide like herons? . . .

Therefore, the pedlar. (But why did they not
avail themselves of his wares?)

(Levertov, *Collected Poems*, 838)

In an exegetical gloss appearing to the right of the poem proper, Levertov makes a midrashic move, imaginatively linking Chagall's image to her Russian-born father's dreamy accounts of a peddler born aloft by a "sackful of wings," noting that although the two men—Chagall and her father—never met, they shared a deep mystical knowing. While hardly explicit, the wings evoke that divine emanation known as the *Shekhinah*. (The Jewish prayer for the dead, for example, asks that the departed find rest "upon the wings of the Shekhinah.") The Shekhinah is a well-known Kabbalistic figure for that feminine aspect of the Godhead who resides closest to "the lower earth"—the region of the human, the temporal, the fully embodied. Well-versed in Jewish mysticism, Paul Levertoff, who, as we will see, becomes known as "the patriarch of Jewish Christian writers," indeed makes the Shekhinah the linchpin in his radical account of the incarnate Jesus, as embedded in the rabbinic idea of the in-dwelling of the divine Presence.[1] Turning back to the poem, we see the underpinnings of this kind of religious appropriation or borrowing laid bare. With a nod toward Hopkins's "The Windhover" ("sheer plod makes plough-down sillion shine"), the poet suggests that "wings" are just what those hopelessly earthbound Jewish villagers need to "glide like herons," rather than "plod[ding]" on "forever by foot." Returning to Chagall's painting, we see this concept made vivid, for the Jewish peddler (assisted by the wings of the Shekhinah) floats so high that he can all but touch the spires of the nearby Cathedral of the Blessed Virgin Mary (!), with these two vivid spiritual presences rendered proximate.

It is a heady formulation, one which Paul fervently believes will help end the treacherously oppositional stance afflicting these two world religions. Yet, despite the "certainty of wings," the poem suggests that Paul's efforts to share this "good news" fail:

You bore such news, so longed-for,
fulfilling a hope so ancient
it had almost become dry parchment. . . .

but when you arrived
they would not listen.
They laughed at you. And then they wept.
But would not listen.

(*Collected Poems*, 838)

Such dismal moments of missed connection haunt Paul throughout his life as a "Jewish Christian" missionary and help shape some of his daughter's deepest personal and aesthetic concerns.

Denise Levertov is sometimes described as a "Jewish poet." Her works appear, for example, in the *Norton Anthology of Jewish American Literature* and *Telling and Remembering: A Century of American Jewish Poetry*. Nonetheless, this rubric or category never seemed, to me at least, especially resonant or helpful. And when you look at the interviews that pose the question of Jewishness to her directly, she politely but firmly deflects the query, saying something along the lines of "well I was an agnostic then," or "I was passionately committed to social justice"—as was her then-husband Mitchell Goodman, a prominent political activist and secular Jew (Greene, *A Poet's Life*, 162). To make matters more confusing, or perhaps more interesting, we should note that after many years spent thinking and writing about doctrinal Christian precepts, she formally converted to Catholicism in 1990—surely a move that would discredit, or at least complicate, her status as a Jew. But now that we have recognized the limits of describing Jewish Christian relations as simply a matter of a "parting of the ways"—for the boundaries between the two are profoundly porous and indeterminate—we may be in a better position, first, to consider what it means to speak of someone like Denise Levertov as a "Jewish" poet (as we increasingly complicate the designation of "Jewishness"), and, second, to explore the aesthetic implications and creative consequences of such fluid affinities. That is, how do her world and her work contribute to our growing understanding of the instabilities informing the connections between Jewishness and Christianity?

"A Christian Chasid"

It took me a while to piece together the significance of Denise Levertov's paternal inheritance. Early in her career, she changed the spelling of the familial "Levertoff" to "Levertov," reportedly so as not to be confused with her older sister Olga, known also for her writing. As a result, I didn't immediately understand that her father was the same Paul Philip Levertoff known as "the patriarch of Jewish Christian writers." That said, her lineage isn't a secret. All the biographies note that her father was born into a Hasidic family and was a descendant of Reb Shneur Zalman of Liadi (founder of Chabad Lubavitch), and that she read Martin Buber's writings on Hasidic thought. But hardly anyone pauses to consider what it means that her father, upon his conversion to Christianity, was a trailblazer who devoted his life to actively crafting a synthetic religious practice reflecting his conviction in Judaism and Christianity as wholly compatible and mutually illuminating.

Declaring himself to be a devoted follower of "Rebbe Yeshua of Nazareth" (aka Jesus), Paul lives out his life as "a lone Chasid in a Christian world" (Levertoff, 3). For many of us, the very notion of a "Christian Chasid" might register as an oxymoron, if not an abomination. But from a certain scholarly vantage, Paul can be simply accused of traveling to the outer limits of Hasidic theology—at least as construed by Martin Buber, the great Jewish philosopher responsible for reintroducing Hasidism to Western thought. In the opening pages of *Love and the Messianic Age* (a collection of Levertoff's writings on "Christian-Chasidic theology"), we read: "according to daughter, Denise Levertov, Martin Buber drew inspiration from Levertoff's attempt to communicate the Chasidic world—inspiration that resulted in his popular *Tales of the Hasidim*" (11–12). In light of this claim, it behooves us to consider Shaul Magid's thoroughgoing account of Buber's deep interest in Christian thought. Writing in *Hasidism Incarnate: Hasidism, Christianity, and the Construction of Modern Judaism*, Magid shows us how one of the most strictly devout movements in traditional Judaism must be understood within the context of Christian theology, as glossed by Buber, who argues that it was Jesus who introduced the possibility of believing in "an indwelling God, who can be addressed in an unmediated relationship" (121). Unlike the prophets of Israel who imagined that such intimacy was a distant promise, Jesus asserts that such a "reconciliation" was an immediate possibility, fully available in "the here and now" (121). This principle of "incarnational thinking" courses throughout Buber's rendition of Hasidism, linking Jesus's teaching to that of the Baal Shem Tov, Hasidism's foremost teacher and proponent. It is an arresting claim—one which we might imagine would enrage the black-hatted *Hasidim* in Williamsburg or Mea Shearim.[2] But it is also one that helps us appreciate Hasidism as both an antinomian response to what Buber understood to be an urgent spiritual crisis and an incredibly creative and vibrant phenomenon with real spiritual appeal. From Magid's perspective, Hasidism should be understood not merely as one among several other strains of traditional Jewish practice, but also as part of a counternarrative, a potentially disruptive presence, akin to "the crazy aunt in the attic"—an eccentric theological development that many modern Jewish thinkers find irrelevant in their otherwise sweeping accounts of "authentic" Judaism (Magid, 174).[3]

If Hasidism is like a "crazy aunt," then Paul Philip Levertoff is surely one of her more eccentric offspring—and exceptionally well-suited to this study. Depending on which biographical snippet one reads, Levertoff is variously identified as a "Hasidic Jewish scholar and translator," a "prominent religious scholar," "an ordained Anglican priest," and "an apostate." Denise herself gives a range of responses attesting to the complex nature of her father's religious identity. In 1965, she offers this short, rather cryptic account: "My father was essentially a European and then he was a Jew who had become a Christian and finally an Anglican priest. This was a very strange *uncategorizable* sort of fact" (Sutton, *Conversations*, 4; emphasis mine). Twelve years later, she revises this linear narrative, offering deeper insights both into her father's intricately crafted spiritual alliances and into what those alliances meant for her family:

> Even though my father had become a Christian, and of course an Anglican Priest, he always emphasized that he was a "Jewish Christian." He emphasized the fact that Jesus and the disciples were Jews. To him Christianity was really a fulfillment of the messianic hope. He and my mother, who was Welsh, certainly instilled in me and my sister a great deal of pride in being Jewish, although the Jewish community did not consider us so. We were apostates in their eyes. They thought of my father either a traitor or just crazy. (Estess, *Conversations*, 89)

"A traitor or just crazy": such was Levertoff's reputation for many years. One of Denise's biographers, Donna Hollenberg, recounts how the editors of the first English translation of the *Zohar* (published by Soncino Press) were loath to include his name among the other translators, wary of his outlier status. It is perhaps only because of Beatrice, his wife, who insisted upon the attribution, that we even know of his involvement with this groundbreaking project. To be sure, more than sixty years after Levertoff's death, scholars are now reassessing his approach to Hebrew-Christianity, newly appreciative of his religious hybridity and his deep capacity to see sameness without eliding difference, to see bridges, where others would see walls.[4] As Shalom Goldman explains, Levertoff's insistence on this hyphenated identity sets him apart from other "Hebrew Christian missionaries" who typically sought to recruit Jewish converts to Christianity, requiring them to abandon one faith for another, to embrace a new religion at the cost of another (4). Levertoff understood Judaism and Christianity as "two phases of one and the same religion—of God-manhood—or to use a more abstract expression, two moments of one and the same Divine-human process" (Levertoff, *Love and the Messianic Age*, 7; cited in Wolfson, 286–87).[5]

Careful to "work both sides of the aisle," Levertoff sought to draw Christians closer to Judaism, even as he worked to help Jews overcome their fear of Christianity. We might think of Levertoff's approach to interfaith negotiations as akin to translation—a complex strategy central to understanding Jewish Christian textual encounters (Seidman). But unlike a project such as the recent *Christianity in Jewish Terms*—a fascinating effort to help Jews overcome their fear of the Christian Other by recasting such foundational concepts as "incarnation" or divine embodiment into more palatable terms such as "the imaginal body of God"—Levertoff is intent on collapsing difference altogether, no matter how far the reach. In *Love and the Messianic Age*, for example, he expands upon the Christian notion of fellowship (otherwise known as *Koinonia*, or communion, as realized through the Eucharist) as described in John 1:3–6, by equating it with *achdut*, the Hasidic notion of seeking unity with God through prayer and study, altogether bypassing such formidable (and potentially alienating) concepts such as the Eucharist. Not content merely to help mitigate whatever anxieties his Jewish audience may suffer upon engaging Christian tropes or doctrines, Levertoff seeks to help them discover how Christianity is actually part of their own spiritual DNA. To this end, he rejects standard notions of "conversion," which emphasize repudiating one's immoral past as a step toward embracing a "true faith," in favor of distinctly Jewish notions of *teshuvah*—returning, repentance, or spiritual homecoming. That is, a turn to Christ is glossed as a return to righteousness and spiritual alignment, wholly recognizable concepts to one versed in Jewish thought. Nor did he restrict himself to theological compositions. Levertoff is known for writing the very first modern Hebrew book about Jesus, titled *Hayei Yeshu'a ha Mashiah u-fo'alav (The Son of Man: A Survey of the Life and Death of Jesus Christ)*—which drew the attention of the novelist Sholem Asch, who would eventually write his own Christological trilogy (Quiñónez, 24). Moreover, in an effort to expand the then-nascent canon of modern Hebrew letters, Levertoff translated Augustine's *Confessions* (originally written in Latin) into Rabbinic Hebrew.

Paul Philip Levertoff was driven. This tireless commitment plays out in his clerical practice as well as in his writings. Twice a month on Saturday/Shabbat afternoons, those who attended the "Hebrew Christian Church" would have had the opportunity of participating in a wholly unique rendition of the Eucharistic Mass, called *Seder Kedush D'Seudah D'Malcha Kadeesha* or "The Order of Service of the Meal of the Holy King." Replete in a *yarmulke* (a skullcap), a *tallit* (a prayer shawl), and a cassock (a Christian clerical robe), Reverend Levertoff (identified in the liturgy as "HaCohen"—Hebrew for the High Priest) would conduct a Hebrew-language service including such ancient Hebrew prayers as *Yidid Nefesh* (a beloved fourteenth-century *piyyut* or liturgical hymn) along with traditional Anglican hymns translated into Hebrew—all in the interest of making "Christian worship" "plainer and less alien to the Jewish mind." He delivered his sermons either in English or in Yiddish—depending on the congregational makeup ("Works and Needs," 3).[6]

Above all, Levertoff works to counteract what he sees as a major misconception afflicting the Jewish world: the stereotype of the *shtetl* Jew hunched over his studies, shrouded in darkness and oblivious to the light. To this end, he insists that the "key note of Chasidic piety" is "joy"—a claim he shores up with a line from a Pauline epistle, "Rejoice, and again I say unto you rejoice," again placing Judaism and Christianity on a seamless continuum (57). Indeed, numerous accounts—as relayed by his wife Beatrice, as well as by both of his daughters, Olga and Denise—have Paul breaking into a little Hasidic jig upon meeting up with various family members, or upon receiving good news. But Levertoff's borderzone experience seems to be as much colored by frustration and despondency as by radiance and joy. A perpetual outsider, his work makes both the Jews and the Christians uneasy. Donna Hollenberg, one of Denise's biographers, recounts how the poet's father was awarded an honorary Lambeth Doctorate of Theology only after her mother had appealed directly to the Archbishop of Canterbury on her husband's behalf, explaining that "it would mean an enormous lot to him that the Jews should realize that the Church recognizes his work." The Archbishop's response is decidedly mixed, for even as he recognizes Levertoff's scholarly prowess, he can't help but comment that "[his is] not perhaps a very balanced mind" (27). Paging through the many articles and bulletins Levertoff wrote in his capacity as Vicar of the Holy Trinity Church, one gets a much deeper sense of the intense emotional volatility engendered by his calling. A short essay called "Work and Needs" (1924) starts off with Rev. Levertoff filled with "despair" as he trudges toward his church, his "spirit oppressed with the weight of the almost superhuman task" facing him. His dark mood lifts when, during the service, he hears "Jews rumbling out Hebrew responses." But Monday finds him "played out and again depression sets in." This rollercoaster of a piece ultimately ends on a muted high note, concluding with a plea for funds so that he can publish new editions of such Hebrew works as his biographies of Jesus and of St. Paul—which had factored in the conversion of such illustrious figures as Hans Herzl, son of Theodore Herzl, "founder of Zionism," whom Levertoff had baptized in 1924. (What Levertoff doesn't know is that six years later, in 1930, Hans would take his own life—a tragedy that will become an occasion to grieve not only his death, but also the mental distress suffered by a host of others claiming this hybrid identity.) In a 1931 paper presented at the "17th Annual Conference of the Hebrew Christian Alliance of America," dedicated to the memory of Hans Herzl, Mark John Levy (a founding member of the Alliance) opens with a litany of loss detailing the afflictions of those who languish in isolation, failing to find a place in a "Christian circle of loving fellowship" ("Hebrew Christianity," 8).[7] Several years later, Olga, Levertoff's older daughter, offers a similar account, citing this "pathetic and terrible story" as an example of the profound loneliness suffered by those who, upon identifying as Jewish Christians, find themselves socially adrift, cut "off from the Community" (*Wailing*, 121). Life in the borderzone is difficult.

This chronically unfulfilled longing to forge connections, personal and theological, sounds throughout Denise's recounting of her father's religious life. A few years after writing "Wings in the Pedlar's Sack," she revisits this formative narrative and tale of psychic origin, this time in prose. Bearing the rather offhand title, "A Minor Role," the essay reads a bit like a fairy tale or a myth, with the poet highlighting how her father's turn toward Christianity is, from the outset, marked by danger and uncertainty. She begins by imagining the young Paul (né Feivel) as he navigates a liminal space, moving through a hazardous landscape. Stopping to play on a day "when winter and spring struggle with one another," young Feivel—then a boy of eight or nine—engages in a "forbidden game," traversing the half-frozen "wide swift Dnieper River" by leaping from "floe to floe, riding the ice down-stream for short distances. . . . If a floe split beneath a rider's feet, or if he missed his footing and fell between two of the heavy, moving masses into the black reawakened water, woe betide him" (*Tesserae*, 4). It is a prescient scene because, as we know, Feivel is destined to spend his life negotiating choppy waters, navigating the narrows. On this occasion, even though he suffers no physical danger, spiritual peril awaits. Continuing on his way home, he finds a scrap of paper with Hebrew writing, and—like any good Yeshiva *bucher* (boy)—he picks it up, assuming that it belongs to a sacred text. And it does—just not one that he recognizes. But Feivel is immediately enthralled by this fragment (from, as it turns out, the Gospel of Matthew), whose contents suggest that there is a world other than the one he knows, a world with an alternate narrative—in which the young instruct their elders, and where the new counters the old.[8] Much like Augustine, a major figure in Levertoff's spiritual journeying, he happens upon the perfect sacred text precisely at the right moment. Remarkably enough, instead of either being terrified by the "Christian Other" or being caught up in the throes of self-annihilating desire, Levertoff (at least as his daughter describes it) experiences a profound moment of self-knowing—a recognition born out some years later when he reads the Gospels in a "Gentile and utterly secular atmosphere" and discovers that "this book of the Christians seemed more his than theirs." That is, instead of encountering radical otherness, Paul's reading experience offers up a profound encounter with a version of the self that was heretofore unknown. Operating outside the parameters of what Shaul Magid calls the "Christian gaze" (a coercive cultural force that polices religious difference), young Feivel is thrilled by a "story about a boy like himself"—and is undeterred by his father, who throws the textual fragment into the stove, a gesture that invokes all kinds of associations with haunting loss and totalitarian repression.

Of course, the story doesn't end here. A precocious child born to a prestigious Belarusian family, Feivel attends the Volozhin Yeshiva in Lithuania. Upon receiving rabbinical ordination, he successfully appeals to his family for permission to attend the University of Königsberg. There he discovers a "world of cafés and open lectures . . . a world where Jews and Gentiles mingle in bewildering freedom." Taking full advantage of this rich brew, Levertoff immerses himself in the Gospels (reading them in both German and Hebrew translations)—a textual encounter that his training in the Kabbalah makes him especially well-suited to—and rapidly concludes not only that Jesus is the true Messiah, but that, again, "this book of the Christians seemed more his than *theirs*" (aka the Gentiles)! In the grips of this new knowing, and "shining with faith," he hurries back to Belarus so that he can share the "good news" with his family. This time, the response is much harsher: his family is horrified. When Feivel refuses to buckle, they conclude that their son must be mad, locking him in his bedroom. Feivel—soon to be baptized Paul—escapes, returning to Königsberg. He never sees his family again. But he also never gives up on the possibility of connection. Paul dedicates his synthetic account of what he calls "Hasidic writings; with special reference to the Fourth Gospel" (*Love and the Messianic Age*), to his father Shaul Levertoff, a prominent member of a Chasidic dynasty in Belarus, citing from John: "An Israelite in whom there is no guile" (John 1:47)—a reference to Nathanael, a Jew who recognizes Jesus as "the King of Israel." Paul, it seems, held out hope to the end.[9]

These narratives of loss and ruptured relations, driven by Paul's unflagging commitment to suturing together two disparate religious traditions, make for a complex family legacy. Life in the Levertoff household was sometimes unpredictable, even when it came to matters of religious education. Writing in an unpublished essay, Denise recalls how "there were periods when we had family prayers each morning, but then, for reasons unknown, the practice would be discontinued." More generally, she concludes that her parents, "despite their own profound belief and commitment, were . . . , one might say, laissez-faire to the point of neglect" since both were thoroughly preoccupied with Paul's scholarship and missionizing endeavors (2). Of the two daughters, Olga, the eldest, seems to have suffered the most—at least outwardly.

Her father's "favorite," Olga devoted the early part of her adult life to disseminating Paul's vision, a project culminating in her 1933 monograph *The Wailing Wall*. Written with two audiences in mind, Olga seeks to both "help Jews discover the truth of Christianity" and convince Christians of the spiritual gifts Judaism offers. A self-proclaimed "daughter of an apostate," Olga, who has a flair for melodrama, begins by depicting a cluster of Jews huddled together in grief:

> A grey wall stands beneath a burning sky. When evening's shadows darken it, grey figures gather near and darken it too with many sorrows. They mourn and weep, touching it as though for comfort. (1)

Seizing upon Jerusalem's crumbling "Wailing Wall," which she variously depicts as a "ruined heap," an "ancient partition," "a grey wall," and a "prison wall" as her central metaphor, Olga mourns a people spiritually crippled by an isolationist predisposition; for this stony pile shuts out "from Jewry light and life." But Jews are not the only ones who are invested in this edifice, since this "barrier, a wall of separation between two worlds," reflects a condition of mutual animosity. Both Jews and Christians insist upon maintaining what she understands to be a fiction of absolute, unassailable difference. Her position is akin to that of a double agent. To her Christian readers, she reveals that no Gentile realizes "the immense antipathy that the Jews have to the Christian doctrine of Incarnation" and that most Jews "hate Christianity like a mother who has given birth to a traitor." Her Jewish readership, however, learns that Jesus himself was a victim of anti-Semitism and thus wholly worthy of a relationship grounded in empathetic identification.

Olga works to disentangle Christianity from the swell of anti-Semitism by reassuring her fellow Jews that Christ also "suffers with his people." Answering those Jews who would then ask about the roots of anti-Christianity, a hostility arguably directed toward one of their own, she cites "Dr. Martin Buber": "Only Galuth—that is, exile-psychology—is responsible for the fact that we have allowed such a movement as Christianity, which originated in our midst, to be torn out from our history.... We must overcome the superstitious terror with which we have regarded the Nazareth movement, a movement which we must place where it properly belongs—in the spiritual history of Israel" (50). Anticipating Magid's work by nearly ninety years, Olga notes that the steady suppression of Hasidism ("i.e., the mystical movement of the 18th century") is partly to blame for Judaism's programmatic resistance to incarnational thought: "official Judaism has always been ashamed of the strong vein of mysticism which has always run through it, dismissing Hasidism as a sort of Dervish sect bent on ecstasy and attempting to attain a state of elevation by mechanical means" (35). When it comes to answering those Christian readers who might wonder what is to be gained by venturing into Jewish thought, Olga—her father's acolyte—invokes the *Zohar*, the foremost "guide to the intricacies of Jewish thought." There, readers would discover soaring hymns (extrapolated and rendered by Paul Levertoff) dedicated to the "Shekhinah's splendor"—an emanation that is sure to enrich their devotion to Christ (39–40).

For all of Olga's passionate focus, there is a constant undertow of sorrow and isolation—a strain of feeling that becomes more pronounced as she considers her own identity position. Even while insisting upon her Jewishness, she confesses to a singularly awkward stance, presenting her readers with this syntactic convolution: On the one hand, she does "not feel closer to the Jews whom I meet than to the Gentiles." On the other hand, she continues, "I feel, to be sure, that I am far nearer to them than any Gentiles could be." Vigilantly opposed to "passing," Olga mourns a world where merely tolerating Jewishness (even for Jewish Christians) is a point of pride, citing an exchange with the "wife of a Jewish-Christian missionary" who proudly remarks, "My children know that their father is a Jew, . . . but they don't mind" (101). The passage concludes with Olga giving up on the hope of any "rapprochement between the Jewish and Christian worlds," since such efforts seem to end up with Christians seeking to "turn moderately good Jews" (presumably like the aforementioned children) into "thoroughly bad Gentiles": those who, at worst, actively promote anti-Semitism, or at best, do nothing to prevent it.

Time brings little in the way of succor. Thirty years after *The Wailing Wall* was published, Olga belatedly commemorates her father's death with "The Ballad of My Father." Written shortly before her death, the poem was never published—until 1967, when Denise places it at the end of her volume *The Sorrow Dance*. Read within the context of the rest of the collection (comprising open-form elegiac lyrics, including "To Olga," Levertov's own lament for her sister), "Ballad," a doggedly metrical poem comprised of seven quatrains interlaced with six rhyming couplets, stands out as a peculiar act of complex displacement (or ventriloquism). Speaking perhaps to Denise's own ambivalence, this is an inscrutable move, rife with possibilities. Contrary to whatever the title might suggest, "Ballad" is hardly a joyful tribute to a beloved parent. To be sure, the opening line "Yachchilderalum, putzele mutzele" (a bit of nonsensical, faux Yiddish) sets us up for a warmhearted song of praise. But such expectations evaporate quickly, and what follows is a chilling dialogue between the now-deceased Paul and his "disciples"—a throng of Holocaust victims—whom he queries: "why is your footzele burnt to the bone?" They explain: "Hail, dear Rabboni! [our teacher] We would not leave you lonely! / We come from the limepit where / millons were thrown." Historical catastrophe gives way to Christological apocalypse, with *The Revelation to John* looming large in subsequent stanzas, as the poet (again, Olga) sings: "He danced. . . . For an end of strife, for eternal life, for behold / I make all things new" (Revelation 21:5). With its regular rhythms and reliable rhymes, "Ballad" might seem to hold out the promise of a longed-for reconciliation. But the final stanza suggests otherwise:

> Yachchiderlaum, putzele mutezele –
> Now if I couldzele I'd speak to you true:
> But your dance it is ended and all the tears expended—
> So sleep on and take your rest, my father, my Jew. (272)

In this haunting leave-taking, made somehow worse with its hollow-sounding use of the faux-Yiddish "couldzele," Olga casts her many years of dedicated service to the "Hebrew Christian" cause in doubt, gesturing toward all kinds of misaligned efforts, repressed thoughts, and buried questions.[10] These doubts are affirmed by a terrible reality: in the wake of the Holocaust, a tragic disaster arguably fueled and abetted by Christian anti-Semitism, the dream of a hybrid religion born out of mutual appreciation and spiritual recognition, withers.

For all of their conviction, both Paul and his daughter Olga discover that the Jewish Christian borderzone is an often inhospitable landscape fraught with uncertainties, disappointments, and psychic ruptures precipitated by failed relational encounters. The theological aftershocks and implications of these sorts of traumas might be understood as iterations of what Martin Buber would call a *Vergegnung* or a "mismeeting"—a word he coins to describe what happens when real meetings between persons—*Begegnung*—go wrong (Friedman, *Life and Work*, 5).

Buber was exceptionally prolific: his bibliography contains over one hundred entries, ranging from monographs and essays to lengthy philosophical studies. But as scholars have long recognized, much of this vast body of work centers on a few large issues and concerns to which he returns repeatedly, carrying each one forward into the next stage of his thinking. The precept "I-Thou" is perhaps the most widely known of these foundational ideas, encapsulating his insights into meaningful human existence as a by-product of a dialogic encounter between oneself and others—both human and divine. This concept informs his famous "conversion," his turn away from Jewish mysticism toward Hasidism, as he determines that the former focuses on unifying "the self with the all-self," while the latter directs one's attention to the sacred meanings manifest in the connections *between* persons, and between "the divine life" and "here where we stand" (Buber, *Origin*, 42).

That is, according to Buber, Hasidism calls for a radical reconsideration of the person and her ongoing connectedness to the divine—a concept rooted in Buber's study of Christianity (and, as we will see, also central to Denise Levertov's aesthetic objectives). This encounter with an Other—who is not the Self—helps Buber reexamine his own religious heritage and recognize that movements and ideas cast as marginal, or arcane/irrelevant, must be made central (thus launching a bold critique of rabbinic Judaism). Remarkably enough, Buber is careful *not* to cover his conceptual tracks. Even as he mines the depths of Hasidism to uncover its essential belief in the sacramental value of the material world, he doesn't erase the role Christianity plays in spurring his investigation. Nor does he view the wisdom to be gained from this movement (Hasidism) as belonging exclusively to Jews.

Buber's vital encounter with Christianity is a strong instance of what he might call a "real encounter" or meeting—a seminal concept of his rooted in a formative childhood memory. Abandoned by his mother at the age of three, Buber recalls standing out on the balcony of his grandparents' house with a neighbor's daughter. Looking down at the street, this "big girl" tells the young Buber, "No, she will never come back." He then continues:

> I know that I remained silent but also that I cherished no doubt of the truth of the spoken words. It remained fixed in me; from year to year it cleaved ever more in my heart, but after more than ten years I had begun to perceive it as something that concerned not only me, but all men. . . . I suspect that all I have learned about genuine meeting in the course of my life has its first origin in that hour on the balcony. (Friedman, *Life and Work*, 4)

Twenty years later, his mother comes to visit Buber, who is now married with children. The reunion is profoundly disappointing: "I could not gaze into her still astonishingly beautiful eyes without hearing the word *Vergegnung*"—again, his term for "mismeeting" or "misencounter" to designate "the failure of a real meeting between men" (Friedman, 4). Rather than serving as an open wound or an irrecoverable loss to be perpetually mined à la Proust, this trauma becomes the cornerstone for his lifelong commitment to promoting the value of a life lived in dialogue with an Other who is not the Self. This principle of being, most clearly articulated in the seminal work *I and Thou*, also shapes his account of Hasidism, with its singular emphasis on the need to craft a connection, "a genuine relation" with all beings—human and divine.

Turning back to the poems of Denise Levertov, we find evidence of a steady interest in Hasidism (especially in her early works, where allusions to Buber's *Tales of the Hasidim* figure largely; see Hallisey). But there is more to be learned from this linking than thematic soundings. Buber's account of meetings and mismeetings provides a strong frame for thinking about the poet's own protracted longing for connection, so often unrealized or met with disappointment. This frame is especially helpful when it comes to reading those poems explicitly animated by her relationship with her father, Paul Levertoff, and more broadly those born out of deep spiritual restlessness, chronicling her long search for spiritual fulfillment and her many years of spiritual restlessness.

Four years after her father's death, Denise describes performing a dance of her own in homage to her father. Taking its title from Christian doctrine, "In Obedience" acknowledges Paul Levertoff's sovereign authority. But unlike Olga's dark ballad in which filial affection dominates, Denise's poem is marked by distance and ambivalence. It begins with a found text, a letter from her mother announcing that "the dread word has been spoken" (75). But rather than responding directly either to her mother or to the "dread word" (cancer perhaps?), Levertov first turns her attention elsewhere, seeking out the cusp between the revealed and concealed as manifest in the natural world—the "almost invisible spider," the "almost visible spiral" sketched out in a bird's song—as a way, perhaps, of both distracting herself from and approaching the pain. Then, stirred by sudden resolve, the poem faces her impending loss, announcing, albeit reluctantly: "let there be more joy!—if that / is what you would have." Meeting her father on his terms, the poet dances solo in her garden, "for joy, only for joy / while you lie dying." But the encounter is decidedly flawed; instead of setting her steps to a Yiddish folk tune, as was Olga's wont, Denise hums a few lines from one of her staunchly Anglican mother's favorite texts, *The Pilgrim's Progress*, identifying herself as "Mr. Despondency's daughter." As if this implicit slight was not enough, the poet coldly concludes: "Let my dance / be mourning then, / now that I love you too late" (75). Once again, Buber's powerful insights into the wounds precipitated by moments of "mismeeting" come to mind.

It is perhaps in search of more stable ground that Levertov takes steps toward disentangling herself from her father's messy legacy—for the region of Hebrew-Christianity is riddled with mismeetings. Ultimately, she formally converts to Catholicism. But this decision comes after having spent many years crafting poetry that probes the possibilities of connection between persons, histories, and the divine. Writing in "The Poet in the World" (1967), one of many craft statements she produced during her career, Levertov claims E. M. Forster's well-known adage "Only connect"—an "aesthetic statement" with "moral" obligations—as a poetic mantra. Typically Forster's epigraph is understood as a modernist mandate warning of the perils of isolation, but within the context of this discussion, it registers also as a variation on a truth central to Buber's rendering of Hasidism, as relayed in *The Way of Man: According to the Teachings of Hasidism* (a book that Levertov cared for and knew well). Citing the movement's founder, the Baal-Shem Tov, Buber urges his readers to develop a "genuine relation to the beings and things in whose life we ought to take part." One who seeks "holy living" must be "in relationship to the world in which he has been set, at the place on which he stands" (Buber, 43–44).

Yet instead of crafting poems that fulfill this mandate, Levertov gives us a poignant set of failed efforts—attesting to just how hard it is to "connect." In "At the Edge" (1960), for example, she wistfully reflects, "How much I should like to begin / a poem with And—"—an elusive longing that remains conspicuously unresolved, since the poem ends in irrecoverable deletion and fracture: "but whom / no And may approach suddenly" (116). Even "O Taste and See," a widely celebrated ode to the imagination, begins in disappointment: "The world is / not with us enough" (playing on Wordsworth's famous sonnet). Although the rest of the poem seeks to remedy this condition, the damage is done. The savage use of enjambment (line break) makes the terrible sense of loss and deprivation especially hard felt, as the line seems to extend an offer of all kinds of possibility ("The world is . . ."), only to have it immediately wrenched away with a negation ("not with us"). As we will see, this is not an isolated expression. In poem after poem, we find a speaker seeking to forge connections (between persons, histories, or between spiritual and material realms of being) that remain frayed or unresolved. That is, during this stage of her career, poetry doesn't serve as a place of connection so much as a place where the *longing* for connection is articulated.

In an especially kind and openhearted essay, the poet Eavan Boland, who taught with Levertov at Stanford during the 1980s, notes how—contrary to Levertov's loud, highly public proclamation about the necessity of community—her best poems move toward "dispossession rather than possession" (184). Remarking upon "A Map of the Western Part of the County of Essex in England," an early poem that helped make Levertov's reputation as a lyric poet, Boland notes how, at a moment when the lyric emerges as an occasion for actively claiming one's origins, Levertov probes her unresolved sense of distance and displacement.[11] Even after twenty years of US citizenship, a place where she is "less a stranger . . . than anywhere else, perhaps," she feels closest to other homesick immigrants ("All the Ivans dreaming of their villages / all the Marias dreaming of their walled cities"), "picking up fragments of the New World slowly, / not knowing how to put them together nor how to join."

Insofar as "A Map" tracks the poet's efforts in connecting to place, it names an interest central to other poems from the same volume, *The Jacob's Ladder* (1961), including the three poems that are most frequently anthologized as "Jewish": "Illustrious Ancestors," "The Thread," and the titular poem "The Jacob's Ladder," all of which are similarly interested in questions of connection. Gathered together and neatly identified, we understand why these three poems are often approached as examples of what fellow poet Jerome Rothenberg (a good friend of Levertov at the time) might call "ancestral" verse—poetic investigations of one's ethnic-religious heritage (Hallisey, 265). But guided, as it were, by "A Map," we see that Levertov's inquiries are driven by something other than an interest in family origins, or even a sense of the ethical obligation to excavate one's ethnicity in the interest of complicating/diversifying the landscape of American letters (like her contemporaries Adrienne Rich and Muriel Rukeyser). In general, Jewish ethnic identity as a secular enterprise doesn't hold her attention much. Instead, these poems, which surely complicate the term "Jewish," constitute Levertov's most explicit effort to explore what this Jewish Christian heritage means for her poetically.

"Illustrious Ancestors," a tribute to Levertov's spiritual inheritance, clearly names the project. The opening account of the legendary Rav Zalman (again, an ancestor of Chabad fame), based on several different stories (featuring different Rabbis) relayed by Buber in his *Tales of the Hasidim*, is linked here to the story of Angell Jones, a Calvinist mystic and tailor who was known for sewing bits of scripture into "coats and britches"—and an ancestor on the side of the poet's Welsh-born mother, Beatrice Spooner-Jones. The two sides of the family are more similar here than different: reading these narratives as complementary rather than contentious (both Rav Zalman and Angell Jones take a practical approach to spiritual matters), Levertov locates her poem—like the prayers, the passionate studying, or the handiwork of her ancestors—in the space in-between, suturing together what too often is set apart, often to destructive ends. "Thinking some line still taut between me and them," the poet seeks to make poems at once honoring the Rav's pragmatism and Jones's ethereal attentiveness. Refusing to set one family off from another, the poem presents as a single unit, without any stanzaic breaks. Nonetheless, such connections *are* hard to make, as dramatized by the poet's use of space and enjambment. Generally speaking, Levertov—a disciple of William Carlos Williams—is extremely attentive to line break as the site of meaning. In "Illustrious Ancestors" the line is drawn "taut" indeed. For, even as the poem is a contiguous whole, the conspicuous use of white space calls attention to the effort. The large chunks of white space (appearing to the left of the page rather than the right) make for a certain kind of anxiety as our eyes travel over unmarked expanses seeking syntactic resolution. The same kind of drama informs the extravagant enjambment linking together the two patriarchs: "He used / what was at hand—as did / Angell Jones of Mold" (83).

"Illustrious Ancestors" ends with "the tailor" (aka Angell Jones) in mid-stitch, pausing "with his needle in the air"—a fittingly soft end to a poem that places a premium on connections rather than on conclusions or closure. A few years later, Levertov picks up this dangling strand in pursuit of her own unspecified spiritual inquiry. Curiously enough, considering her reputation as a "lyric" poet, Levertov uses the standard "I" sparingly. But "The Thread" finds the poet willing to risk considerably more, to put herself on the line, so to speak. This vulnerability is marked in the use of very short lines (none is longer than eight syllables, unlike the long and loose, prosy lines of "Illustrious"). Prosodically, this is the line of uncertainty, change, and transformation—an openness marked also by the questions peppered throughout: "Was it / not long ago this thread / began to draw me? Or / way back Was I / born this way with its knot about my neck, a bridle?" Amidst a cluster of images devoted to connection (threads, elastic, cobwebs), one stands out in particular: that of a fishing line, as the speaker notes that "no barbed hook / pierced and tore me," bringing to mind perhaps a Christological account of conversion ("I will make you fishers of men"; Matthew 4:19). But other shadings and meanings may also be at play—as I discovered upon learning that some recent editions of liberal High Holiday prayerbooks (*machzorim*) now include "The Thread" (along with some other contemporary poems). The Conservative *machzor (Lev Shalem)*, for example, offers the poem as an alternative to the traditional *viddui* (confessional sequence), highlighting those aspects of the poem that engage the idea of *teshuvah*, of returning to God. Yet from a certain vantage, this framework amplifies rather than mutes the volume on those aspects of the poem which register as Christian. For this linking between teshuvah/repentance and turning/conversion recalls Paul Levertoff's hybrid account of repentance, which owes much to Hasidic teachings emphasizing repentance as a spontaneous soulful awakening, rather than as the product of a long arduous process of focused introspection—accounts which, in turn, have much in common with Christian notions of conversion (*Love*; cited in Wolfson, 310). To encounter "The Thread" while immersed in High Holiday prayer opens up the possibility of relinquishing proprietary or exclusionary claims to engaging with well-entrenched "Jewish" ideas—such as that of teshuvah/repentance—in wholly new ways, thanks to its hybrid theology. Interpolated thus into the High Holiday liturgy, "The Thread" serves as a compelling example of how poems, invested in their own in-betweenness, can infiltrate even the most stalwart of sacred spaces, hence expanding the Jewish Christian borderzone.

While "The Thread" finds the poet-speaker perched on the edge of the borderzone, other poems from the same volume show the poet venturing further into the "space in-between." "A Letter to William Kinter of Muhlenberg" (not to be found in any anthology of Jewish verse), for example, finds the poet in motion—riding on a bus back to New York from a trip to Muhlenberg

College—an occasion marked by meeting and mismeeting. Hosted by Professor William Kinter, whom she addresses as Zaddik (a "holy man" in Jewish mystical and Hasidic texts)—a displaced incarnation of her father perhaps—she describes two instances of imperfect sighting, beginning with the "Stations of the Cross" (a series of small paintings hanging in the student chapel). Even as she fails to apprehend "what the almost abstract / tiles held," the Christian image affords access to a differently charged spiritual landscape, offering a glimpse or a "shadow of what might be seen," should she give herself over to the "Imagination's / holy forest," the domain of Jewish mysticism, through which "the Zohar's dusty / shimmering roads" lead (44). Even though neither region holds her attention, the journey "between" has itself a bracing effect, as she later writes about this poem to her friend and fellow poet Robert Duncan: "I had a brief but quite wonderful experience—of *in-sight*" (*Letters*, 268).

On another occasion, however, Levertov exercises her visual acuity to stay fully present in the "space in-between." In 1960, while visiting the Church of Santo Domingo in Oaxaca, Levertov comes upon a "Jacob's Dream," a fresco that engenders the poem "The Jacob's Ladder." Unlike some ekphrastic poems which either register frustration with the limits of their linguistic art or override the "otherness" of the visual image, "The Jacob's Ladder" instances a "true meeting" with an aesthetic Other (see W. J. T. Mitchell, https://complit .utoronto.ca/wp-content/uploads/COL1000-Week11-Nov25_WJT_Mitchell.pdf). A beautifully sturdy poem, "The Jacob's Ladder" is comprised of five stanzas, five lines each. While it certainly displays the same affinity for enjambment that Levertov generally favors, the effect is softened by the relative regularity of line length constituting each stanza. As a result, the emphasis is on the act of seeing, as directed toward the Other, rather than on the viewer or the "self" articulating the experience. The space requisite for a "true meeting" to unfold is clearly defined, as the speaker/viewer begins by dismissing any prior representations of this well-known scene that might comprise the encounter, including perhaps Blake's luminous watercolor, by describing the fresco thus: "The stairway is not / a thing of gleaming strands. . . . it is of stone." (This focus on pure materiality owes something to her engagement with Objectivist poets such as George Oppen, and perhaps to Hasidic thought which places a premium on concrete being.) For Levertov, this attentiveness leads to a deeper appreciation of the tension between what is known and unknown, the revealed and the concealed. The hard materiality of "rosy stone" owes its "glowing tone of softness" to the instability, the "doubting/night gray," of the surrounding sky. Only after the stairway, "the ladder," is taken in fully does the poet then attend to the man who is slowly on the ascent:

and a man climbing
must scrape his knees, and bring
the grip of his hands into play. The cut stone
consoles his groping feet. Wings brush past him.
The poem ascends.

At this point, the poem's borderzone status comes into focus. While the poem is called into being by a Catholic image (a specific anchoring confirmed with the title's definite article, "The"), it is linked also to a Hasidic framework by way of a passage Levertov finds in the second volume of Buber's *Tales of the Hasidim*, which she uses for the epigraph of *The Jacob's Ladder*. Ascribed to Rabbi Moshe of Korbyn in response to the well-known episode from the book of Genesis, Chapter 28 in the Hebrew Bible, in which Jacob ("he") dreams of a ladder ascending to heaven, we read in this epigraph (from Buber):

> That "he" is every man. Every man must know: I am clay. . . . but "the top of it reached to heaven"—my soul reaches to heaven; "and behold the angels of God ascending and descending on it"—even the ascent and descent of the angels depend on my deeds.
>
> (*The Jacob's Ladder*, ii)

This passage by Buber speaks beautifully to Shaul Magid's account of Buber's innovative insights into Hasidism's efforts to "recentralize the person" (rather than the book) "in the place of the world" (123). Rabbi Moshe teaches that the angels' mobility depends upon what is human. Yet, with his scraped knees and "groping hands," this "man" also points toward the passage in the Book of John where Jesus folds his own story into that of Jacob's: "And he said to him, 'Very truly, I tell you, you will see heaven opened and the angels of God ascending and descending upon the Son of Man'" (John 1:51). With this radically inclusive (hybrid) image, Levertov gestures toward one of her father's more provocative formulations. As Paul Levertoff argues: "the mystery of the Cross—the mystery of the Word made flesh, the divine becoming *human* in the *person* of Christ, may actually be embedded in Hasidic/Kabbalistic thought." Elliot Wolfson, a Kabbalah scholar with his own keen interest in the Jewish Christian borderzone, takes up Levertoff's account, explaining that "the first disciples of Jesus saw in him 'a visible manifestation of God, a soul, in which the Divinity dwells, Jewishly expressed, the Shekhinah'" (who, of course, has wings; Wolfson, "Paul Philip Levertoff," 99). At the site of this evocative cross-religious encounter, the poem—a metonymic iteration of the poet/self (who is otherwise not named)—makes itself known. Urged on by "Wings" that "brush past" as "the man" arduously pursues the divine, the poem (itself a material incarnation) "ascends" on its own sacred journey, connecting the human and the spiritual, the below and the above, the Son and the Father (or, in this case, the daughter and the father), Jewishness and Christianity.

With "The Jacob's Ladder," Levertov begins to excavate a space for a "poetics of the in-between," grounded in her capacity to patiently apprehend that which she sees, external to herself. But before she can go much further, the enterprise is preempted by what she calls "political anguish"—an intense pressure to respond poetically to the grim news that begins to pour out of Vietnam daily (Lacey, 151). With a handful of exceptions, including an effort to affirm her vision by way of articulating an "I-Thou" relationship with her cat (see "The Cat as Cat"), Levertov abandons lyric meditations in favor of aggressively didactic poems, pitching herself against American indifference (Hollenberg). The next fifteen years (1967–82, more or less) find her on the frontlines of poetic activism, bearing witness to an onslaught of catastrophes including not only the Vietnam War, but also the Detroit riots of 1967, the rise of nuclear armament, and the terrible famine that savaged Biafra—a tidal wave of historic upheaval that overwhelms her penchant for cautious, precise naming. To be sure, politics can either make or break a poet. The pressure to bear witness, to stir readers to action, and perhaps even to identify an alternative narrative that counters or mitigates the damage, makes for a serious challenge—especially if events conspire against or even disable one's aesthetic tenets. Such is the position in which Levertov finds herself in the winter of 1966—in the midst of America's "first televised war." As we have seen, her poetics depends upon a certain confidence in her visual acuity; so many early poems celebrate acts of seeing objects external to the self (paintings, subway posters), then showing what can become known. But in "Advent 1966," the procedure is disabled. The scene is one of profound disequilibrium: poised to immerse herself in a period of sacred reflection (Advent), the poet is distracted as the horrifically "real" images of Vietnamese children scorched by napalm overtake and obliterate the spiritual possibilities extended by Robert Southwell's marvelously strange metaphoric rendering of Christ's sacrifice, known as the "Burning Babe." Southwell recalls how, while gazing into a fire on Christmas Eve, "A pretty Babe all burning bright did in the air appear . . ." only then to "melt into a bath to wash them [men] in my blood." In Levertov's account, this redemptive vision is occluded by image upon image "the flesh on fire / . . . wholly human." Derailed thus from what is, traditionally, a spiritually restorative journey ahead, the poet finds herself going into an aesthetic tailspin:

> . . . because of this my strong sight,
> My clear caressive sight, my poet's sight I was given

that it might stir me to song,
is blurred.
There is a cataract filming over
my inner eye. Or else a monstrous insect
has entered my head, and looks out
from my sockets with multiple vision. (343)

Working her way through this rather melodramatic, high-pitched moment clotted with alliteration and grotesque images, the poet concludes that her ocular gifts must be rescinded in the face of political realities, as she will not be permitted "to look elsewhere." It is a dark place for one who depends so much on her "clear caressive sight" (that is, seeing as an act of intimate connection) both to chart her aesthetic course and to claim her poetic presence.

Aggravating what is already a hardwired distrust in the human other, this choice costs Levertov dearly, both aesthetically and relationally, because this turn toward the political precipitates the infamous "break-up" between Levertov and fellow poet Robert Duncan. After more than twenty-five years of passionate epistolary exchange (their letters constitute a 700-page volume), the longtime friends part ways over what Duncan calls the vacuous "moralizing" afflicting Levertov's "naïve" political verse.[12] They part ways in 1971. After nearly two years of silence, Duncan tries to restore the connection with a warm letter responding to a newly published collection, expressing relief that these new poems promise a return to "the central concourse of the human stream we have always been united in" (713). But "Denny," as she signs herself, rebuffs him soundly, writing that he "waited too long" and that "Any kind of relationship can die of undernourishing and abuse" (716). The episode is among the most dramatic and best-chronicled in a long career characterized by a series of what Buber might call "mismeetings"—personal, professional, pedagogic, and romantic encounters that end in ragged disappointment, abrupt resignations, or just plain hurt.[13] Ultimately, the task of understanding the psychodynamics informing Levertov's history of ruptured encounters is best left to biographers. What interests me is how this chronic condition of distrust and disappointment becomes the grounds of a theological position that allows her to embrace, or maybe just to become reconciled to, conditions of unknowing and uncertainty—a legacy of her father's exhaustive and exhausting commitment to living in a world wedged between two religious traditions.

For much of her adult life, Levertov had a fitful relationship with Christianity. On and off, she would go to churches of different denominations, depending on where she lived and her affinity for the particular clerical leadership. But with her mother's death in 1978, the poet begins a slow and steady turn toward Catholicism. It is almost as if she was unable to craft her own religious identity until wholly free of both her father's manic, hyper-intellectual religious graftings and her mother's steadfast but unarticulated "faith" (see "Work That Enfaiths"). Not surprisingly, she proceeds cautiously with an "agnostic mass" honoring the Day of St. Thomas Didymus (1982), a six-part poem titled "Mass for the Day of St. Thomas Didymus" fashioned after the liturgical structure. The occasion suits a poet whose art has long depended on visual acuity, for St. Thomas is known best for grounding his faith in hard physical evidence (it is to him, of course, that we owe the phrase "Seeing is believing"). Colloquially known as "Doubting Thomas," the apostle's investment in concrete truths speaks to Levertov's resistance to easy notions of reliable Divine justice that quickly crumble under the sorrowful weight of lived reality. Even while contemplating a more clearly boundaried religious framework than the one she inherited, Levertov fastens on a theology grounded in uncertainty. A few years later, on the eve of her conversion, Thomas again figures large. Walking down the street, the poet witnesses a "small man / gray but vivid" crying out, as his disabled child suffers through a seizure, "Lord, I believe, help thou / mine unbelief." It is, indeed, a moment of meeting as the poet, feeling a "flash of kinship," identifies him as her "twin." Like St. Thomas, who plunged his hand into Jesus's open wound, she says retrospectively: "I needed / blood to tell me the truth" (844–46).

But in 1982, Levertov still has a ways to go toward conversion. Levertov starts her Mass with the "Kyrie," a direct appeal to God's mercy (*Kyrie Eleison*: "Lord have mercy"). However, the best Levertov can do is direct her awkward petition toward a vaguely identified Other with a conspicuously high apostrophic address (she usually eschews such rhetorical flourishes): "O deep unknown, guttering candle," to whom she declares that "our hope" lies not only in "the unknown," but "in our unknowing" (gesturing perhaps toward St. John of the Cross who comes to the "Cloud of Unknowing" by way of Christian mysticism). Praise follows petition, as the newly positioned poet counterintuitively celebrates gifts rendered by the concealed, the unseen: "Praise / the invisible sun burning beyond / the white cold sky, giving us light and the chimney's shadow." But this unspiritual unfolding is not without its challenges. As her "Mass" reaches its conclusion, a theological crisis erupts, for she can't shrug off the "deft infliction . . . of hell by human hands," and she is utterly "baffled" as to why "The word / chose to become / flesh" (676). In other words, why would anyone want to be human? At last, this hardwired disaffection for the human condition that colors so much of her career comes to the fore.

Yet as tradition dictates, the "Mass" remains incomplete without the *Agnus Dei* (the "Lamb of God"). Here, in the sixth and final part of the poem, Levertov arrives at something like a resolution, which evokes Buber's account of the dialogic relation between God and humanity, even as the frame is unequivocally Christian. Exercising her poetic authority, Levertov begins by objecting to the founding metaphor whereby Jesus is likened to the "Lamb of God." As she sees it, "this pretty creature . . . leaper in air for delight of being" is wholly ill-suited to a God who is expected to "take away the Sins of the World."[14] Incredulous, she pursues the matter further, with a rhetorical query: "Omnipotence has been tossed away, reduced to a wisp of damp wool?" Faced with the prospect of retiring the (Hebraic) idea of an all-powerful Godhead in favor of a distinctly more fragile incarnation (the Christian lamb), the poet initially resists—for the trade-off means forgoing a chance at effortless redemption. But the poem ends with her taking up the challenge attendant upon this theological realignment. Stirred into action by a "shivering God," the poet hesitatingly offers the creature the only thing at hand: "Let's try / if something human still / can shield you." That is, faced with a God who is genuinely in need of Others, the poet must claim her humanity—and forge a connection to an Other in a way that had long eluded her.

Doubt, then, rather than faith, is her portal. Sudden blinding radiance, incandescent illumination, perfect clarity: these are the terms often linked to "conversion." Levertov's experience, however, is strikingly otherwise. At one point during her slow turn, she offers an "Oblique Prayer," pointedly rejecting iconic narratives such as St. John's *"dark / night of the soul"* or Paul's desert sojourn, instead finding herself in an indeterminate space, "gray, / a place / without clear outlines." Instead of gifting her with a world defined by stability, Catholicism seems to provide a platform for engaging some hard truths about human limitations. With this insight, she works her way toward relinquishing prior expectations of secure borders, asking: "Is it / part of human-ness / to enter /no man's land?"

But her forays into the space in-between are not always so tentative or cautious. In "Standoff," the poet takes an aggressive approach, striding into the Jewish Christian borderzone, insisting upon humanity's right to a relation to the divine:

Assail God's hearing with gull-screech kniveblades.

Cozen the saints to plead our cause claiming,
grace abounding
God crucified on the resolve not to displume
our unused wings
hears: nailed palms
cannot beat off the flames of insistent sound,

strident or plaintive,
nor reach to annul freedom—

nor would God renege.
Our shoulders ache. The abyss
gapes at us.
When shall we dare to fly? (768)

Her conviction is buoyed both by Christian doctrine, with its own strong valuation of the embodied being, and by Hasidism (again, à la Buber), which also maintains that realizing one's full human potential is requisite to accessing the divine. In what takes the form of a sharp, relatively spare set of couplets, the speaker stakes her claim. At the outset, she briefly considers enlisting "the saints"—those who occupy a liminal space in between the human and the divine—to advance her cause. But she quickly realizes that no such intermediary is necessary, for an incarnate, fully embodied God (imaged here as Christ on the Cross) is capable of fully taking in, of "hearing" the human longing for intimate relationship with the divine Other—an intimate relationship to be facilitated with the help of "wings." The image brings us back full circle to her father Paul's conception of the Shekhinah, that "glorious fullness," as contiguous with the "Person of Christ." After a lifetime of ambivalent and angry estrangement, the poet prepares to don the very wings in which her father had so much faith—and to meet the "abyss," a region of irresolvable uncertainty, which Buber calls "holy insecurity"—an evocative term to which I will return in my next and final chapter.

But to take leave of Levertov here would be to shift the focus away from her principal contribution to understanding the spiritually and emotionally charged challenges posed by the Jewish Christian borderzone. For more than any other writer I consider, Levertov knows what it means to live in a hybrid space where both religions are accorded authority. Indeed, so many of her poems bear witness to emotional complexities attendant upon this state of being, specifically naming the problem of connection—theologically and personally. It is thus with pleasure and perhaps relief, or maybe surprise, that we find that—on the threshold of conversion—she is able to revisit this longing and say, "Lord, not you, / it is I who am absent," and then to wonder what it might take to focus her own "flickering mind" on "you the unchanging presence" (825). Here, the use of the lowercase "you," the most intimate of pronouns, is striking. Instead of evoking the lofty "You," the abstract Other who so often stays at a theoretical remove, she works to name and acknowledge responsibility for the chronic distance, disappointment, and distrust underwriting so many of her poetic encounters.

Levertov died in December of 1997. Up until the end, she was in a state of "theological confusion." In November, a month before her death, she thought about leaving the Church, beset with questions "not about God," but "about specifically Christian[ity] with its exclusivity" (Hollenberg, 442). Even after having long left the Jewish Christian borderzone as crafted by her father, she still finds boundaried institutions making her uneasy. Yet these last months also bring instances of what Martin Buber calls "grace"—a term he uses to describe spontaneous meetings when "The I not only encounters its Thou but is discovered by it. . . . It comes and passes, addresses and is gone, discovers and vanishes" (Arthur Cohen, *Martin Buber*, 52). After many years, Levertov revists this old scene of mismeeting in "Moments of Joy":

> A scholar takes a room on the next street
> the better to concentrate on his unending work, his word,
> his world. His grown children
> feel bereft. He goes and comes while they sleep. . . . (1010)

Much of the poem is given over to fantasy, the resolution of a long-held ache. Paul Levertoff, the "scholar" in the poem, had indeed pursued his religious vision often at his family's expense. But in this poem, published posthumously, the past is remade. The unnamed "child" wakes to find her beloved father "clearly there to protect / as he had always done." Joyfully she calls out "Abba" (Hebrew for "father"), reaching for "the old, intimate name / from the days of infancy." In turn, the "old scholar, the father / is deeply glad to be found." The fantasy, as it were, ends here, with father and child united in a moment of mutual recognition—again, a moment of grace. But the poem itself continues—as the poet-speaker leaves off wistfully imagining to conclude: "That's how it is, Lord, sometimes; / You seek and I find" (101). With a variation on Matthew 7:7 ("Seek and ye shall find"), as well as perhaps on the children's game, Levertov steps out as her father's daughter, taking her place, even if only briefly, in the Jewish Christian borderzone—a space in-between where the divine and the human are contiguous (and of a piece).

6
Coda: Holy Insecurity

[T]he prophets of Israel always aimed to shatter all security and to proclaim in the opened abyss of the final insecurity the unwished-for God who demands that his Human creatures become real . . . and confounds all who imagine that they can take refuge in the certainty that the temple of God is in their midst
—Buber, from Preface to *Daniel*, 29

You must transcend ever anew into the transforming abyss, ever anew vowed to the holy insecurity
—*Daniel*, 99

"Holy Envy." Much of this book has been devoted to teasing out the implications of this provocative locution, especially as played out in poetry. We have seen how this anxiety-ridden position can be activated when someone looks over the proverbial fence and sees that someone else's religion promises aesthetic resources and opportunities that may otherwise be scarce, or construed as desirable and unavailable. Moreover, we have seen how not only envy of but desire for a religious Other can make for a considerable amount of aesthetic fallout. This concept presumes a certain degree of religious stability—for if boundaries are to be traversed, they must be stable, or at least operative. But in these last pages, I want to briefly explore—or at least name—another way of configuring a relationship with the religious Other, grounded in the recognition that such boundaries are inherently fluid and porous. This model begins with another evocative locution—what Martin Buber calls "holy insecurity."

Throughout much of his life, Martin Buber garnered controversy. Dismayed by his anarchic take on *halacha* (Jewish law), the standard bearers of institutional Judaism viewed him with suspicion. And then there was his avowed respect and fondness for Jesus, whom the philosopher famously embraces as "my great brother"—which only aggravated the matter (*Two Types of Faith*, 12). At a moment (the early twentieth century) when Jewish scholarship was largely invested in affirming absolute religious difference, Buber's penchant for bridge-building by way of identifying religious contiguities was deemed disruptive, indeed dangerous. But as scholars have become more attuned to the complexities coloring the relationship between Judaism and Christianity, subsequent notions of precisely what constitutes *Jewish thought* have expanded—and Buber's contributions have become the subject of renewed attention. That said, resistances and blind spots persist. Even as *I and Thou* is now celebrated as a masterwork of Jewish philosophy, and even as Buber's accounts of Hasidism as a major theological innovation figure large in new interpretations of Jewish religious thought, certain works are routinely dismissed as, categorically, "not Jewish" (see Mendes-Flohr; Friedman). Such is the case when it comes to talking about Buber's early "philosophic poem," *Daniel: Dialogues on Realization* (1913). To be sure, it is a peculiar little book. Barely one hundred pages long, it comprises five rather stiff, highly self-conscious "dialogues" (which actually register as monologues animated occasionally by a question or comment), exploring such philosophic abstractions as "meaning," "reality," and "unity." A highly eclectic text, *Daniel* reflects Buber's commitment to crossing not only disciplinary but religious boundaries in the interest of arriving at a deeper understanding of what it means to be human. For in these pages we find not only traces of Nietzsche and the German mystic Jakob Böhme, but also a fair amount of Chinese philosophy, interspersed with Christian imagery. Nearly paralyzed by his fear of "the abyss," Daniel (the fictional protagonist), for example, longs "for comfort like the dying Christ for the communion" (86). But such respite eludes him. For, as Buber comes to understand it, "all true living" is fundamentally dangerous. That is, living with one's whole being means cultivating an ongoing willingness to descend "anew into the transforming abyss" to "risk your soul ever anew." This willingness is requisite to entering God's kingdom, which does not hold out a promise of wholeness, a sense of arrival, or of unity. Rather, it is a "kingdom of danger and risk," a region evocatively called "the kingdom of holy insecurity" (97–99).

In his late twenties, Buber discovers the world of Hasidic thought, drawn particularly to its vision of a life characterized by *devotio*—a perspective grounded both in an ongoing recognition of everyday holiness and of the fundamental fragility of our ability to keep that recognition in sight. Buber finds his way into this world by way of stories: the tales or "legends" of such great Rabbis and teachers as Rabbi Nachman (of Breslov) and the Baal-Shem Tov (Rabbi Israel Ben Eliezer). It is in a retelling of one of these early stories, "The Rabbi and His Son," that Buber first describes the world as a "narrow ridge" or a bridge spanning a great abyss (Friedman, 43). Writing in his introduction to Buber's seminal study, *The Origin and Meaning of Hasidism*, Maurice Friedman, an early authority and champion of Buber's work, highlights the concept, explaining that Buber ultimately rejected gnostic/mystical traditions, including that of the Kabbalah, since they are founded upon a belief in a secure and ultimately knowable (if only by a few) world order. By contrast, Hasidism understands that the world offers no guarantees, and that to live in "the Face of God" means to live in a perpetual state of "holy insecurity." While meeting with the Divine takes place "in the concrete" (meaning that it is of this world), the meeting itself is momentary, and such encounters must constantly be pursued and renewed. What Friedman doesn't tell us—at least not by way of conventional documentation or citation—is that many of these core ideas are initially worked out in *Daniel*, a theologically restless text that brings together a wide range of religious and philosophic traditions. That is, while Buber ultimately makes a strong case for "holy insecurity" as a cornerstone of Hasidism, he first came to this understanding while crafting a text strikingly adrift in a sea of religious diversity. Perhaps more than any other text of his (and Buber was prolific), *Daniel* reflects Buber's conviction that, as Arthur Cohen explains, religious dogma obstructs spiritual growth: for "he (God) withdraws at precisely the moment when man, in his thirst to hold fast to God, seeks to tie him to liturgical continuity. . . . The Holy will not be contained" (Cohen, 56–57).

"On Meaning: Dialogue in the Garden," the third of the five dialogues constituting *Daniel*, dramatizes just how traumatic this discovery can be. An old friend named Reinhold comes to Daniel enormously distressed. He begins by telling Daniel about growing up "secure with the security" of one who believes he is sovereign and all-powerful. All of this changed when, on a seaside vacation, Reinhold set out alone in his rowboat; it was a beautiful night, the waters were calm, there was nothing to fear. But upon returning, he finds himself paralyzed with fear; his sense of security is shattered, as he peers into "the abyss"—Buber's signature term for a state of perpetual unknowing (85–86). Reinhold finds himself estranged from both "the mind-knowers," those who are confident that the world can be tamed through the intellect, and "the God knowers," those who maintain that the abysses can be mitigated, indeed eliminated, through faith. Reinhold comes to Daniel seeking comfort, which comes in the way of hard truth, as Daniel tells Reinhold that his discovery is far from aberrant or fleeting. Instead, it marks the start of a new way of being from which there is no retreat. "All living with the whole being and unconstrained force means danger; for there is no thing . . . that thus known does not reveal its bottomless abyss." The task is not to shirk from this danger, but to "risk your soul ever anew" and "descend into the transforming abyss," for danger leads to "the Kingdom of God," which is "a kingdom of danger, of risk, . . . of opened spirit and of deep realization, the kingdom of holy insecurity."

Toward a Poetics of "Holy Insecurity"

Conceptually expansive, *Daniel* is rhetorically a bit of a letdown. Style belies content, for even as Buber insists on uncertainty as a primal feature of daily existence, the text itself is rigidly constructed and highly self-conscious. Filled with long declamatory monologues and uninspired clichés depicting churning seas and perilous cliffs, *Daniel* marks an early stage in Buber's efforts to write out of a place defined by both direct speech and vatic poetry (Mendes-Flohr, "Buber's Rhetoric," 23). Ten years later, with the publication of *I and Thou*, Buber comes closer to realizing his aesthetic objectives, giving us a more fractured text dramatizing the fragility underwriting both human and divine encounters. Nonetheless, the notion of "holy insecurity" is folded into his larger philosophic construct.

So I want to ask: What might a poetics of holy insecurity look like? And what might the responses it garners tell us about our collective investment in religious boundaries? Both questions, of course, merit full consideration. But for now, as a way of beginning the conversation, I want to consider Leonard Cohen's ecumenical prayer, "Hallelujah," and some of the ways in which it has been received and claimed by disparate religious traditions.

Cohen died in the late fall of 2016, and was buried in Montreal at Shaar Shomayyim, his family's congregational cemetery. A month after his death, a memorial marking the end of *sheloshim*—the initial thirty-day period of mourning—was held at Cohen's local shul, Ohr Ha Torah in Los Angeles. There, Cohen's good friend, the renowned writer and editor Leon Wieseltier, offered a tribute, remarking: "Leonard was never more Jewish than in his lifelong engagement with the figure of Jesus," citing Cohen's great song "Suzanne," in which Cohen gives us a Jesus "broken . . . forsaken, almost human." Immediately, Buber, who famously embraced Jesus as his "great brother," comes to mind. Cohen, however, roamed even more widely afield than the philosopher—at least in practice. After studying for three years at the Mount Baldy Zen Center in California, Cohen was formally ordained as a Buddhist monk. But as he understood it, this affiliation did not compromise or diminish his attachment to Judaism. A year after becoming a monk, he addresses the matter drolly yet firmly: "Anyone who says / I'm not a Jew / Is not a Jew. . . . So say: Eliezer, son of Nissan . . . a.k.a / Jikan the Unconvincing / Zen monk, / a.k.a / Leonard Cohen" (411).[1]

In "'New Jerusalem Glowing': Songs and Poems of Leonard Cohen in Kabbalistic Key," Elliot Wolfson takes us some way in understanding Cohen's contribution to a new iteration of Jewish aesthetics,[2] showing how his lyrics are animated by a desire for mystical union, even while knowing that such unity is so very fleeting. While explicitly recognizing that Cohen draws on Zen Buddhism, Christianity, and Jewishness in assembling a repertoire of symbols and tropes that will help him name his longings, Wolfson focuses primarily on Cohen's engagement with Lurianic Kabbalah. Diving deep into Cohen's lyrics, Wolfson gives us a Jewish mystic—a poet who finds shards of light among the brokenness of being. It is a strong, important account. Yet this focus necessarily downplays the theological restlessness that informs so much of Cohen's work—as well as perhaps diminishes the profound humanity underwriting his lifelong interest in making poems that seek, as Buber puts it, to "breach the barriers of solitude" and to build "a bridge across the abyss" (*I and Thou*). This is the Cohen who in *The Book of Mercy* (1986) identified himself as lost and adrift, a "singer in the lower clouds" (1). It is also the Cohen we hear but a few years later, in what is probably his most well-known, widely discussed, and widely covered song, "Hallelujah."

The standard version of the song (as it appears in *Stranger Music*, an authorized selection of his songs and poems) is only four stanzas long, notably shorter than most of Cohen's other lyrics. Striking a self-consciously defiant stance, the speaker engages in a disaggregated internal monologue structured as a dialogue with the Self, whom he addresses as "You" (that is, even as he addresses a "You," there is no identifiably distinct Other). In this way, the utterance bespeaks a deep longing to engage an Other, even knowing that this effort may be futile. This is the abyss Cohen negotiates with his fragile offering—a "holy," "broken" song of praise, "Hallelujah"—a mournful variation on a doxology, a kind of liturgical speech that theologian Walter Brueggemann describes as a "world-making" or a constitutive act (Brueggemann, *Israel's Praise*, 29). For praise is not merely an act of address; rather it actively constructs a theological framework within which God can be met. This "Hallelujah" is especially hard-won. Cohen spent years wrestling with the lyrics, discarding nearly eighty other variations until settling on the four stanzas that constitute the standardized version included in *Stranger Music*.[3] This final version is strikingly nonsectarian: other than a brief gesture toward Psalms by way of a reference to "David . . . the baffled king," there is nothing to suggest that Cohen is speaking within a fixed religious tradition. Despite the absence of theological markers, or perhaps because of it, "Hallelujah" has been claimed by at least three world religions—Buddhism, Christianity, and Judaism—some a bit more aggressively than others. That is, Cohen gives us a highly mutable text, which paradoxically seems to elicit a desire to tie it down, or tether it to a discrete religious tradition.

Before he died in 2016, Cohen lived to see his song celebrated by the Zen teacher James Ishmael Ford as "one of the great Western Buddhist hymns, even if the words are all about David, king of sinners." Then upon his death, *The Tablet*—an international Catholic weekly—published a piece honoring Cohen, identified as "a Canadian Jew turned Zen Buddhist," for restoring "meaning to 'Hallelujah,'" a liturgical utterance that had lost its luster. Intent on placing the song firmly within the Catholic tradition, the author focuses particularly upon one performance: "Then there is the 'holy dove': when Allison Crowe sang it ['Hallelujah'] she was quite clear what Cohen was singing about; she substituted the words 'Holy Ghost.'"[4] Radiating certainty, this claim emphatically resists the fragile instability of the song—a quality dramatized by the handful of "alternative" stanzas attached to the end, inviting the reader/auditor/singer to choose between "the holy, or the broken Hallelujah"—or "a cold" and "broken, Hallelujah." As it turns out, Crowe's version is but one of several efforts seeking, even more pointedly, to claim the song for a Christian audience. Jake Hamilton (2009), for example, sings of "God's . . . Son there broken, beaten for me," while Cloverton (2012) offers "A Hallelujah Christmas," which celebrates a "baby boy / Who's come to earth to bring us joy."[5]

Such is the cultural moment into which Daniel Kahn steps when, in 2016, he uploads his own take on what has been described as "the great prayer of the modern age" (Light, 228). As if provoked by these Christianizing efforts, Kahn offers a sustained, rather *chutzpadik*, effort to take what began as an ecumenical expression and mark the lyric as a decidedly *Jewish* production. Kahn, an American-born poet and musician known for his contributions to the ongoing revival of Klezmer music—a genre derived from the Jewish Eastern European musical tradition—responds confidently when asked about his wildly successful version (a viral sensation, at least in Jewish quarters):

> Hallelujah is essentially a Yiddish song Leonard Cohen wrote in English, by which I mean it's Jewish. It's like the Song of Solomon, the double working of devotion to God and devotion to a lover, the juxtaposition of eroticism and spirituality. These are all, to my opinion, very Jewish themes. To do it in Yiddish makes sense.[6]

The banner at the bottom of the video simply reads "Leonard Cohen's 'Hallelujah'—in Yiddish," suggesting that what follows is merely a translation. But actually Kahn (who looks like a healthy, rather buff incarnation of Tevye the Milkman, resplendent in a dark vest and fiddler cap) gives us what he calls a "trapadation"—a fusion of translation and adaptation. Amplifying a narrative frame toward which Cohen merely gestured, Kahn's "Hallelujah" buffers Cohen's raw, ragged, *cri de coeur* by giving us a full-blown midrash on the tortured tale of King "Dovid" (in Yiddish) and his troubled affair with Bathsheba. It is a move designed to pull the song back from a religious no-man's-land and firmly assert its Jewish pedigree. But even more interesting is how Kahn wields Yiddish in the service of shoring up the very boundaries that Cohen seeks to test, by exploiting its function as a *lehavdel loshn*, a "differentiation language"—a strain of vocabulary deployed in the interest of setting "insiders" apart from "outsiders." Kahn starts off slowly, calling David's song a *mishibayrach*—a term referring specifically to the traditional prayer for healing, rendered in the subtitles simply as "prayer" (*Ha mavein Ya vin*, "Those who understand will understand"). Then in the fourth stanza, taking full advantage of Cohen's "additional verses" where Eros meets Agape, Kahn firmly overwrites the Christological reference to the "holy dove" (the very image that in Crowe's version becomes the "Holy Ghost") by recalling how "the Shekhinah"—a Kabbalistic term for the feminine incarnation of the divine—"glowed in our blood." Then the Yiddishisms really begin to pile up, all left untranslated: Cohen's "pilgrim who's seen the light" becomes a *mensch*; "David's" desire burns "hot through every letter, from *alef, beys*," bringing the song to a triumphant conclusion: "Though all is lost / I will praise *Adonai* / And cry like a *L'Chaim*, Hallelujah." And with that, Kahn emphatically dispels all vestiges of spiritually charged uncertainty, or what Buber might call "holy insecurity," that may have called Cohen's mutable song into being in the first place.[7]

So, you may ask, why dwell on a text—Kahn's rendition—that I find so unsatisfying, even off-putting? What is of interest? My answer begins with Rita Felski's account of how reading can be at once self-affirming and unnerving. In any given text, we can discover a version of ourselves that surely we recognize, but don't much care for. Felski memorably likens this sort of reading experience to "seeing an unattractive, scowling, middle-aged person coming into a restaurant, only to suddenly realize that you have been looking into a mirror behind the counter and this unappealing person is you. Mirrors don't always flatter" (48). Indeed. For in the course of sorting through my impatient account of Kahn's concerted effort to tie down Cohen's borderless text, I began to think about my own resistance to "holy insecurity," a space characterized by religious fluidities—and to consider just how disconcerting and unsettling such spaces can be.

Early on in this project, I had occasion to attend a Passover *seder* (a ritual holiday meal) hosted by Brigham Young University—the flagship university owned by the Church of Latter-day Saints. To be sure, such an event is hardly unique. Every year, churches, restaurants, and assorted non-Jewish organizations, provide opportunties for non-Jews to participate in some version of this ritual meal. Indeed in an article exploring the phenomenon, Lauren Davidson cheekily describes Passover as "the Jewish festival that non-Jews love to observe" (*Atlantic*, April 14, 2014). "Observe" is indeed the operative word, for on the one hand, it can mean to attentively notice; on the other hand, it can also mean to actively fulfill or participate in a religious or legal form of obligation. The latter sense of the word plunges us into that messy phenomenon known as "cultural appropriation"—an act entailing the "inapproppriate or unacknowledged adoption of the customs, practices, ideas of one people or society by members of another and typically more dominant people or society" (Oxford Dictionary). This "seder" which I attended activated both senses of the word "observe": for what began as a thoughtfully designed educational experience ultimately crossed over into discomforting territory—even as it afforded yet another lesson in the complex contours of the Jewish Christian borderzone.

Sponsored by Brigham Young University's program in Religious Education, these "seders"—a series of events which are always sold out—are eagerly atttended mostly by Church members and a scattering of Messianic Jews. I enter a large ballroom, packed with participants. After being directed to an empty seat at an otherwise full table, I turn my attention to the PowerPoint presentation in progress, "Passover at the Time of Gamliel and Jesus." (Second Temple Judaism holds special appeal for Mormons, who see themselves as inheriting and extending the Temple tradition, as a "Latter-day" Kingdom of Zion.) At this point, even as I squirm a bit at the idea of the seder as a museum exhibit, I can recognize the pedagogic value—and try to settle into the moment.

Then things take a disorienting turn, as the leader/teacher announces that the lecture is over and dons what he explains is a *"kippah"* (a skullcap worn by many Jews during prayer, and by Orthodox Jewish males at all times). I stiffen as the leader tells the assembled to pour "two fingers" of "wine" (or in this case, grape juice, since Latter-day Saints don't drink alcohol) and proceeds to say the *bracha* (the blessing) in Hebrew, including the sacred name *Adonai Eloheinu*: a non-Jew prays to the Jewish God as part of a performance. While I didn't fully recognize it at the time, this was the moment when the event stopped being strictly educational and became culturally/religiously problematic.[8] Looking back over my notes later, I see that I had scrawled: "This isn't yours, it's mine." The borderzone can be a lonely place—saturated with silence and loss.

Now it is time to eat. My tablemates pepper me with questions: "Do you know this all by heart?" "Have you been to a seder before—you seem to know what you are doing" (and I thought I was being so discreet). "Is this what *real* seders are like?" I don't dissemble, but do explain that at my house seders are considerably noisier and messier. Then I ask them about their interest in attending such an event. The answers are varied, but share a common theme: *we* identify with *your story*; we, too, struggled to be free; we, too, have food constraints. Listening to these responses, I start thinking about the limits of analogy. Is abstaining from alcohol or beverages in the Mormon tradition equivalent to Jewish dietary laws? And what about comparing a recent historically verifiable event—a grueling trek undertaken by nearly three thousand Mormons over a period of four years, pushing handcarts from the Midwest to the West in search of religious freedom—to a mythic account chronicling more than two hundred years of slavery brought to an end by divine intervention?

Before I can reflect further about the kinds of questions that arise when religions come in contact, I overhear my neighbor musing: "It is funny that the Jews don't understand that Passover is really all about Jesus. After all, they were saved because of the Blood of the Lamb on the doorpost." At this point the borderzone threatens to become a combat zone; in retrospect, I could have benefited from the sturdy wisdom of Amy-Jill Levine (an indefatigable warrior on the frontlines of Jewish Christian relations), who is wary of church-sponsored seders, despite their educational benefits. At the very least, I would have been better prepared for what followed. As Levine understands it, many such occasions are problematic on at least two counts. First, often designed as "feel-good" events, such "performances" help foster a romanticized relationship to Jewishness, thus absolving participants from the obligation to pursue hard, but necessary, conversations about Christian anti-Semitism.[9] Second, in the interest of crafting a compelling narrative, these events tend to elide history by presenting the Passover seder *as if* an iteration of the Last Supper—a misconception that has been firmly disproved by any number of scholars.[10] Actually, it isn't even fully clear that the Last Supper was a Passover meal (it is not in *John*, which, according to Levine, is the most historically reliable of the gospels[11]).

While the leader (and "author") of the "seder" I attended certainly made an effort to note how the ritual changes over time (the back cover of the occasion's "haggadah" includes a chronology), the performance itself soft-pedals history. After the *afikomen* has been found (and redeemed for one of BYU's famous mint brownies), the leader dramatically marks the end of the "Jewish" seder by taking off his *kippah*, announcing: "Now I want to tell you why YOU should care about the Passover seder." Bypassing the gospel of John in favor of

Luke, the leader gestures toward an image of Jesus at table with the apostles and cites: "Then he took bread, and when he had given thanks, he broke it and gave it to them, saying, 'This is my body, which is given for you. . . .'" (22:19). "Seders, like this, help us build a bridge to our Jewish friends," the leader declares (so, I think darkly, appreciation of the religious other *is* at stake); "but more importantly," he continues, "Jesus instituted the sacrament, and on this occasion we gather to celebrate not just his resurrection, but this time of redemption. For we know that Elijah appeared to Joseph Smith to sanctify the building of the first temple. He—Elijah—is with us." I look quickly at my tablemate (the same one who insisted that Passover is really all about Jesus) and, without my asking, he says: "1836, Ohio, Elijah appeared in a vision." Then the leader asks us all to stand and welcome Elijah: "for Christ has risen and redemption is at hand." A student opens the ballroom door, and we turn in her direction. The leader raises the fourth cup—Elijah's cup, the cup of redemption—now rebranded as the cup of resurrection; we are all silent. For a full minute, we are silent. The seder is over. As I am leaving, I ask my neighbor (the same one) how he felt during that long silence, which was both so full and so empty. Meeting my gaze, he says: "Holiness. I felt holiness."

Later, I write about this experience for an online magazine (*Faith Counts*), recounting how, despite all of the religiously problematic and invasive moves, that last moment lingers with me. I think of my own seders (and those of my friends) and how the moment when we open the door for Elijah is usually filled with giggles or silly pranks (as if to cover up our discomfort). For if anyone believes—really believes—that the Messiah might arrive, they keep it to themselves. I describe feeling a pang of "holy envy," acknowledging how my own lively, sometimes raucous, *sedarim* rarely allowed space for such quiet, explicitly faith-affirming moments.

But now, as my study of this complex emotional response to the religious Other comes to a close, I realize that because I had spent the evening so intent on safeguarding my own religious boundaries, noting with irritation every moment that the leader trespassed onto *my* "territory"—that I had missed an opportunity to peer over the edge into an "abyss" and to venture into a place of "holy insecurity."

Notes

Preface

1. My own experience presenting these poems to interfaith groups suggests that this fear is unfounded; rather than silencing participants, these texts invite deeper and more honest exchanges—about religious similarities, differences, and longings—welcome departures from the usual niceties.

1. Holy Envy: Writing in the Jewish Christian Borderzone

1. Not only has Jewish studies, as a discrete discipline, changed significantly, allowing for more in the way of cross-religious inquiry, but—as documents such as "Dabru Emet: A Jewish Statement on Christians and Christianity" (2000) suggest—the broader Jewish community (at least its more liberal constituency) is less wary of the Christian Other.

2. See Paula Fredriksen, "What a Friend We Have in Jesus," *Jewish Review of Books* (Spring 2012): 2; and Michael Peppard, "A Moment in Our Shared History," *Tablet,* July 7, 2012.

3. Daniel Boyarin, "Nostalgia for Christianity: Getting Medieval Again," *Religion and Literature* 42 (Summer 2010): 49–76.

4. The "Jewish Jesus" has been the subject of at least two important studies: Neta Stahl's *Other and Brother: Jesus in the 20th-Century Jewish Literary Landscape*; and Matthew Hoffman's *From Rebel to Rabbi: Reclaiming Jesus and the Making of Modern Jewish Culture.*

5. "Divine Beauty from Van Gogh to Chagall and Fontana," Palazzo Strozzi, exhibit review by Alexandra Korey, https://www.theflorentine.net/2015/09/10/divine-beauty-from-van-gogh-to-chagall-and-fontana/.

6. I am indebted here to Dean Franco's useful comments on this chapter, as well as to his own discussion about the transient nature of borders in his book *The Border and the Line: Race, Literature, and Los Angeles*, 21–24.

7. Saul N. Zaritt explores this lost prospect in his essay "Maybe for Millions, Maybe for Nobody: Jewish American Writing and the Undecidability of World Literature." Later in this study, I consider Louis Zukofsky's hope for Yiddish as an emancipatory tongue.

8. Jakobson, *Six Lectures on Sound and Meaning*.

2. Lives of the Saints: Mina Loy and Gertrude Stein

1. See, for example, Rachel Adler in "'To Live Outside the Law You Must Be Honest': Boundaries, Borderlands, and the Ethics of Cultural Negotiation."

2. Cristanne Miller gives a full account of Loy's turn to Jewishness in *Cultures of Modernism: Marianne Moore, Mina Loy, and Else Lasker-Schuler* (168–173).

3. According to Burke (16), "Mina came to suspect that her mother's religion was based less on theological principles than on her concern with other people's opinions."

4. This figure is discussed extensively by Matthew Hoffman in *From Rebel to Rabbi: Reclaiming Jesus and the Making of Modern Jewish Culture*.

5. This reading draws extensively upon my essay "Divine Women, Fallen Angels: The Late Devotional Poetry of Mina Loy."

6. Feinstein elaborates fully on Stein's Jewishness in a new book, *Gertrude Stein and the Making of Jewish Modernism*.

7. Shreiber, "A Time to Eat" (work in progress).

8. Of the two, it is Alice—also born Jewish—who actively professes desire for the religious Other. Not only is she thoroughly enthralled with Spain, but Catholicism itself calls to her. Indeed, after Stein's death, Alice would formally convert, claiming that she was merely reaffirming her faith since she had been baptized as a child! (or so she claimed; see Janet Malcolm).

9. Ulla Dydo suggests that the sorrow occasioned by the impending death of Stein's good friend, the painter Juan Gris, is part of this emotional mix (188).

10. This move surely complicates her status as a stalwart secularist. Although she is hardly a believer, she is wholly interested in the world—including all of its rhythms and formulations. Following Ben Friedlander's provocative reading, we might recognize Stein as a first "child of Paul," insofar as she identifies as Jewish, eschews traditional practices, and welcomes "Gentiles" to her projects. She emerges thus as a true "antinomian" (Jewish) poet, not only because she is fearless when it comes to operating outside the parameters of grammar, but also outside the parameters of religion.

3. Hiding in Plain Sight: Louis Zukofsky, Shame, and the Sorrows of Yiddish

1. The King James Bible continues to be a touchstone for all kinds of self-avowedly Jewish poets, including Jacqueline Osherow and Peter Cole. It will be interesting to

see what kind of impact Robert Alter's acclaimed new translation of the entire Hebrew Bible has on English-language Jewish poetry.

2. I would like to thank Charles Bernstein for this image.

3. See, for example, Jonathan Ivry in "'[A]ll / things began in Order to / end in Ordainer': The Theological Poetics of Louis Zukofsky from 'A' to X," *Texas Studies in Literature and Language* 51 (2009): 203–22.

4. See Peter Quartermain's discussion of Zukofsky's efforts to craft a "poetry allied to speech" (90–103).

5. See Jonathan Freedman's comprehensive account of *The Waste Land*'s cultural impact, in *The Temple of Culture: Assimilation and Anti-Semitism in Literary Anglo-America*, 177–82.

6. This geological metaphor comes from Naomi Seidman's lectures on "Freud's Yiddish Languages"; I thank her for sharing this unpublished work with me. Zukofsky scholarship has further benefited recently from the work of two younger scholars, both of whom are deeply familiar with Yiddish; see Sarah Ponichtera and Ariel Resnikoff.

7. See, for example, Naomi Seidman's essay "The Language of the New Testament and the Translation of the Bible," in *The Jewish Annotated New Testament*, 699–702.

8. Merle Bachman offers an excellent account of the vitality and sense of possibility characterizing American Yiddish poetic culture in the 1920s in her essay "An Exotic on East Broadway: Mikhl Licht and the Paradoxes of Yiddish Modernist Poetry." Her insights into how poets such as Licht and Glatstein (both Zukofsky's contemporaries) viewed Yiddish as wonderfully in keeping with America's propensity for linguistic experimentation, help illuminate Zukofsky's interest in Yiddish as a rich poetic resource (Bachman, in Miller and Morris, *Radical Poetics*, 79–102).

9. See Shreiber, "Passover in the Jewish Christian Border Zone."

10. Even as the primary meaning of "speech" belongs to Hebrew—the language of prayer—it is possible to take the line as one more jab at those who are wont to celebrate Yiddish as "speech," thus denying/downplaying its mongrel vitality.

11. Craig Dworkin offers a detailed account of the status of this wall in 1929 when "A" 4 was being drafted.

12. Strong examples of such readings are conspicuous in the 2010 collection, *Radical Poetics and Secular Jewish Culture*, in which Zukofsky's presence is invoked by poets Charles Reznikoff, Rachel Blau DuPlessis, and Bob Perlman. More recently, poet-critic Ariel Resnikoff offers a wonderfully detailed account of Zukofsky's Yiddish-inflected poetics in his dissertation "Home Tongue Earthquake: The Radical Afterlives of Yiddishland" (2019). In these pages, Resnikoff explicitly links contemporary avant-garde Jewish American poetics to Zukofsky's own innovative strategies.

13. As Resnikoff notes, Yiddish is a starting point for a number of writers working in the early part of the twentieth century, including Henry Roth and Louis Zukofsky. As my readers may recall, Roth casts Yiddish in a nostalgic light—a world to be ultimately left behind as David, the young would-be poet/writer, seeks entry into a

bigger, markedly Christianized world, in search of new aesthetic possibilities. Zukofsky takes an importantly different approach, seizing upon Yiddish, a cauldron of linguistic multiplicities—as a "starting point" for his own poetics. That is, he seeks to take the essential vibrancy and agility of his mother tongue forward as he works his way into a larger literary world (Resnikoff, 85). To be sure, Resnikoff's reading is part of a larger project exploring how a discrete set of twentieth-century writers refused monolingual constraints, preferring instead to craft a "translingual poetics." His account of Zukofsky's deep and ongoing relationship to Yiddish marks the next step in the changing landscape of both Jewish literary studies and of widespread accounts of modernism. While Zukofsky has long been celebrated for his "radical" poetics, only rather recently have emerging scholars like Resnikoff and Ponichtera, trained in both Yiddish and comparative modernism, been thus equipped to make strong, thick, and well-substantiated cases for the important role Yiddish plays in shaping Zukofsky's exceptionally intricate and agile approach to language. These efforts benefit from a conversation, now several decades in the making, initiated and extended by poet-critics such as Charles Bernstein and Stephen Fredman, who have long urged us to listen to how "decentered" or "marginal" languages such as Yiddish help foster linguistic innovation. Moreover, these efforts reflect the transformative work of critics such as Chana Kronfeld, whose breakthrough study *On the Margins of Modernism: Decentering Literary Dynamics* demonstrates how adding such "minor" literatures as Yiddish and Hebrew to the mix requires a comprehensive remapping of modernism's contours.

4. Unholy Envy: Karl Shapiro and the Problem of "Judeo-Christianity"

1. Norman Finkelstein, in his recent volume *Like a Dark Rabbi: Modern Poetry and the Jewish Literary Imagination* (2019), begins with a discussion of Karl Shapiro, a poet whose stance toward religion he describes as at once "proud and regretful." Although the book appeared only after I had drafted my own discussion, Finkelstein's account importantly contributes not only to our understanding of Shapiro, but to the role secularism plays in the construction of the Jewish American identity.

2. Andrew Gross, in a long essay exploring Shapiro's take on identity, distinguishes between individualism and identity, arguing that Shapiro aligns himself with the former.

3. Wilson's reading has since been discounted, since contemporary Bible scholars such as Menachem Kister note that although the scrolls may have been either written or copied down during Jesus's lifetime, they cannot be claimed as expressions of proto-Christianity (*JANT*, 711).

4. See Mark Silk's discussion, "Notes on the Judeo-Christian Tradition in America."

5. Shapiro's *A Prosody Handbook* (1965, co-authored with Robert Beum) attests to this conviction.

6. I wonder if Lenny Bruce would consider this distinction a suitable addition to his famous bit on "Jewish" versus "Goyish": "Kool aid is Goyish, black cherry soda very Jewish."

7. Uncannily enough, this position resonates with the Kabbalistic reading of circumcision as prerequisite to any significant visionary experience (see Shaye Cohen, *Why Aren't Jewish Women Circumcised?*, 44–45).

8. The quote in the preceding section heading is from the Introduction in *Poems of a Jew*.

5. The Certainty of Wings: Denise Levertov and the Legacy of Her Hebrew-Christian Father

1. In this way, Levertoff makes manifest the very kind of cross-religious suturing that Arthur Green details in "Shekhinah, the Virgin Mary, and the Song of Songs," showing how the cult of the Virgin, associated with such appealing notions as "love, beauty, and simple piety," helped inspire Jewish articulations of a feminine godhead (28).

2. Some Jewish scholars such as Arthur Green are also made a bit queasy by Magid's study, suspecting him of wanting to dismantle religious boundaries altogether (*Stanford Review* 2014).

3. Focusing on Buber's early essay "Christ, Hasidism, and Gnosis," Magid shows how Hasidism—unlike Kabbalah, a gnostic tradition which arguably introduced the idea of an incarnational Godhead to Jewish thought—promoted a more democratic, inclusive vision (120–22).

4. See, for example, essays by Jorge Quiñónez, Shalom Goldman, and Elliot Wolfson.

5. While Levertoff's position is surely unique, his commitment to correcting the dominant narrative which insists upon casting Judaism and Christianity in an antagonistic relationship can be read within the context of other figures, as described by Shaul Magid in his essay "Loving Judaism Through Christianity: The Cases of Elijah Zvi Soloveitchik and Oswald Rufeisen."

6. See the Denise Levertov Papers, M0601, Box 33, Folders 5–8 in the Department of Special Collections, Green Library, Stanford University.

7. See also Anne Perez's essay "Apostasy of a Prince: Hans Herzl and the Boundaries of Jewish Nationalism."

8. More than likely Feivel found a page from Shem Tob's fourteenth-century Hebrew translation of the Gospel, which circulated throughout Europe.

9. It is an interesting choice, since the Gospel of John is known at once as the most "Jewish," as well as the most "anti-Jewish," of the Gospels (*JANT*, 172).

10. Indeed, Olga ultimately moves out of the Jewish-Christian borderzone altogether, renouncing the first half of this hyphenated identity to become what she calls a "Christian Socialist."

11. See also Romana Huk's discussion of how poems describing epiphanic arrivals are often undercut by a sense of loss or failure. In this same essay, Huk takes note of Levertov's efforts to "fold her developing interests in incarnational Christianity back into her Jewish roots" (in "'Nothing / Like a Real Bridge': Rae Armantrout and Denise Levertov," 61).

12. Donna Hollenberg offers a short but nuanced account of the many factors leading up to the rupture, including theological differences as well as Duncan's psychoanalytically charged reading of Levertov's opposition to the war as symptomatic of unacknowledged psychic ruptures (283–85).

13. See Donna Hollenberg's collection, *Denise Levertov in Company: Essays by Her Students, Colleagues, and Fellow Writers*, for a fuller account of the poet's personal and professional history.

14. *Agnus Dei, qui tollis peccata mundi, ora pro nobis*: "Lamb of God, who taketh away the sins of the world, pray for us."

Coda: Holy Insecurity

1. In a long interview with Arthur Kurtzweil, Cohen explains his sense of the compatibilities and affinities between Zen Buddhism and Judaism more fully: https://www.leonardcohenfiles.com/arthurkurzweil.pdf

2. Readers should also take note of Aubrey Glazer's book-length study of Cohen as a post-secular "Jewish (and beyond)" mystic.

3. See Janet Maslin, "Time Passes, but a Song's Time Doesn't," *New York Times*, December 9, 2012, https://www.nytimes.com/2012/12/10/books/the-holy-or-the-broken-by-alan-light.html.

4. Catherine Pepinster, "Leonard Cohen: Poet of Lyrical Grace," *The Tablet*, November 17, 2016, https://www.thetablet.co.uk/features/2/9193/leonard-cohen-poet-of-lyrical-grace.

5. I wish to thank an anonymous press reader of this book manuscript for calling attention to that larger cultural/interreligious context informing my discussion of Kahn.

6. Larry Yudelson, "A New and Very Yiddish Hallelujah," *Jewish Standard*, November 17, 2016, https://jewishstandard.timesofisrael.com/a-new-and-very-yiddish-hallelujah/.

7. I am indebted to Eric Selinger's account of Kahn's version of Cohen's song in his paper, "Fartaytsht un Farbesert: Leonard Cohen, Daniel Kahn, and the Yiddish 'Hallelujah,'" https://www.researchgate.net/publication/331982287_Fartaytsht_un_Farbesert_Leonard_Cohen_Daniel_Kahn_and_the_Yiddish_Hallelujah.

8. Writing in *Appropriate: A Provocation*, Paisley Rekdal describes a somewhat comparable incident, helping me to recognize its appropriative elements and thus name the source of my discomfort (32–33).

9. In fairness, I must note that the Latter-day Saints are singularly hospitable to Jews and historically have worked very hard to educate themselves about Judaism.

10. See, for example, David Freidenreich, who writes that it is simply "anachronistic" to call the Last Supper a Passover seder—a ritual meal that "developed after the destruction of the Temple" (*JANT*, 652).

11. Amy-Jill Levine, "Holy Week and the Hatred of the Jews: How to Avoid Anti-Judaism This Easter," ABC Religion and Ethics, April, 1, 2021, https://www.abc.net.au/religion/holy-week-and-the-hatred-of-the-jews/11029900.

Works Cited

Adler, Rachel. "'To Live Outside the Law You Must Be Honest'—Boundaries, Borderlands, and the Ethics of Cultural Negotiation." *Reconstructionist* 68, no. 2 (Spring 2004): 4–15.
Altmann, Alexander. "'Homo Imago Dei' in Jewish and Christian Theology." *Journal of Religion* 48, no. 3 (1968): 235–59. JSTOR, www.jstor.org/stable/1202149. Accessed March 11, 2016.
Amishai-Maisels, Ziva. "Chagall's 'White Crucifixion.'" *Art Institute of Chicago Museum Studies* 17, no. 2 (1991): 138–53, 180–81.
Anzaldúa, Gloria. *Borderlands/La Frontera: The New Mestiza*. Introduction by Norma E. Cantú and Aída Hurtado. San Francisco: Aunt Lute Books, 2012.
Armstrong, Tim. "Loy and Cornell: Christian Science and the Destruction of the World." In *The Salt Companion to Mina Loy*, edited by Rachel Potter and Suzanne Hobson. Cromer, UK: Salt Publishing, 2010.
Asch, Sholem. *The Apostle*. Translated by Maurice Samuel. New York: G. P. Putnam's Sons, 1943.
———. *Die Mutter*. Warsaw: Kultur Liga, 1925.
———. *The God of Vengeance: Drama in Three Acts*. Translated and introduced by Isaac Goldberg; preface by Abraham Cahan. Boston: Stratford, 1918.
———. *Mary*. Translated by Leo Steinberg. New York: Carroll and Graf, 1985.
———. *The Nazarene*. Translated by Maurice Samuel. New York: G. P. Putnam's Sons, 1939.
———. *One Destiny: An Epistle to the Christians*. Translated by Milton Hindus. New York: G. P. Putnam's Sons, 1945.
Bachman, Merle. *Recovering "Yiddishland": Threshold Moments in American Literature*. New York: Syracuse University Press, 2008.
———. "An Exotic on East Broadway: Mikhl Likht and the Paradoxes of Yiddish Modernist Poetry." In *Radical Poetics and Secular Jewish Culture*, edited by

Stephen Paul Miller and Daniel Morris, 79–102. Tuscaloosa: University of Alabama Press, 2010.
Bakhtin, M. M. *Rabelais and His World*. Bloomington: Indiana University Press, 1984.
Baldwin, James. *Collected Essays*. New York: Library of America, 1988.
Benjamin, Walter. "A Child's View of Color." In *Walter Benjamin: Selected Writings*, edited by Marcus Bullock and Michael W. Jennings, vol. 1, 50–52. Cambridge, MA: Harvard University Press, 1996.
Bennington, Geoffrey, and Jacques Derrida. *Jacques Derrida*. Translated by Geoffrey Bennington. Chicago: University of Chicago Press, 1993.
Bernstein, Charles. *A Poetics*. Cambridge, MA: Harvard University Press, 1992.
———. *Pitch of Poetry*. Chicago: University of Chicago Press, 2016.
———. "Introduction." *Louis Zukofsky: Selected Poems*. New York: Library of America, 2006, xiii–xxvii.
Bernstein, Irving. *The Lean Years: A History of the American Worker, 1920–1933*. New York: Penguin, 1966.
Bhabha, Homi. *The Location of Culture*. London: Routledge, 1994.
Bloom, Harold. "The Sorrows of American-Jewish Poetry." *Commentary*, 53, no. 3 March 1972, 69–74.
Boyarin, Daniel. *Border Lines: The Partition of Judaeo-Christianity*. Philadelphia: University of Pennsylvania Press, 2004.
———. *Dying for God: Martyrdom and the Making of Christianity and Judaism*. Stanford, CA: Stanford University Press, 1999.
———. *The Jewish Gospels: The Story of the Jewish Christ*. New York: New Press, 2012.
———. "Nostalgia for Christianity: Getting Medieval Again." *Religion and Literature* 42 (Summer 2010): 49–76.
———. *A Radical Jew: Paul and the Politics of Identity*. Berkeley: University of California Press, 1994.
Brueggemann, Walter. *Israel's Praise: Doxology against Idolatry and Ideology*. Minneapolis, MN: Fortress Press (Paperback Edition), 1988.
Buber, Martin. *Daniel: Dialogues on Realization*. Translated with introduction by Maurice Friedman. New York: Holt, Rinehart and Winston, 1964.
———. *I and Thou*. Translated by Walter Kaufmann. New York: Simon and Schuster, 1970.
———. *The Origin and Meaning of Hasidism*. Translated with introduction by Maurice Friedman. New York: Horizon Press, 1960.
———. *Tales of the Hasidim*. Translated by Olga Marx. New York: Schocken, 1947.
———. *Two Types of Faith: A Study of the Interpenetration of Judaism and Christianity*. Translated by Norman P. Goldhawk. New York: Harper and Row, 1951.
———. *The Way of Man: According to the Teachings of Hasidism*. London: Routledge, 2020.

Burke, Carolyn. *Becoming Modern: The Life of Mina Loy.* New York: Farrar, Straus and Giroux, 1996.
Bynum, Caroline Walker, and Paula Gerson. "Body-Part Reliquaries and Body Parts in the Middle Ages." *Gesta* 36, no. 1 (1997): 3–7. JSTOR, www.jstor.org/stable/767274. Accessed July 24, 2021.
"Catholic Encyclopedia." *NewAdvent.org.* www.newadvent.org/cathen.
Celan, Paul. *Selected Poems and Prose of Paul Celan.* Translated by John Felstiner. New York: W. W. Norton, 2001.
Chagall.com. www.chagallpaintings.com/over-vitebsk/.
Chametzky, Jules. *Norton Anthology: Jewish American Literature.* New York: W. W. Norton, 2001.
Cohen, Arthur. *Martin Buber.* New York: Hillary House, 1957.
Cohen, Leonard. *Stranger Music: Selected Poems and Songs.* New York: Vintage, 1994.
———. *The Book of Mercy.* Toronto: McClelland and Stewart, 1986.
Cohen, Shaye J. D. *Why Aren't Jewish Women Circumcised? Gender and Covenant in Judaism.* Berkeley: University of California Press, 2005.
"Dabru Emet: A Jewish Statement on Christians and Christianity." *New York Times: Sunday,* September 10, 2000.
Damon, Maria. "Gertrude Stein's Jewishness, Jewish Social Scientists, and the 'Jewish Question.'" *Modern Fiction Studies* 42, no. 3 (Fall 1996): 489–506.
Davidson, Lauren. "Passover, the Jewish Holiday for Gentiles." *Atlantic* (April 14, 2014). https://www.theatlantic.com/national/archive/2014/04/passover-the-jewish-holiday-for-gentiles/360608/.
Derrida, Jacques. *Writing and Difference.* Translated and introduced by Alan Bass, Chicago: University of Chicago Press, 1978.
Duncan, Robert. *The Letters of Robert Duncan and Denise Levertov.* Edited by Robert J. Bertholf and Albert Gelpi. Stanford, CA: Stanford University Press, 2004.
DuPlessis, Rachel Blau. "Midrashic Sensibilities: Secular Judaism and Radical Poetics (A Personal Essay in Several Chapters)." In *Radical Poetics and Secular Jewish Culture,* edited by Stephen Paul Miller and Daniel Morris, 199–224. Tuscaloosa: University of Alabama Press, 2010.
Dworkin, Craig D. *Dictionary Poetics: Toward a Radical Lexicography.* New York: Fordham University Press, 2020.
Dydo, Ulla E., and William Rice. *Gertrude Stein: The Language That Rises: 1923–1934.* Northwestern University Press, 2003.
Feinstein, Amy. *Gertrude Stein and the Making of Jewish Modernism.* Gainesville: University Press of Florida, 2020.
Feldman, Irving. "*Poems of a Jew,* by Karl Shapiro." *Commentary,* November 1958. www.commentarymagazine.com/articles/irving-feldman/poems-of-a-jew-by-karl-shapiro/.
Felstiner, John. "'Clawed into Each Other': Jewish vs. Christian Memory in Paul Celan's Tenebrae." *Triquarterly* 87 (Spring/Summer 1993): 193–203.

———. *Paul Celan: Poet, Survivor, Jew*. New Haven, CT: Yale University Press, 1995.
Fiedler, Leslie A. *Olaf Stapledon: A Man Divided*. New York: Oxford University Press, 1983.
Finkelstein, Norman. *Like a Dark Rabbi: Modern Poetry and the Jewish Literary Imagination*. Cincinnati: Hebrew Union College Press, 2019.
Franco, Dean J. *The Border and the Line: Race, Literature, and Los Angeles*. Stanford, CA: Stanford University Press, 2019.
Fredriksen, Paula. "What a Friend We Have in Jesus." *Jewish Review of Books*. Spring 2012.
Fredman, Stephen. *A Menorah for Athena: Charles Reznikoff and the Jewish Dilemmas of Objectivist Poetry*. Chicago: University of Chicago Press, 2001.
Freedman, Jonathan. *The Temple of Culture: Assimilation and Anti-Semitism in Literary Anglo-America*. New York: Oxford University Press, 2000.
Freidenreich, David M. "Food and Table Fellowship." In *The Jewish Annotated New Testament: New Revised Standard Version Bible Translation*, edited by Amy-Jill Levine and Marc Zvi Brettler. Second Edition. 650–53. Oxford: Oxford University Press, 2017.
Friedlander, Ben. "Letter to the Romans." In *Radical Poetics and Secular Jewish Culture*, edited by Stephen P. Miller and Daniel Morris, 418–38. Tuscaloosa: University of Alabama Press, 2010.
Friedman, Maurice. *Martin Buber's Life and Work*. New York: F. P. Dutton, 1981.
Frost, Elizabeth. "Mina Loy's 'Mongrel Poetics.'" In *Mina Loy: Woman and Poet*. Edited by Keith Tuma and Maeera Shreiber, 149–80. Orono, ME: National Poetry Foundation, 1998.
Frymer-Kensky, Tikva, et al. "Dabru Emet: A Jewish Statement on Christians and Christianity." *Institute for Islamic Christian Jewish Studies*. icjs.org/dabru-emet-text/.
Fuchs, Thomas. "The Phenomenology of Shame, Guilt, and the Body in Body Dysmorphic Disorder and Depression." *Journal of Phenomenological Psychology* 33, no. 2 (2002): 223–43.
Gadamer, Hans-Georg. *Gadamer on Celan: "Who Am I and Who Are You?" and Other Essays*. Translated and edited by Richard Heinemann and Bruce Krajewski; introduced by Gerald L. Bruns. New York: State University of New York Press, 1997.
Gilman, Sander L. *Jewish Self-Hatred: Anti-Semitism and the Hidden Language of the Jews*. Baltimore, MD: Johns Hopkins University Press, 1986.
Glatstein, Jacob. "Mozart." Translated by A. Z. Forman. http://poemsintranslation.blogspot.com/2012/06/jacob-glatstein-mozart-from-yiddish.html.
Glazer, Aubrey. *Tangle of Matter and Ghost: Leonard Cohen's Post-Secular Songbook of Mysticism(s) Jewish and Beyond*. Brookline, MA: Academic Studies Press, 2017.
Glenn, Susan A. *The Jewish Cold War: Anxiety and Identity in the Aftermath of the Holocaust*. Ann Arbor, MI: Jean and Samuel Frankel Center for Judaic Studies, 2015.

Gold, Michael. *Jews Without Money*. New York: H. Liveright, 1930.
Goldstein, Laurence. *The American Poet at the Movies: A Critical History*. Ann Arbor: University of Michigan Press, 1994.
Goody, Alex. *Modernist Articulations: A Cultural Study of Djuna Barnes, Mina Loy, and Gertrude Stein*. New York: Palgrave Macmillan, 2007.
Green, Arthur. "Shaul Magid. Hasidism Incarnate: Hasidism, Christianity, and the Construction of Modern Judaism." *Studies in Christian-Jewish Relations* 10, no. 1 (2015). ejournals.bc.edu/index.php/scjr/article/view/9120/8220.
Greene, Dana. *Denise Levertov: A Poet's Life*. Urbana: University of Illinois Press, 2012.
Gross, Andrew. "Liberalism and Lyricism, or Karl Shapiro's Elegy for Identity." *Journal of Modern Literature* 34, no. 3 (Spring 2011):1–30.
Grossman, Allen R., and Mark Halliday. *The Sighted Singer: Two Works on Poetry for Readers and Writers*. Baltimore, MD: Johns Hopkins University Press, 1992.
Hahn, Cynthia. *The Reliquary Effect: Enshrining the Sacred Object*. London: Reaktion, 2017.
Hallisey, Joan. "Denise Levertov's 'Illustrious Ancestors': The Hasidic Influence." In *Denise Levertov: Selected Criticism*, edited by Albert Gelpi, 260–67. Ann Arbor: University of Michigan Press, 1993.
Harshav, Benjamin. *The Meaning of Yiddish*. Stanford, CA: Stanford University Press, 1999.
Harshav, Benjamin, et al. *Sing, Stranger: A Century of American Yiddish Poetry: A Historical Anthology*. Stanford, CA: Stanford University Press, 2006.
Heschel, Susannah. "Jesus in Modern Jewish Thought." In *The Jewish Annotated New Testament: New Revised Standard Version Bible Translation*, edited by Amy-Jill Levine and Marc Zvi Brettler, 736–40. Second Edition. Oxford: Oxford University Press, 2017.
Hirsch, Emil G. *My Religion and the Crucifixion Viewed from a Jewish Standpoint*. New York: Arno Press, 1973.
Hobbins, John. "Krister Stendahl's Three Rules of Religious Understanding." *Ancient Hebrew Poetry*. ancienthebrewpoetry.typepad.com/ancient_hebrew _poetry/2010/05/krister-stendahls-three-rules-of-religious-understanding.html.
Hoffman, Matthew. *From Rebel to Rabbi: Reclaiming Jesus and the Making of Modern Jewish Culture*. Stanford, CA: Stanford University Press, 2007.
Hölderlin, Friedrich. "Patmos." Translated by Scott Horton. *Harpers.org*. harpers .org/2007/07/patmos/.
Hollander, John. "The Question of American Jewish Poetry." In *What Is Jewish Literature?*, edited by Hana Wirth-Nesher. Philadelphia: Jewish Publication Society, 1994.
Hollenberg, Donna Krolik. *A Poet's Revolution: The Life of Denise Levertov*. Berkeley: University of California Press, 2013.
Hopkins, Gerard Manley. *Gerard Manley Hopkins*. Edited by Catherine Phillips. New York: New York University Press, 1995.

Huk, Romana. "'Nothing / Like a Real Bridge': Rae Armantrout and Denise Levertov." In *Denise Levertov in Company: Essays by Her Students, Colleagues, and Fellow Writers*, edited by Donna Krolik Hollenberg, 53–70. Columbia: University of South Carolina Press, 2018. Project MUSE, muse.jhu.edu/book/59175, Accessed January 16, 2019.

Ivry, Jonathan. "'[A]ll / things began in Order to/end in Ordainer': The Theological Poetics of Louis Zukofsky from 'A' to 'X.'" *Texas Studies in Literature and Language* 51 (2009): 203–22.

Jakobson, Roman. *Six Lectures on Sound and Meaning*. Cambridge, MA: MIT Press, 1981.

James, William. *The Varieties of Religious Experience*. Cambridge, MA: Harvard University Press, 1985.

Johnson, Kimberly. *Made Flesh: Sacrament and Poetics in Post-Reformation England*. Philadelphia: University of Pennsylvania Press, 2014.

Julius, Anthony. *T. S. Eliot, Anti-Semitism, and Literary Form*. New York: Thames and Hudson, 2003.

Kaufmann, David. "The Praying Atheist: A Look at the Poetry of Karl Shapiro." *Forward*. April 22, 2005. forward.com/culture/3345/the-praying-atheist-a-look-at-the-poetry-of-karl-shapiro.

Kazin, Alfred. "The Jew as Modern Writer." *Commentary*, April 1966. www.commentarymagazine.com/articles/alfred-kazin-2/the-jew-as-american-writer. Accessed December 15, 2020.

Kermani, Navid. *Wonder Beyond Belief: On Christianity*. Translated by Tony Crawford. Cambridge: Polity, 2019.

Kister, Menachem. "The Dead Sea Scrolls." In *The Jewish Annotated New Testament: New Revised Standard Version Bible Translation*, edited by Amy-Jill Levine and Marc Z. Brettler, 710–14. Second Edition. Oxford: Oxford University Press, 2017.

Klein, Melanie. *Envy and Gratitude and Other Works, 1946–1963*. New York: Delacorte/Seymour Lawrence, 1975.

Klingenstein, Susanne. *Jews in the American Academy, 1900–1940: The Dynamics of Intellectual Assimilation*. New Haven, CT: Yale University Press, 1991.

Klink, Joanna. "You. An Introduction to Paul Celan." *The Iowa Review* 30, no. 1 (2000): 1–18. doi:10.17077/0021-065X.5234.

Koren, Sharon Faye. "A Christian Means to a Conversa End." *Nashim: A Journal of Jewish Women's Studies and Gender Issues* 9 (Spring 2005): 27–61. JSTOR, www.jstor.org/stable/40326617.

Korey, Alexandra. "Divine Beauty from Van Gogh to Chagall and Fontana." Palazzo Strozzi, exhibit review.

Kristeva, Julia. *Strangers to Ourselves*. Translated by Leon S. Roudiez. New York: Columbia University Press, 1991.

Kronfeld, Chana. *On the Margins of Modernism: Decentering Literary Dynamics*. Berkeley: University of California Press, 1996.

Lacan, Jacques. *The Seminar*. Edited by Jacques-Alain Miller, vol. 11. New York: W. W. Norton, 1998.

Lambert, Joshua N. *Unclean Lips: Obscenity, Jews, and American Literature*. New York: New York University Press, 2013.
Leighton, Christopher M. "Christian Theology After the Shoah." In *Christianity in Jewish Terms*, edited by Tikva Frymer-Kensky et al., 36–48. Boulder, CO: Westview Press, 2000.
Levertoff, Olga. *The Wailing Wall*. Morehouse Publishing Co., 1937.
Levertoff, Paul P. *Ben-ha-adam: Ḥaye Yeshuʻa Ha-Mashiaḥ U-Feʻulay*. ʻEdut le-Yisʼraʼel, 1911.
———. *Love and the Messianic Age*. Vine of David, 2009.
Levertov, Denise. *Collected Poems*. Edited and annotated by Paul A. Lacey and Anne Dewey; introduced by Eavan Boland. New York: New Directions, 2013.
———. Denise Levertov Papers, M0601, Box 33, Folders 5–8 in the Department of Special Collections, Green Library, Stanford University.
———. *The Jacob's Ladder*. New York: New Directions, 1961.
———. *The Sorrow Dance: Poems*. New York: New Directions, 1967.
———. *Tesserae: Memories and Suppositions*. New York: New Directions, 1995.
———. "Work That Enfaiths," *CrossCurrents* 40.2 (Summer 1990): 150–59.
Levertov, Denise, and Jewel S. Brooker. *Conversations with Denise Levertov*. Jackson: University Press of Mississippi, 1998.
Levine, Amy-Jill. "Holy Week and the Hatred of the Jews: How to Avoid Anti-Judaism This Easter." April 1, 2021. https://www.abc.net.au/religion/holy-week-and-the-hatred-of-the-jews/11029900.
Levine, Amy-Jill, and Marc Zvi Brettler. *The Jewish Annotated New Testament: New Revised Standard Version Bible Translation*. Second Edition. Oxford: Oxford University Press, 2017.
Levy, Mark John. *Workings of an English Jewish Christian Heart*. London: Operative Jewish Converts' Institution, 1892.
Lieberman, Chaim. *The Christianity of Sholem Asch: An Appraisal from the Jewish Viewpoint*. New York: Philosophical Library, 1953.
Light, Alan. *The Holy or the Broken: Leonard Cohen, Jeff Buckley, and the Unlikely Ascent of "Hallelujah."* New York: Atria Books, 2013.
Loy, Mina. *The Last Lunar Baedeker*. Edited and introduced by Roger L. Conover; note by Jonathan Williams. Asheville, NC: Jargon Society, 1982.
Magid, Shaul. *Hasidism Incarnate: Hasidism, Christianity, and the Construction of Modern Judaism*. Stanford, CA: Stanford University Press, 2015.
———. "Loving Judaism through Christianity: The Cases of Elijah Zvi Soloveitchik and Oswald Rufeisen." *Common Knowledge* 26, no. 1 (January 2020): 88–124. Project MUSE, muse.jhu.edu/article/749022. Accessed October 12, 2020.
Medwick, Cathleen. *Teresa of Avila: The Progress of a Soul*. New York: Doubleday, 2001.
Mendes-Flohr, Paul. "Buber's Rhetoric." In *Martin Buber: A Contemporary Perspective*. New York: Syracuse University Press, 2002.
Meyer, Steven. *Irresistible Dictation: Gertrude Stein and the Correlations of Writing and Science*. Stanford, CA: Stanford University Press, 2001.

Miller, Cristanne. *Cultures of Modernism: Marianne Moore, Mina Loy, and Else Lasker-Schüler: Gender and Literary Community in New York and Berlin.* Ann Arbor: University of Michigan Press, 2005.

Miron, Dan. "God Bless America: Of and Around Sholem Asch's East River." In *Sholem Asch Reconsidered*, edited by Nanette Stahl. Beinecke Rare Book and Manuscript Library, 2004.

Mitchell, W. J. T. "Ekphrasis and the Other." In *Picture Theory: Essays on Verbal and Visual Representation*. Chicago: University of Chicago Press, 1994. complit.utoronto.ca/wp-content/uploads/COL1000-Week11-Nov25_WJT_Mitchell.pdf.

Moore, Deborah Dash. "Jewish GIs and the Creation of the Judeo-Christian Tradition." *Religion and American Culture: A Journal of Interpretation* 8, no. 1 (Winter 1998): 31–53. JSTOR, www.jstor.org/stable/1123913.

Ngai, Sianne. *Ugly Feelings*. Cambridge, MA: Harvard University Press, 2005.

Norich, Anita. "Sholem Asch and the Christian Question." In *Sholem Asch Reconsidered*, edited by Nanette Stahl, 252–53. Beinecke Rare Book and Manuscript Library, 2004.

———. *Writing in Tongues: Translating Yiddish in the Twentieth Century*. Seattle: University of Washington Press, 2013.

Novak, David. *Jewish-Christian Dialogue: A Jewish Justification*. New York: Oxford University Press, 1989.

O'Collins, S.J., Gerald, and Edward G. Farrugia, S.J. *A Concise Dictionary of Theology*. New York: Paulist, 2000.

Ovid and George Sandys. *Ovid's Metamorphosis Englished, Mythologized, and Represented in Figures*. Lincoln: University of Nebraska Press, 1970.

Ozick, Cynthia. "Envy: Or Yiddish in America." In *A Cynthia Ozick Reader*, edited by Elaine M. Kauvar. Bloomington: Indiana University Press, 1996.

Peers, E. Allison. *Studies of the Spanish Mystics*. New York: Macmillan, 1951.

Peppard, Michael. "A Moment in Our Shared History." *Tablet*, July 5, 2012.

Perez, Anne. "Apostasy of a Prince: Hans Herzl and the Boundaries of Jewish Nationalism." *AJS Review* 42, no. 1 (2018): 89–110. doi:10.1017/S0364009418000077.

Perloff, Marjorie. "English as a Second Language: Mina Loy's 'Anglo-Mongrels and the Rose.'" In *Mina Loy: Woman and Poet*, edited by Keith Tuma and Maeera Shreiber. Orono, ME: National Poetry Foundation, 1998.

Phillips, Robert. "The Art of Poetry XXXVI: Karl Shapiro." *Paris Review* 28, no. 99 (1986): 182–216.

Plate, S. Brent. *Walter Benjamin, Religion, and Aesthetics: Rethinking Religion Through the Arts*. New York: Routledge, 2004.

Ponichtera, Sarah. "Louis Zukofsky: Building a Poetics of Translation." *In geveb*. December 16, 2019. ingeveb.org/articles/louis-zukofsky-building-a-poetics-of-translation.

Pound, Ezra, and Louis Zukofsky. *Pound/Zukofsky: Selected Letters of Ezra Pound and Louis Zukofsky*. Edited by Barry Ahearn. New York: New Directions, 1987.

Pratt, Mary Louise. "Arts of the Contact Zone." *Profession*, 1991, 33–40. JSTOR, www.jstor.org/stable/25595469.

Probyn, Elspeth. *Blush: Faces of Shame*. Minneapolis: University of Minnesota Press, 2005. JSTOR, www.jstor.org/stable/10.5749/j.ctttt6tj.
Quartermain, Peter. *Disjunctive Poetics: From Gertrude Stein and Louis Zukofsky to Susan Howe*. Cambridge: Cambridge University Press, 1992.
Quiñónez, Jorge. "Paul Phillip Levertoff: Pioneering Hebrew-Christian Scholar and Leader." *Mishkan* 37 (2002): 21–34.
Rekdal, Paisley. *Appropriate: A Provocation*. New York: W. W. Norton, 2021.
Resnikoff, Ariel. "Home Tongue Earthquake: The Radical Afterlives of Yiddishland." PhD diss., Philadelphia: University of Pennsylvania, 2019.
Ross, Alex. "Bach's Holy Dread." *New Yorker*. December 26, 2016.
Roth, Henry. *Call It Sleep*. New York: Noonday Press, 1993.
Rubin, Louis D., Jr. "Karl Shapiro 1913–2000: He Took His Stands." *Sewanee Review* 109, no. 1 (Winter 2001): 108–19. JSTOR, www.jstor.org/stable/27548970. Accessed December 9, 2020.
Rubin, Steven J. *Telling and Remembering: A Century of American Jewish Poetry*. New York: Beacon, 1997.
Scarry, Elaine. *The Body in Pain: The Making and Unmaking of the World*. New York: Oxford University Press, 1985.
Schäfer, Peter. "The Jew Who Would Be God." *New Republic*. May 18, 2012. newrepublic.com/article/103373/jewish-gospels-christ-boyarin.
———. *The Jewish Jesus: How Judaism and Christianity Shaped Each Other*. Princeton, NJ: Princeton University Press, 2012.
———. *Jesus in the Talmud*. Princeton, NJ: Princeton University Press, 2007.
Schimmel, Harold. "ZUK. YEHOASH DAVID REX." *Paideuma* 7, no. 3 (Winter 1978): 559–69. JSTOR, www.jstor.org/stable/24725174. Accessed December 9, 2020.
Schonfield, Jeremy. *Undercurrents of Jewish Prayer*. The Littman Library of Jewish Civilization, 2008.
Schor, Esther H. *Emma Lazarus*. New York: Nextbook, 2006.
Schultz, Kevin. *Tri-Faith America: How Catholics and Jews Held Postwar America to Its Protestant Promise*. New York: Oxford University Press, 2011.
Schwartz, Regina M. *Sacramental Poetics at the Dawn of Secularism: When God Left the World*. Stanford, CA: Stanford University Press, 2008.
Scroggins, Mark. *The Poem of a Life: A Biography of Louis Zukofsky*. Shoemaker and Hoard, 2007.
Seidler, Meir. "Reading Chad Gadya through the Kaleidoscope of Time." In *Religious Stories in Transformation: Conflict, Revision and Reception*, edited by Alberdina Houtman et al. Boston, MA: Brill, 2016.
Seidman, Naomi. *Faithful Renderings: Jewish-Christian Difference and the Politics of Translation*. Chicago: University of Chicago Press, 2006.
———. "Judaism Unbound, Episode 204: Confronting Yiddish Shame." www.judaismunbound.com/podcast/episode-204-naomi-seidman.
———. "The Language of the New Testament and the Translation of the Bible." In *The Jewish Annotated New Testament: New Revised Standard Version Bible*

Translation, edited by Amy-Jill Levine and Marc Z. Brettler, 699–702. Second Edition. Oxford: Oxford University Press, 2017.
Selinger, Eric. "Fartaytsht un Farbesert: Leonard Cohen, Daniel Kahn, and the Yiddish 'Hallelujah.'" February 2019. https://www.researchgate.net/publication/331982287_Fartaytsht_un_Farbesert_Leonard_Cohen_Daniel_Kahn_and_the_Yiddish_Hallelujah.
Shandler, Jeffrey. *Adventures in Yiddishland: Postvernacular Language and Culture.* Berkeley: University of California Press, 2005.
Shapiro, Karl. *Coda: Last Poems.* Edited by Robert Phillips. Huntsville, TX: Texas Review Press, 2008.
———. *Essay on Rime.* New York: Reynal and Hitchcock, 1945.
———. *In Defense of Ignorance.* New York: Random House, 1960.
———. "Modern Poetry as Religion." *American Scholar* 28, no. 3 (Summer 1959): 297–305.
———. *Person, Place, and Thing.* New York: Reynal and Hitchcock, 1942.
———. *Poems of a Jew.* New York: Random House, 1958.
———. *The Poetry Wreck: Selected Essays, 1950–1970.* New York: Random House, 1975.
———. *Selected Poems.* Edited by John Updike. New York: Library of America, 2003.
———. *V-Letter and Other Poems.* n.p. 1944.
Shapiro, Karl, and Robert L. Beum. *A Prosody Handbook.* New York: Harper and Row, 1965.
Shreiber, Maeera. "Divine Women, Fallen Angels: The Late Devotional Poetry of Mina Loy." In *Mina Loy: Woman and Poet,* edited by Keith Tuma and Maeera Shreiber, 467–83. Orono, ME: National Poetry Foundation, 1998.
———. "Passover in the Jewish Christian Border Zone." FaithCounts.com. faithcounts.com/passover-in-the-jewish-christian-border-zone/.
———. *Singing in a Strange Land: A Jewish American Poetics.* Stanford, CA: Stanford University Press, 2007.
Silk, Mark. "Notes on the Judeo-Christian Tradition in America." *American Quarterly* 36, no. 1 (Spring 1984): 65–85. JSTOR, www.jstor.org/stable/2712839. Accessed December 4, 2020.
Smith, Richard H. *Envy: Theory and Research.* Oxford: Oxford University Press, 2008.
Stahl, Neta. *Other and Brother: Jesus in the Twentieth-Century Jewish Literary Landscape.* New York: Oxford University Press, 2013.
Stein, Gertrude. *The Autobiography of Alice B. Toklas.* New York: Vintage, 1960.
———. *Everybody's Autobiography.* Cambridge, MA: Exact Change, 2014.
———. *Geography and Plays.* Boston: Four Seas Company, 1922.
———. *Lectures in America.* New York: Vintage, 1975.
———. *The Making of Americans: The Hersland Family.* Preface by Bernard Faÿ. New York: Harcourt, Brace, 1934.
———. *Portraits and Prayers.* New York: Random House, 1934.

———. "A Radio Interview." *Paris Review* 116 (Fall 1990), www.theparisreview.org/miscellaneous/2282/a-radio-interview-gertrude-stein. Accessed July 12, 2020.
———. *A Stein Reader*. Edited and introduced by Ulla E. Dydo. Evanston, IL: Northwestern University Press, 1993.
———. *Tender Buttons: Objects, Food, Rooms*. Los Angeles: Sun and Moon Press, 1991.
———. *Useful Knowledge*. New York: Payson and Clarke, 1928.
———. *Wars I Have Seen*. New York: Random House, 1945.
———. *Writers at Work: The Paris Review Interviews*. Edited by Malcolm Cowley. New York: Viking, 1958.
Stein, Gertrude, and Amy Feinstein. "The Modern Jew Who Has Given Up the Faith of His Fathers Can Reasonably and Consistently Believe in Isolation." *PMLA* 116, no. 2 (March 2001): 416–28. JSTOR, www.jstor.org/stable/463528.
Stevens, Wallace. *Collected Poems*. New York: Knopf, 1954.
Stewart, Susan. *Poetry and the Fate of the Senses*. Chicago: University of Chicago Press, 2002.
[Tanakh]: *JPS Hebrew-English Tanakh: The Traditional Hebrew Text and the New JPS Translation*. 2nd ed., Jewish Publication Society, 1999.
Taylor, Barbara B. *Holy Envy: Finding God in the Faith of Others*. New York: HarperOne, 2019.
Thomson, Virgil, Gertrude Stein, et al. *Four Saints in Three Acts: An Opera to Be Sung*. New York: Random House, 1934.
Tuma, Keith. "Mina Loy: Notes on Religion." In *A Sulfur Anthology*. 1990. Edited and introduced by Clayton Eshleman, 403–7. Middletown, CT: Wesleyan University Press, 2016.
———. "Mina Loy's 'Anglo-Mongrels and the Rose.'" In *Mina Loy: Woman and Poet*. Edited by Keith Tuma and Maeera Shreiber, 181–202. Orono, ME: National Poetry Foundation, 1998.
Umansky, Ellen. "Ray Frank." *The Encyclopedia of Jewish Women*. jwa.org/encyclopedia/article/frank-ray.
———. *From Christian Science to Jewish Science: Spiritual Healing and American Jews*. New York: Oxford University Press, 2005.
Welsh, Andrew. *Roots of Lyric: Primitive Poetry and Modern Poetics*. Princeton, NJ: Princeton University Press, 1978.
Wilson, Edmund. "The Scrolls from the Dead Sea." *New Yorker*. May 14, 1955, 45–121.
Wineapple, Brenda. *Sister Brother: Gertrude and Leo Stein*. New York: G. P. Putnam's Sons, 1996.
Wirth-Nesher, Hana. *Call It English: The Languages of Jewish American Literature*. Princeton, NJ: Princeton University Press, 2006.
Wolfson, Elliot R. "Judaism and Incarnation: The Imaginal Body of God." In *Christianity in Jewish Terms*, edited by Tikva Frymer-Kensky et al., 239–54. Boulder, CO: Westview Press, 2000.

———. "New Jerusalem Glowing: Songs and Poems of Leonard Cohen in a Kabbalistic Key." *Kabbalah: Journal for the Study of Jewish Mystical Texts* 15 (2006): 103-52.

———. "Paul Philip Levertoff and the Popularization of Kabbalah as a Missionizing Tactic." *Kabbalah: Journal for the Study of Jewish Mystical Texts* 27 (2012): 269-320.

"Would You Be Different? Madame Loy Shows How." *The Pittsburgh Press*. April 3, 1921, 2. Newspapers.com. www.newspapers.com/clip/15430648/mina-loy-fashion-designs.

Yuval, Israel Jacob. *Two Nations in Your Womb: Perceptions of Jews and Christians in Late Antiquity and the Middle Ages*. Berkeley: University of California Press, 2006.

Zangwill, Israel. *The Melting Pot: Drama in Four Acts*. London: Forgotten Books, 2015.

Zaritt, Saul N. "Maybe for Millions, Maybe for Nobody: Jewish American Writing and the Undecidability of World Literature." *American Literary History* 28, no. 3 (August 2016): 542–73.

Zukofsky, Louis. *"A."* New York: New Directions Publishing, 2011.

———. "Program: 'Objectivists' 1931." In *Prepositions +: The Collected Critical Essays*. Foreword by Charles Bernstein; additional prose edited and introduced by Mark Scroggins. Lebanon, NH: University Press of New England, 2000.

Index

achdut (seeking unity with God), 113
Adler, Rachel, 144n1 (chap. 2)
affect. *See* emotions
Akiva, Rabbi, 7, 19
Albertus Magnus, 33
Alexander, Philip, 2
Alter, Robert, 145n1
American Scholar (journal), 82
Amidah (core of Jewish prayer), 23
anti-absorption, 25
anti-Semitism: American literary culture and, 81–82; Asch's response to, xiii; Celan's response to, 11–12; Christianity identified with, xiv, 92, 117–19; at Columbia University, 66; Eliot's, 96; Holocaust as culmination of, 93; Jewish interpretations of Jesus in response to, 8, 19, 108; Loy and, 31, 32; Pound's, 61; Self-Other dynamic in, 7, 8; Shapiro and the Bollingen affair, 80–83; Stein and, 41; stereotypes associated with, 31, 38, 96, 114; Tenebrae services associated with, 13
Anzaldúa, Gloria, vii–viii
Art Institute of Chicago, 7
Asch, Sholem: and America, 20; and anti-Semitism, xiii; career of, 9; criticisms of, 9–10, 16, 20; and English language, 9, 20; and the Jewish Christian borderzone, xiii, 8–9, 16–20; and Paul Levertoff, 113; life of, 8–9; and Yiddish, xiii, xiv, 9–10, 20
Asch, Sholem, works: *The Apostle*, 9; *Die Mutter*, 73; *The God of Vengeance*, 9; *Mary*, 9; *The Nazarene*, 9, 17–20; *One Destiny*, 16, 20
assimilation, 92

Auden, W. H., 81, 89
Augustine, 88, 115; *Confessions*, 35, 113
avant-garde: Jewish writers and, 32, 54–55, 58; Joyce's *Finnegans Wake* as exemplar of, 22; language use by, 93; Loy and, 28, 32; Stein and, 42; Zukofsky and, 145n12

Baal Shem Tov (Rabbi Israel Ben Eliezer), 111, 121, 135
Bach, Johann Sebastian, xiv, 2, 65, 72–73, 76–77; "St. Matthew Passion," 65, 66–67, 72
Bachelard, Gaston, 37
Bachman, Merle, 77, 145n8
Bakhtin, Mikhail, 74–75
Baldwin, James, "Stranger in the Village," 79
Baptism, 104–5
Barnstone, William, 62
Beckett, Samuel, 93
Beinecke Rare Book and Manuscript Library, Yale University, 34
Benedict XIV, Pope, 13
Benjamin, Walter, 36
Bergson, Henri, 29
Bernini, Gian Lorenzo, "The Ecstasy of Saint Teresa," 47, 51
Bernstein, Charles, 25, 54–55, 145n2, 146n13
Bhabha, Homi, viii, 7, 19
Bible. *See* Hebrew Bible; King James Bible
Blake, William, 125
Bloom, Harold, 89
Bloomgarden, Solomon ("Yehoash"), 25, 57, 63–65, 72–73, 75; "Among the Trees," 73; "*Bakhr Esh-Shaytan*," 64; "On the Ruins," 64

163

INDEX

body: Christian conceptions of, 34–35, 37–38; Christian Science and, 34–35; Loy and, 34–35, 37–40; Shapiro and, 102–5; Yiddish associated with, 79. *See also* incarnation; materiality
Böhme, Jakob, 134
Boland, Eavan, 122
Bollingen affair, 80–83, 88
borderlands, vii–viii, x
borderzones: affect associated with, x–xi; background of concept of, vii–viii; poems as, xii; religious, x–xiii. *See also* Jewish Christian borderzone
boundaries: holiness as a form of, xiii; Jews and, viii–ix; poetry and, xi–xii
Boyarin, Daniel, xi, 2–4, 68; *Border Lines*, 4; *Dying for God*, 4; *The Jewish Gospels*, 5; *A Radical Jew*, 4
Brettler, Marc, vii, 1
Breuer, Josef, 49
Brigham Young University, 139–40
Brooks, Cleanth, 82
Bruce, Lenny, 147n6 (chap. 4)
Brueggemann, Walter, 137
Buber, Martin: controversy associated with, 134; and Hasidism, 110–11, 119–23, 126, 131, 134–35; and holy insecurity, xv, 131, 133–36, 139; and the Jewish Christian borderzone, 119–23, 134–39; on Judaism and Christianity, xv, 111, 117, 119–20, 134, 136; life of, 120; and mismeetings, xv, 119–21, 128, 132; relationship as focus of work of, xv, 119–20, 130, 132, 137
Buber, Martin, works: "Christ, Hasidism, and Gnosis," 147n3; *Daniel: Dialogues on Realization*, 134–36; *I and Thou*, 120, 134, 136; "On Meaning: Dialogue in the Garden," 135–36; *The Origin and Meaning of Hasidism*, 135; *Tales of the Hasidim*, 111, 120, 123, 126; *The Way of Man*, 121
Buddhism, 136–38
Bunyan, John, *The Pilgrim's Progress*, 121
Burke, Carolyn, 28, 40
Byron, George Gordon, Lord, "Hebrew Melodies," 63

Cahan, Abe, 9
carnival (Bakhtinian), 75
Catholicism: art of, 43; cardinal sins of, 87; concepts of, 28, 40, 53; and Leonard Cohen's "Hallelujah," 138; Denise Levertov's conversion to, 110, 121, 128–32; liturgy of, 12–13; and reliquaries, xvi–xvii; and saints, 44–49; and Tri-Faith America, 83–84. *See also* saints

Celan, Paul, xiii, 11–16, 20; "Tenebrae," 11–16
Chabad Lubavitch, 110
Chagall, Marc, 8, 19; "Over Vitebsk," 108–9; "The White Crucifixion," 8, 19, 65, 108–9
Chambers, "Ricky," 64
Chambers, Whittaker, 58, 64
charms, 107
cheder (Talmud Torah school), 21, 56
Cheng, Vincent, x
Christians/Christianity: and anti-Semitism, xiv, 92, 117–19; and the body, 35, 37–38; Dead Sea Scrolls and, 90–92, 146n3; Hasidism and, 111; Holocaust linked to, 11, 65, 93, 119; Jewish attractions to, xiv, 23; Jews' rejections of, 10–11; and Leonard Cohen's "Hallelujah," 138; as Other to Jews, x–xi, 3–5, 23, 54, 56, 65–66, 73–74, 101, 115; as Other to Muslims, 43; Paul Philip Levertoff and, 109–21; Shapiro and, 71; Zukofsky and, xiv, 56, 58–60, 64–77. *See also* Catholicism
Christian Science, 34–35, 38
Church of Jesus Christ of Latter-day Saints, 140–42, 148n9
circumcision, 99, 101–4, 147n7 (chap. 4)
Clinchy, Everett, 84
Cloverton, "A Hallelujah Christmas," 138
Cohen, Arthur, 135
Cohen, Shaye, 147n7 (chap. 4)
Cohen, Leonard, 136–39; *The Book of Mercy*, 137; "Hallelujah," xv, 136–39; *Stranger Music*, 137
Cole, Peter, 144n1 (chap. 3)
Columbia University, 58, 66
Commentary (journal), 89
Confirmation, 97–98
Conservative Judaism, 32, 124
contact zones, viii
conversion, 32, 110, 112–14, 121, 124, 128–32
Couperin, François, *Leçons de Ténèbres*, 14
Crowe, Allison, 138
cultural appropriation, 140
Curie, Marie, 29
Czernowitz Conference, 71

"Dabru Emet," 143n1 (chap. 1)
Damon, Maria, 41
Dante Alighieri, *La Vita Nuova*, 76
David (biblical king), 138–39
Davidson, Lauren, 140
Day of St. Thomas Didymus, 129
Dead Sea Scrolls, 90–92, 146n3
Der Jude (*The Jew*; journal), 32
Derrida, Jacques, 62, 76, 104

desire for the Other: Boyarin and, 3–5; Christianity and, 66; envy as manifestation of, 87–88; in human–God relationship, 130–31; Lacanian notion of, 56; Leonard Cohen and, 137; Levertov and, xv, 42, 131; Loy and, 42; Paul Philip Levertoff and, 115; in Roth's *Call It Sleep*, 23; Shapiro and, 101; Zukofsky and, xiv, 56, 58, 65–66, 73–74, 79
Deuteronomy, Book of, 14, 71, 106
Dickinson, Emily, 15
Didymus, Thomas, 129
Docetism, 37
Donne, John, 91
Doubting Thomas, 129
Duncan, Robert, 125, 128, 148n12
DuPlessis, Rachel Blau, 3, 54, 145n12
Dworkin, Craig, 145n11
Dydo, Ulla, 40, 46, 51, 144n9

Easter, 66, 69–70
Eddy, Mary Baker, 34
Elijah (prophet), 142
Eliot, T. S., 3, 10, 22, 59–60, 64–65, 71, 81, 82; "Bleistein with a Cigar," 96; "Burbank with a Baedeker," 96; "Dirge," 96; "The Hollow Men," 59; *The Waste Land*, 22, 60, 64, 77, 82
emotions: associated with borderzones, x–xi; associated with Jewish Christian borderzone, 4–5; literary studies and, 85–86; in response to the Other, xii–xiii; rhyme in relation to, 100; Stein and, 52–53. *See also* envy; shame
envy: defined, 87; in interfaith exchange, xv, 1, 86; psychoanalytic theories of, 87–88; shame linked to, 100–101; Shapiro and, xv, 71, 86–88, 95–101, 103; spoiling of desired object as one response of, 87, 97. *See also* holy envy
Erskine, John, 58, 60
Essenes, 90–91
Eucharist, 23, 37, 44, 95–96, 105, 113. *See also* transubstantiation
Exodus, Book of, 75, 106
Ezekiel, Book of, 105

Fadiman, Clifton, 58
Faith Counts (magazine), 142
Feinstein, Amy, 41
Feldman, Irving, 89
fellowship, Christian, 113, 114
Felski, Rita, 139
Felstiner, John, 12–16
Fiedler, Leslie, 3, 20–21

Finkelstein, Norman, 146n1
First Hebrew Congregation, Oakland, 41–42
Ford, Ford Madox, 29
Ford, James Ishmael, 138
foreigner, Kristeva's concept of, 31, 56, 67–68, 74, 76
Forster, E. M., 121
Forward, The (*Forverts*; newspaper), 9, 89
Francis, Pope, 7
Franco, Dean, 144n6
Frank, Rachel ("Ray"), 41–42
Fredman, Stephen, 61, 146n13
Fredriksen, Paula, 2
Freedman, Jonathan, 82, 145n5
free verse, 89, 91
Freidenreich, David, 149n10
Freud, Sigmund, 49, 87, 102
Friedlander, Ben, 144n10
Friedman, Maurice, 135
Frost, Robert, 76
Fuchs, Thomas, 99–100
Futurism, 32, 33

Gadamer, Hans-Georg, 13–14
gaze of the Other, 88, 98–99
Geiger, Abraham, *The Original Text and Versions of the Bible*, 6
Genesis, Book of, 29, 104, 126
Gilman, Sander, 61
Ginsberg, Allen, 82
Glatstein, Jacob, xiii, 10–11, 16, 58, 65–66; "Good Night, World," 10–11; "How Much Christian," 11; "Mozart," 65
Glazer, Aubrey, 148n2
God: humanity in relation to, 14, 18, 29–30, 36–37, 104, 111, 119, 130–31; Jews/Israel in relation to, 14, 85. *See also* incarnation; Shekhinah
Gold, David, 21
Gold, Mike, 69
Goldman, Shalom, 112
Goldsmith, Kenneth, 93
Goldstein, Laurence, 98
Goodman, Mitchell, 110
Gospel of John, vii, 29, 75, 113, 141, 147n9
Gospel of Luke, 142
Gospel of Matthew, 62, 67–68, 115, 132
grace, 94, 132
Great Books course, 58–59, 60, 66
Green, Arthur, 147n1, 147n2
Greenberg, Uri Zvi, 8
Gris, Juan, 45, 144n9
Gross, Andrew, 88, 146n2
Grossman, Allen, xii, 95

Haggadah, 25–26, 141
halacha (Jewish law), 27, 134
Hamilton, Jake, 138
happiness, saints as embodiment of, xiv, 44
Harshav, Barbara, 10
Harshav, Benjamin, 10, 63, 108
Hasidism: Buber and, 110–11, 119–21, 123, 126, 131, 134–35, 147n3; and holy insecurity, 135; and incarnational thinking, 18, 111, 126; Levertov and, 125–26, 131; and materiality, 125; and mysticism, 113, 117, 119–20; Paul Philip Levertoff and, 110–11, 114, 116, 124; radical eccentricity of, 111
Hebrew Bible, viii, 14, 54, 63, 104, 145n1
Hebrew Christian Alliance of America, 114
Hebrew-Christianity, xv, 109–21
Hebrew language, ix, 21, 41, 56, 68, 71–72, 78, 145n10
Herrick, Robert, 60
Herzl, Hans, 114
Herzl, Theodore, 114
Heschel, Susannah, "Jesus in Modern Jewish Thought," 6
High Holidays, 124
Himmelfarb, Martha, 2
Hirsch, Emil, 6–7, 19
Hoffman, Matthew, 143n4
Hölderlin, Friedrich, "Patmos," 15
Hollander, John, 54
Hollenberg, Donna, 112, 114, 148n12, 148n13
Hollywood, 98
Holocaust: Celan and, 11–16; Christianity linked to, 11, 65, 93, 119; non-Jews' discussion of, xi; Olga Levertoff's "The Ballad of My Father" and, 118–19
holy envy: as affirmation of differences, xiii, 2, 142; Boyarin as case study in, 4–5; interfaith exchange based on, 1–2, 86; origin of term, xii; tolerance contrasted with, 1, 2, 86; Zukofsky and, 56
holy insecurity, xv, 133–39, 142
hooks, bell, 98
Hopkins, Gerard Manley, 15; "The Windhover," 99, 109
Huk, Romana, 148n11
Hulme, T. E., *Speculations*, 82

Ignatius of Loyola, Saint, 35, 47–48, 50
incarnation, xiv, 14, 36–37, 109, 111, 117, 126, 131, 147n3
interfaith exchange: challenges inherent in, x–xii, 2, 11, 69–70; criticisms of, 33–34; cultivation of, 1–2, 36–37, 69; envy as feature of, xv, 1–2, 86; Tri-Faith America and, 83–84
Introspectivists, 10, 58

Isaiah, Book of, 22–24, 62, 104
Islam, 17
I-Thou, 119, 127, 132

Jakobson, Roman, 22
James, Henry, 60
James, William, 44, 48–50, 52–53
JANT. See Jewish Annotated New Testament
Jerome, 23
Jesus: in Asch's *The Nazarene*, 18–19; Buber and, 111, 134, 136; Celan's "Tenebrae" and, 14; in Chagall's "White Crucifixion," 8, 19, 108; his words on the cross, 7, 19, 68; as image of God, 104; incarnation of, 36–37, 109, 111, 126; Jewish characteristics of, 6–8, 19, 62, 68, 106, 113; Jewish interpretations of, 5–8; as Lamb of God, 130; Leonard Cohen and, 136; Loy and, 33–35, 38; Passover Seder and, 141–42; Paul Philip Levertoff and, 111, 113, 114, 116; in Reni's "Crucifixion," 43; Shapiro and, 85, 106; Stein and, 46; Teresa of Avila and, 51; Zukofsky and, 60, 67–68. See also Jewish Jesus
Jewish American literature: characteristics of, 21; Levertov and, 110; Stein and, 28, 40–41; Zukofsky and, 56
Jewish Annotated New Testament (*JANT*), vii, 1–2
Jewish Christian borderzone: Asch and, xiii, 8–9, 16–20; Buber and, 119–23, 134–39; Celan's "Tenebrae" and, 11–16; Chagall and, 8, 19, 108–9; Christian Science and, 34; dangers and disappointments of, xv, 115, 119, 140–42; Dead Sea Scrolls in, 90–92; emotions associated with, 4–5; fluidity of, 2–3, 8, 17, 21, 66, 134, 139; Haggadah and, 25–26; incarnation and, xiv, 36–37; Isaiah and, 22–23; *JANT* in, 1–2; Krensky's "Reliquary II" in, xv–xviii; Leonard Cohen and, 136–39; Levertov and, xv, 110, 120–32; literary modernism and, 3–4; Loy and, xiii–xiv, 27, 31–40; non-Jewish Passover Seders in, xv, 69, 140–42; overview of writers working in, xiii–xv; Passover and Easter in, 69–70; Paul Philip Levertoff and, xv, 34, 109–21; Roth's *Call It Sleep* and, 21–26; scholarly discussions in, 6–7; separations between religions established in, ix, 2–3, 6–8, 10–11, 84–107, 134; Shapiro and, xiv–xv, 84–107; Stein and, xiii–xiv, 42–53; translation in, 11–12; Zukofsky and, xiv, 42, 55–79
Jewish-Christian ideals, 11, 16–17, 19–20
Jewish Christians. See Hebrew-Christianity
Jewish Jesus, 8, 19, 38, 54, 108

INDEX

"Jewish Problem," 80
Jewish Review of Books, 2
Jewish studies, vii, x, 61, 143n1
Job, Book of, 29–30
John of the Cross, Saint, 129–30
Johns Hopkins University, 80–82
Johnson, Kimberly, 95
Jones, Angell, 123
Josephus, 90
Joyce, James, 10, 20, 22; *Finnegans Wake*, 22; *Ulysses*, 18, 22
Judaism: Dead Sea Scrolls and, 90–92; and incarnation, 37; and Leonard Cohen's "Hallelujah," 138–39; and mysticism, 18, 125, 137; Paul Philip Levertoff and, 109–21; racial conception of, 42, 90, 93; Shapiro and, 81, 83, 85–86, 88–107; Stein and, 28, 40–43, 144n10; stereotypes of Jews, 31, 38, 96, 114; and Tri-Faith America, 83–84; women's role in, 27, 41–42, 47, 94. *See also* Conservative Judaism; Hasidism; Reform Judaism; Second Temple Judaism
Judas Iscariot, 33
Judeo-Christianity: Dead Sea Scrolls and, 91–92; popularity of term, 83; Shapiro's opposition to, xiv, 84–85, 91–92, 94, 105; World War II and the emergence of, 83–85; Yiddish culture threatened by, 9
Julius, Anthony, 81, 96

Kabbalah, 36, 109, 116, 126, 135, 137, 139, 147n3, 147n7 (chap. 4)
Kahn, Daniel, 138–39
Kaufmann, David, 89
Kazin, Alfred, 9, 20
Kermani, Navid, 43
Khayyam, Omar, *Rubaiyat*, 63
King, Georgiana Goddard, 48
King James Bible, 54, 144n1
Kinter, William, 125
Kister, Menachem, 146n3
Klein, Melanie, 87–88, 97
Klezmer music, 138
Klink, Joanna, 15
Krensky, Beth, "Reliquary II," xv–xvii
Kristeva, Julia, 31, 56, 67, 74, 76
Kronfeld, Chana, 146n3

Lacan, Jacques, 56, 88, 101
Lambert, Josh, 22
Lamentations, 15
Last Supper, 25, 69, 141, 149n10
Lazarus, Emma, 7
Leighton, Christopher, xi
Levertoff, Beatrice, 112, 114, 128
Levertoff, Olga, 110, 114, 116–19, 147n10; "The Ballad of My Father," 121; *The Wailing Wall*, 116–18
Levertoff, Paul Philip, xv, 34, 109–21, 124, 126, 128–32, 147n5; "The Ballad of My Father," 118–19; *Hayei Yeshu'a ha Mashiah u-fo'alav* (*The Son of Man*), 113; *Love and the Messianic Age*, 111, 113, 116; "Work and Needs," 114
Levertoff, Shaul, 116
Levertov, Denise: connection as theme of works of, xv, 110, 115, 120–31; conversion to Catholicism, 110, 121, 128–32; desire for the Other, xv, 42; and Hasidism, 120; Jewish and Christian elements in life and work of, xv, 110, 123–24, 128–32, 148n11; and the Jewish Christian borderzone, xv, 110, 120–32; life of, and relationship to her father, xv, 110, 112, 114–16, 120–21, 124–25, 128–32; poetic practice of, 122–25; and politics, 127–28, 148n12; spiritual longings and restlessness of, xv, 42, 120–21, 124
Levertov, Denise, works: "At the Edge," 122; "Illustrious Ancestors," 122–23; "In Obedience," 121; *The Jacob's Ladder*, 122, 126; "The Jacob's Ladder," 122, 125–27; "Jewish," 122; "A Letter to William Kinter of Muhlenberg," 124–25; "A Map of the Western Part of the County of Essex in England," 122–23; "Mass for the Day of St. Thomas Didymus," 129–30; "A Minor Role," 115–16; "Moments of Joy," 132; "O Taste and See," 122; "The Poet in the World," 121; *The Sorrow Dance*, 118; "Standoff," 130–31; "The Thread," 122, 124; "To Olga," 118; "Wings in the Pedlar's Sack," 108–9
Levine, Amy-Jill, vii, 1, 141, 149n11
Levy, Mark John, 114
Library of Congress, 80
Lieberman, Chaim, 9–10
literary modernism. *See* modernism
Longfellow, Henry Wadsworth, *Hiawatha*, 57, 63
Lowell, Robert, 81
Lowy, Isaac, 32
Lowy, Julia Bryan, 32
Lowy, Sigmund, 31–32, 35, 38
Loy, Mina: as dress designer, 39; Jewish and Christian elements in life and work of, xv, 27, 30, 32–40, 42; and the Jewish Christian borderzone, xiii–xiv, 27, 31–40; life of, xiv, 27, 30–33, 36, 38, 40; and materiality, xiv, 30, 34–40; and mysticism, 27–28, 30, 36, 38–39; poetic practice of, xi, 31; Stein and, 28–30, 40

Loy, Mina, works: "Anglo-Mongrels and the Rose," xiv, 27, 30–38; "Chiffon Velour," 38–40; "Gertrude Stein," 28–30
Loyola University, Chicago, 98
Luhan, Mabel Dodge, 28
Lurianic Kabbalah, 137
lyric poetry, xi–xii

MacNeice, Louis, 89
Magid, Shaul, 18, 53, 111, 115, 117, 126, 147n2, 147n3, 147n5
Man Ray, 43
Manger, Itsik, 8
marketplace (Bakhtinian), 74–75
Marlowe, Christopher, 60
masturbation, 97–98
materiality: Hasidism and, 125; Levertov and, 125–26, 129; Loy and, xiv, 30, 34–40; Shapiro and, 94, 105; Stein and, xiv, 51–52. *See also* body
McAlmon, Robert, 45
melopoeia (musical qualities of language), 107
Mendele the Book Peddler, 78
Mendelssohn, Moses, 6
Mendes-Flohr, Paul, 134
Menorah Journal, 73
Merezhkovsky, Dmitry, "Sakya Muni," 63
Merrill, James, 82
Messianic Jews, 68, 140
messianism, 16, 23, 91–92, 116
Miller, Cristanne, 32, 144n2
Miron, Dan, 16
mismeetings, xv, 119–21, 125, 128, 132
modernism: Christianizing narrative underwriting, 3, 54, 60, 64, 81, 83, 89; Forster and, 121; Jewish American, 21, 56; and the Jewish Christian borderzone, 3–4; Jewish rejection of, 10–11; Loy's criticism of, 30; Henry Roth's *Call It Sleep* and, 20, 22; Zukofsky's role in, 56
Montaigne, Michel de, 103
Moore, Deborah Dash, 83
Moore, Marianne, 82
Moshe of Korbyn, 126
Mozart, Wolfgang Amadeus, 65
mysticism: Hasidism and, 113, 117, 119–20; Jewish, 18, 125, 137; Leonard Cohen and, 137; Loy and, 27–28, 30, 36, 38–39; nondenominational, 36; and the Other, 119–20; Paul Philip Levertoff and, 109; Teresa of Avila and, 28; women and, 27, 47

Nachman, Rabbi, 135
National Conference of Christian and Jews (NCCJ), 83–84, 91

Nazism, 11, 83–84
NCCJ. *See* National Conference of Christian and Jews
Neolog Dohany Street Synagogue, 32
New Critics, 82
New Haven Historical Society, xv–xvi
New Masses, The (journal), 69
New Testament: *Jewish Annotated New Testament (JANT)*, vii, 1–2; Judeo-Christianity and, 83; Zukofsky and, 58
New York Daily News (newspaper), 68
New Yorker (magazine), 90
New York University, 58, 66
Ngai, Sianne, 93, 96; *Ugly Feelings*, 85–86
Nietzsche, Friedrich, 134
Ninth of Av, 15
Norich, Anita, 9, 11

Objectivists, 125
O'Hara, Frank, 82
Oppen, George, 125
Orchard Street Shul Cultural Project, xv–xvii
Osherow, Jacqueline, 144n1
Other: in Buber's philosophy, 119–20; Christians as, x–xi, 3–5, 23, 54, 56, 65–66, 73–74, 101, 115; dynamic in anti-Semitism of Self and, 7, 8; feelings aroused by, xii–xiii; gaze of, 98–99; Jews as, xi, 61, 66; Jews' fear of, viii–ix; mysticism and, 119–20; self-knowledge resulting from contact with, xii, 56, 69, 79. *See also* desire for the Other
Ovid, 87, 97
Ozick, Cynthia, 54; "Envy: Or Yiddish in America," 77

Passover, 66, 68–70, 72, 140–41
Passover Seders, xv, 69, 139–42, 149n10
Paul, 4, 37, 103–4, 114
Peers, E. Allison, *Studies of the Spanish Mystics*, 47
Pennsylvania mining strike, 67–69
Perlman, Bob, 145n12
Perloff, Marjorie, 31
Philo, 90
Picasso, Pablo, 45
Pittsburgh Press (newspaper), 39
Plate, S. Brent, 34
Pliny, 90
poetics of the in-between, xv
Poetry (magazine), 82
Ponichtera, Sarah, 72, 146n13
Porter, Katherine Anne, 81
postcolonial studies, viii
Pound, Ezra, 59, 61, 73, 76, 82, 88, 107; *Pisan Cantos*, 81

INDEX

Pratt, Mary Louise, viii
prayer, 45–46
Probyn, Elspeth, 101
Proust, Marcel, 120
Psalms, 71, 137

race, Jews as, 42, 90, 93
Reform Judaism, 6, 41
Rekdal, Paisley, 148n8
reliquaries, xvi–xvii
Reni, Guido, "Crucifixion," 43
Resnais, Alan, *Night and Fog*, 15
Resnikoff, Ariel, 32, 75, 145n12, 145n13
Revelation, Book of, 118
Reznikoff, Charles, 145n12
Rhav, Philip, 9
rhyme, 100
Rich, Adrienne, 82, 123
rosary, 105–6
Roth, Henry, xiii, 57, 145n13; *Call It Sleep*, 20–26
Rothenberg, Jerome, 41, 123
Rouault, Georges, 100
Rubens, Peter Paul, 47
Rukeyser, Muriel, 123

saints, xiv, 28, 39, 40, 44–50, 131
Samuel, 2nd Book of, 71
Sartre, Jean-Paul, 7
Saturday Review of Literature (magazine), 81
Scarry, Elaine, 15
Schäfer, Peter, 2, 5; *Jesus in the Talmud*, 5
Schonfield, Jeremy, 106
Schultz, Kevin, 83–84
Schwartz, Regina, 95
scientific racism, 42
Scroggins, Mark, 57, 58
Second Commandment, 60
Second Temple Judaism, 140
Seder Kedush D'Seudah D'Malcha Kadeesha, 113
Seidman, Naomi, 11, 62, 77–78, 145n6, 145n7
Self: dynamic in anti-Semitism of Other and, 7, 8; knowledge resulting from contact with the Other, xii, 56, 69, 79; Other in relation to, 69
Selinger, Eric, 148n7
shame: characteristics of, 78, 99–100; envy linked to, 100–101; Shapiro and, 42, 100–101, 105; Yiddish as source of, 78; Zukofsky and, xiv, 56, 74, 77–79
Shandler, Jeffrey, 77
Shapiro, Karl: and Bollingen affair, 80–83, 88; career of, 80–83; and Dead Sea Scrolls, 91; differentiation of Judaism and Christianity in work of, 84–107; and envy, xv, 71, 86–88, 95–101, 103; and the Jewish Christian borderzone, xiv–xv, 84–107; and Judaism, 81, 83, 85–86, 88–107; and Judeo-Christianity, xiv, 84–85, 91–92, 94, 105; poetic practice of, 89, 91, 93, 100, 102, 107; and shame, 42, 100–101, 105; and ugliness, 96–102; in World War II, 80, 83–85
Shapiro, Karl, works: "The Alphabet," 86, 91–93; "Christmas Eve, America," 85; "The Confirmation," 97–98; "The Crucifix in the Filing Cabinet," 105–7; "The First Time," 100–102, 107; "The Leg," 102–5; "Movie Actress," 98; *Person, Place, and Thing*, 80; *Poems of a Jew*, 83, 84–107; *A Prosody Handbook*, 100; *Selected Poems*, 89; "Sunday: New Guinea," 84; "The Synagogue," 93–94, 97, 105; "Teasing the Nuns," 98–99; *V-Letter and Other Poems*, 80, 83, 84–85, 102
Shapiro, Lamed, 8
Shekhinah (feminine aspect of Godhead), 109, 118, 126, 131, 139
Shema, ix, 7, 19
Shreiber, Maeera, 94–95, 144n5, 145n9
Smith, Joseph, 142
Southwell, Robert, 127
Spinoza, Baruch, 46, 60–61, 74
Spooner-Jones, Beatrice, 123
Stahl, Neta, 143n4
Stein, Gertrude: attractions of Christianity and St. Teresa for, xiv, 28, 40, 42–53; difficulty of poetry of, 15, 44; humor of, 51; and the Jewish Christian borderzone, xiii–xiv, 42–53; and Judaism, 28, 40–43, 144n10; life of, 28, 40–52; Loy and, 28–30, 40; and materiality, xiv, 51–52; "portraits" composed by, 45–46; use of language by, xiii–xiv, 29–30, 44, 50, 93
Stein, Gertrude, works: *The Autobiography of Alice B. Toklas*, 43, 44, 45, 50; "Composition as Explanation," 46; *Everybody's Autobiography*, 50; *Four Saints in Three Acts*, xiv, 28, 43–52; *Geography and Plays*, 44; *The Making of Americans*, 44–45; "The Modern Jew Who Has Given Up the Faith of His Fathers Can Reasonably and Consistently Believe in Isolation," 42; "Patriarchal Poetry," 41; *Prayers and Portraits*, 45; "A Sonatina Followed by Another," 41; "A Sweet Tail (Gypsies)," 30; *Tender Buttons*, 44; *Wars I Have Seen*, 50
Stendahl, Krister, xii, 1, 2, 56, 86
stereotypes, of Jews, 31, 38, 96, 114
Stevens, Wallace, 82; "Sunday Morning," 84
Stewart, Susan, xii
syncretism, 70

Tablet (Jewish magazine), 2, 78
Tablet, The (Catholic weekly), 138
tallit (Jewish prayer shawl), xvi–xvii
Talmud, 5
Tate, Allen, 81
Taylor, Barbara Brown, xii–xiii
tefillin (phylacteries), 106
Temple, destruction of, 15, 71–72
Tenebrae service, 12–13
Teresa of Avila, Saint, xiv, 28, 43, 45–52; *The Life of Teresa of Jesus*, 35, 47; *Spiritual Relation*, 51
teshuvah (repentance), 124
Thomson, Virgil, 44, 46, 49, 50
Toklas, Alice B., 40–43, 45, 48, 144
transatlantic review (magazine), 28–30
translation: Christian mistranslations of Hebrew Bible, 62; in the Jewish Christian borderzone, 11–12, 62–64; Zukofsky and, 63–64
transubstantiation, 37, 95, 105. *See also* Eucharist
Tri-Faith America, 83–84
Trilling, Lionel, 58

ugliness, 96–102
Umansky, Ellen, 34
universalism, 2, 3
University of Königsberg, 116
University of Nebraska, 82

vagina dentata, 101
Vatican II, 13
Vietnam War, 127, 148n12
Volozhin Yeshiva, Lithuania, 116

Wailing Wall, 72, 117
war trios, 83–84
Washington, George, 46
Weinreich, Max, 62
Welsh, Andrew, 107
Wieseltier, Leon, 136
Williams, William Carlos, 59, 82, 123; *Paterson*, 81
Wilson, Edmund, 90–92, 146n3
Wimsatt, W. K., 82
Wineapple, Brenda, 41
Winters, Yvor, 76
Wirth-Nesher, Hana, 21, 22
Wolfson, Elliot, 36–37, 126; "'New Jerusalem Glowing': Songs and Poems of Leonard Cohen in Kabbalistic Key," 137

women: Christian Science and, 34; gaze exercised by, 101; in Judaism, 27, 41–42, 47, 94; as mystics, 27, 47. *See also* Shekhinah
Woolf, Virginia, 60
Word, the (Logos), vii, 29, 75
Wordsworth, William, 122
World War II, 80, 83–85

Yeats, William Butler, 82
Yehoash. *See* Bloomgarden, Solomon
Yiddish: in America, 10; Asch's use of, xiii, xiv, 9–10, 20; the body associated with, 79; as a differentiation language, 62; Hebrew in relation to, 71, 78, 145n10; Leonard Cohen's "Hallelujah" sung in, 138–39; Loy and, 31–32; mixed nature of, 10; negative views of, 61, 71; persistence of, 77–78; polylingual character of, 10, 31, 57, 59; Roth and, 57, 145n13; shame linked to, 78; Spinoza and, 61; spoken nature of, 59; Stein and, 41; writers working in, 8; Yehoash and, 63; Zukofsky's use of, xiv, 41, 56–59, 61–66, 70–79, 145n13
Yidid Nefesh, 113
Yom Kippur, 14
Youngman, Henny, 102
Yuval, Israel, 69

Zalman, Rav, 123
Zalman, Shneur, 110
Zangwill, Israel, *The Melting Pot*, 42
Zaritt, Saul N., 144n7 (chap. 1)
Zen Buddhism, 136–38
Zionism, 16, 114
Zohar, 112, 117, 125
Zukofsky, Chana, 56
Zukofsky, Louis: avant-garde and, 145n12; and Christianity, xiv, 56, 58–60, 64–77; desire for the Other, xiv, 56, 58, 65–66, 73–74, 79; and English language, 58; and Great Books course, 58–59, 60, 66; and the Jewish Christian borderzone, xiv, 42, 55–79; and language, 56–57; life of, 56–58, 65–66; particularism of, 59; shame experienced by, xiv, 56, 74, 77–79; translation of Asch's *Die Mutter*, 73; and Yiddish, xiv, 41, 56–59, 61–66, 70–79, 145n13
Zukofsky, Louis, works: "A," 57, 59, 66–79; *Autobiography*, 57; "Poem Beginning 'The,'" 59–65, 70, 77
Zukofsky, Morris, 56–57
Zukofsky, Pinchos, 56–57

Maeera Y. Shreiber is Associate Professor of English, and former Director of Religious Studies, at the University of Utah, where she teaches and writes about poetry, Jewish American literature, ethnic American studies, religious studies, and interfaith relations. Professor Shreiber is the author of, among other books, *Singing in a Strange Land: A Jewish American Poetics* (Stanford University Press, 2007). She has published in numerous journals, including *PMLA, AJS Review, Prooftexts, American Religion,* and *Genre*, and has been the recipient of numerous awards, including fellowships from Fulbright, the National Endowment for the Humanities, and the Stanford Humanities Center.

www.ingramcontent.com/pod-product-compliance
Lightning Source LLC
Chambersburg PA
CBHW020412080526
44584CB00014B/1292